Make Money Quilting

Sylvia Landman

ALLWORTH PRESS
NEW YORK

W9-CEI-804

08   07   06   05   04   5   4   3   2   1

Published by Allworth Press
An imprint of Allworth Communications, Inc.
10 East 23rd Street, New York, NY 10010

Cover design by Derek Bacchus

Interior design by Sharp Des!gns, Inc., Lansing, MI

Page composition/typography by Integra Software Services, Pvt. Ltd., Pondicherry, India

ISBN: 1-58115-399-6

Library of Congress Cataloging-in-Publication Data:

Landman, Sylvia.
   Make money quilting / Sylvia Landman.
      p. cm.
   Includes index.
   ISBN 1-58115-399-6 (pbk.)
1. Needlework industry and trade.   2. Handicraft industries.
3. Home-based businesses.   I. Title.

   HD9936.5.A2L357 2005
   746.46'068'1—dc22

                                        2004028331

Printed in Canada

Contents

Dedication ··· vii
Acknowledgments ··· ix
Foreword *by Peggy Diamanti* ······································ xi

1 Turning Your Hobby into a Business

Quilting as a Business—How the IRS Sees It ················· 1
Working Where You Live—Confusion of Roles ··············· 2
Separate Business from Personal Tasks ························ 3
Motivation and Self-Discipline ································· 3
Set a Work Schedule *and* Stick to It ························ 4
Defining and Achieving Your Goals ··························· 8
Entrepreneurial Characteristics You Should Have ············ 8
Time Management Skills ·· 9
Get It *All* Done with Action Boards
  and Monthly Action Lists ································· 10

2 A Business Plan for Creative Quilters and Sewers

Business Plans Defined—Plan For Success ·················· 13
Three Reasons to Make a Business Plan ···················· 14
A Road Map to Success ······································· 14
A Business Plan Outline for You ····························· 16

3 Designing for the Quilting and Sewing Market

Defining Original Design ····································· 21
Selling a Design More than Once ···························· 22
Color and Design Trends ····································· 23
Should You Design Only What Is
  Highly Profitable? ·· 24
Protect the Artist Within ····································· 24
The Importance of Playing with New Materials ·············· 25
Nourish Your Creativity ······································ 26
How to Maintain a Stream of Ideas ························· 27
Comments from Professional Designers about
  Selling Patterns and Designs ····························· 27

4

Your Marketing Plan

What Is Special about Your Work? · 34
Turn Your Specialty into a Niche in the Marketplace · · · · · · · · · · 35
Why You Need a *Written* Marketing Plan · · · · · · · · · · · · · · · · · 39
Paying to Get the Word Out · 41
Defining Your Product's Benefits · 43
Your Professional Image · 43
Little-to-No-Cost Promotional Ideas · 47
The Importance of Networking and How to Do It · · · · · · · · · · · 48
Marketing Comments and Advice from
    Quilt Professionals · 51

5

Selling Your Quilts

The Quality of Your Work · 55
Selling at Retail · 56
Selling at Wholesale · 67
Sales Representatives Can Create
    Markets for You · 68
Fairs, Exhibits, and Trade Shows · 68
Selling at Both Retail and Wholesale · · · · · · · · · · · · · · · · · · · 73
Important Annual Quilt Shows · 74

6

Negotiating Contracts

The Importance of Contracts · 75
Interview with Kathleen Bissett · 76
Interview with Ann Anastasio · 77
Interview with BrendaLou Scott, Shop Owner · · · · · · · · · · · · · 78
Letter of Agreement · 81

7

Pricing Quilts, Products, and Services

Pricing Basics · 89
Pricing Methods · 90
When to Adjust Your Prices · 94
How Will I Know When to Raise My Prices? · · · · · · · · · · · · · · · 95
How Can I Compete with Others with Similar
    Products Who Charge Less? · 95
How Can I Increase My Profits? · 95
What Do I Say if Buyers Say My Item
    Costs Too Much? · 96
A Pricing Example · 96
Cathy Hooley's Pricing System · 97
Just for Fun · 99
Woodland Manor's Pricing Schedule · · · · · · · · · · · · · · · · · · · 100
Summary · 102

8 More Ways to Make a Profit

Judy Laquidara: Finish What Other Quilters Start · · · · · · · · · · · 104
Patti Foster: Custom Quiltmaker · 105
Karen McCleary: Maker of Quilt Samples · · · · · · · · · · · · · · · · 106
Marilyn Maddalena: Appraiser, Judge, Historian, Speaker · · · · · · 107
Nancy Kirk: Quilt Restoration · 108
Sylvia Landman: Consultant · 109

9 Writing Magazine Articles

What Type of Designs Should You Try to Sell? · · · · · · · · · · · · · 113
Finding Magazines Interested in Your Topics · · · · · · · · · · · · · · 114
How to Write a Query Letter · 117
What to Expect When You Submit
    Work to Magazine Editors · 117
What Is In the Magazine Contract? · 119
Tear Sheets as Marketing Tools · 121
How to Write Instructions · 122
What Do Magazine Designers Earn? · · · · · · · · · · · · · · · · · · · 123
Turning One Article into a Series · 123
Turning a Series into a Column · 124

10 The Art of Teaching

Defining Teaching Styles · 126
Elements of a Class Description · 128
Planning and Organizing Your Class · 129
Your Teaching Attitude · 136
Problem Areas and Difficult Students · · · · · · · · · · · · · · · · · · · 140
Organizing Your Notes—The Start
    of Your Lesson Plan · 143
Creating Your Lesson Plan · 143
Where Will You Teach? · 148
Setting Fees · 155
Teacher Interviews · 159
Deb Donovan's Lesson Plan · 163
Sample Contract · 166
Teaching Credentials and Qualifications · · · · · · · · · · · · · · · · · 167

11 Taking Care of Business

Naming Your Business · 170
City Business License · 171
Home Occupation Use Permits · 171
Zoning Variances · 171
The Home Office Deduction · 171
Buying Wholesale · 173

Managing Your Cash Flow · 175
Credit Cards · 177
Obtaining Merchant Credit · 177
Employee or Independent Contractor · · · · · · · · · · · · · · · · · · 179

12 Copyright

What is Copyright? · 181
Copyright and Quilters · 183
Fair Use of Copyrighted Material · 183
Works in Public Domain · 184
Copyright Pirates · 185
How to File a Copyright · 186
Myths about Copyright · 186
International Copyright · 188
Resources · 189

Appendixes

Appendix A: Books · 190
Appendix B: Publishers' Books · 193
Appendix C: Periodicals · 196
Appendix D: Organizations · 202
Appendix E: Quilt Suppliers and Distributors · · · · · · · · · · · · · 206
Appendix F: Online Quilting Groups · · · · · · · · · · · · · · · · · · · 232
Appendix G: Other Helpful Web Sites · · · · · · · · · · · · · · · · · · 234
Appendix H: Quilting Software · 235
Appendix I: Government Resources · 236

Index · 238

Dedication

E very author needs a Number One Fan. Such a fan need not be quite as dedicated as the antagonist in Stephen King's thriller *Misery*, but rather reasonably dedicated, supportive, enthusiastic and encouraging. I have such a fan—my very much loved nephew, Rich. He faithfully visits quilting and bookshops to engage in a bit of not-so-subtle name-dropping for his doting aunt. When he visits bookstores, he calmly asks why my book titles are not more prominently displayed. He visits new quilt shops and takes in his own copies of my books and provides a sales pitch as to why the new owner should carry my books in the new shop.

He is neither a crafter nor a quilter, but insists on having a copy of each of my books in a place of honor in his home. Blind to my errors and foibles, he persists in being the most proud and loving of fans, singing my praises even when no one is listening. I can't explain it, but I certainly am pleased that he is *my* Number One Fan. I dedicate this book to Rich. Thank you for your unwavering love, support, and pride in my work. It truly touches me.

Acknowledgments

I am indebted for life to my bridegroom, who bravely married me the day I signed the contract to write this book. Patiently, he made meals while watching the back of my head as I faced the computer seven days a week for eight months. He maintained quiet in his new home so I could write. He lovingly counted the weeks until the manuscript would cease being his competition. For his encouragement as he entered the unfamiliar world of authors and books, he deserves a bouquet of flowers, like those he often brought me when discouraging moments arose with the manuscript. Thank you, Jim. You have my heart and my promise to become a full-time wife now.

I also thank:

Sue Wegert, my "Computer Elf," for consistently coming to the rescue with excellent tips and solutions to help me deal with the mysterious nuances of my computer.

Peggy Diamanti, Alice Thiesen, and Marilyn Maddalena: I am blessed with your friendship.

My students who keep me on my toes with questions and suggestions.

The talented array of quilters who endured my probing questions as I interviewed them for this book—thank you! You have enriched this book with your valuable contributions and taught me so much along the way.

—SYLVIA ANN LANDMAN-RASMUSSEN

Foreword

I met Sylvia at a quilting conference. During our walks to and from classrooms and the dining hall, we found a kindred spirit in one another. I was fascinated to learn that English was her second language; she speaks it better than I do and it is my first and only language. Little bits of information came from her, and finally I discovered she had authored several books and articles. We had a great time together and became good friends.

The next time we met, Sylvia was giving a lecture about copyright. She held her audience spellbound. Sylvia has a delightful sense of humor that makes the driest material fascinating. You hear it and absorb it before you know what has happened, and you enjoy the process. I find her writing much the same: It is succinct and to the point, always answering questions I would have asked, and fine-tuning the answer beyond the question.

I purchased all her books to see what this lady was all about. I was impressed with how knowledgeable she is. She knows the facts in depth, and follows them with documentation.

I am especially excited to read Sylvia's new book, *Make Money Quilting*. Quilting is my work. I teach, design, and work at a local quilt shop. Quilting has been in my life since I was a small child, as both of my grandmothers quilted. I have been quilting since 1974.

Sylvia and I have kept in contact, and I feel honored to be asked to write this foreword. I mulled it over in my mind for months. I wanted to sort through how to express the special feelings I have for Sylvia, both as a friend and as a teacher.

Thank you, Sylvia, for giving me this honor. I hope all who read this book enjoy getting to know this delightful lady as much as I have.

—PEGGY A. DIAMANTI

Turning Your Hobby into a Business

Quilters and crafters enrolled in my college-level small business classes express a common problem as they turn professional. Business matters, especially bookkeeping, receive too little of their attention because these creative people value their artistic interests more. They often continue to think like hobbyists rather than like business owners when starting out. Such thinking challenges them as they make a transition from hobby to for-profit enterprises. They seem surprised to learn that the IRS *requires* business owners to maintain books and records that follow business standards common today.

Novice entrepreneurs often fear they are compromising their creative ethic when actively marketing their products. Quilters can resent the time spent on bookkeeping or correspondence. They want what they perceive as "real work"—working with sewing machines, thread, and fabric.

However, the very business activities they shun are those they must develop if quilting is to become profitable enough to earn a living or supplement existing incomes. Bookkeeping may not be as much "fun" as designing or quilting, yet we must discipline ourselves to learn all we can about accounting, advertising, and marketing to profit from our artistic talents.

Quilting as a Business—How the IRS Sees It

If you want to turn your quilting hobby into a business, you may wonder how to tell when the time is right to begin. Four questions may help you recognize when your hobby may be turning into a business. Did you:

+ Net more than $400 per year from your quilting? Internal Revenue Service statutes say that when a taxpayer *nets* (not grosses) more than $400 per year, she must file a Schedule C with her income tax return to report self-employed income. When a small business shows a profit for three out of five years, a viable enterprise exists.
+ Begin to make your quilting profitable so you could buy fabric, patterns, and books, but find that your income extends to pay other expenses?
+ Find yourself increasing the time you work for others and setting your own projects aside?
+ Find yourself keeping notes or an informal bookkeeping system to track expenses and income?

If so, you have begun a business process.

If your quilting activities show a profit and you see a small business emerging, you have a few decisions to make. Begin by assessing the time you will need to spend developing your business. Is it feasible to add more quilting time to your present work-at-home schedule?

Incorporating a new pursuit into your life requires adjustment. Consider your work style and personality as you explore the possibility of creating a business. Many people prefer to work around others, to give and receive regular feedback about group interests. Does this describe you? If so, you may want to rethink starting your business at home, where you will often work in solitude. Many creative people enjoy working alone; others deplore it. Does this lifestyle suit you? If you have answered "yes" to the previous questions and still feel determined to explore converting your quilt hobby to a small business, consider what the IRS has to say.

The IRS is the definitive guide on tax issues and deductions affecting your business, and it requires your quilt business to show a clear "profit motive." This means you must make every effort to make a profit and pay taxes on income you earn.

To turn your hobby into a business and prove you aim to make a profit, you must:

+ Maintain a general business ledger to document deductible expenses and income. You may use very expensive systems, or a small notebook. The IRS accepts computer-generated spreadsheets too.
+ Keep invoices and receipts in good order to affirm your expenses and income.
+ Make regular business transactions.
+ Set aside time devoted to your business.
+ Prove that you follow general business practices such as advertising, bank accounts, legal licenses, and permits, and that you create a business name.
+ Show a profit three out of five years or present solid evidence of your effort to do so.

When the IRS determines that your business shows a profit, you have no problem identifying your activities as "business." However, the IRS can declare your business as a hobby—an activity not engaged in for profit—if you do not follow general business practices.

Even if you list your quilting activities as a hobby, if you generate income from them, you must still add a Schedule C to your annual returns and pay taxes on the earnings. Business owners can deduct losses, but hobbyists can only deduct expenses equal to the amount of income generated. The IRS offers many free booklets to help you establish a profitable business. You can order them by mail or download them from the IRS Web site.

Working Where You Live—Confusion of Roles

Working from home is here to stay. Books, newsletters, and catalogs today dedicate themselves to home-based workers. Magazine articles explore the number one question: "How do you separate personal time from business tasks when you work where you live?"

Friends may say: "How lucky you are to stay at home and work!" or "By the way, are sewing, quilting and other crafts really *work*? It must be so easy," or "Isn't it like getting paid to play?"

Quilters hear these questions often and we *know* it is hard work. We love it, but what gets in our way that makes working from home so complicated? Here are a few reasons.

Society programs us to associate home with family, rest, relaxation, and everyone's favorite, housework. Think of the old adage, "A man's/woman's home is his/her castle." Conversely, society also programs us to expect that working at a job site means leaving home interests behind each day.

Commuting from home office to kitchen takes seconds. There is not much time to switch identities. No wonder it is tough to have a clear picture of who we are at a given moment. Several generations have been socialized to this clean-cut separation, but it has not always been so. Before the industrial revolution, working from home was the norm. The butcher, the baker, and the candlestick maker lived upstairs and worked downstairs. It is difficult today for an entire new generation to learn how to do the same without the benefit of role models long gone.

Separate Business from Personal Tasks

Today, we are drawn to work where we live, but often one of two extremes prevails. Home workers either relax too much, giving most of their attention to home/family issues, or they become workaholics at home. It is easy for newer workers to squander time on unaccustomed, unrestricted domestic relaxation. When the day runs short, they hurry to squeeze in professional duties in too little time.

Overzealous workers, on the other hand, cannot stop working at what they love. Quilting and sewing work is so accessible at home, they allocate most of their attention and energy to it and try to squeeze in domestic concerns in the time remaining. It is not surprising that families object to this, which then brings stress and resentment to the situation.

Neither extreme works well. Both cause guilt, frustration, and a sense of underachievement. Making a clear distinction between home and business obligations is not easy. However, it is essential if one wants to succeed. Left unattended, the problem can get out of hand, lower our efficiency, increase frustration, and make us wonder if working from home is such a good idea after all. You bet it is! If we learn to give each task its due time, there is nothing better!

Motivation and Self-Discipline

The secret of success is to focus on who we are and what we do. We must then mix in a large dose of time management and self-discipline. We need a system to keep personal tasks separate from professional ones so we can still get it all done. But how?

Get Your Tasks in Order

Start with two sheets of paper. Label the first "Household Tasks," the other, "Professional Tasks." Over a week's time, list every activity consuming your time on the proper sheet. Do not leave anything out if you want a realistic schedule. Check often to be sure you have not overlooked anything. Add activities you find yourself doing regularly that you overlooked when writing on the list.

Observe Your Energy Level As You Work

Identify your body's "prime time." When are you most alert and eager to work? What time of day does your energy peak? You will work more efficiently if you assign prime time and high-energy periods to income-producing tasks. Leave mindless tasks such as household cleaning or laundry for when your energy is low. Such tasks require less of you and may require you to learn to do home tasks at a different time of day from before you brought your career home to live.

Schedule Your Work Week

At the beginning of the third week, take another sheet of paper. Divide it into five vertical columns, one for each weekday. Fold this sheet in half horizontally to crease. Begin to prioritize from your master list. Distribute professional tasks evenly throughout the week on the upper section, and put homemaking tasks on the lower portion by writing them on the proper portion of the list. Remember your prime time as you pluck each activity from the master list. Schedule each day remembering there is no one watching you. Committed self-employed artists and quilters must motivate themselves. Try the new schedule for another week.

At the end of a week, if you find you simply cannot accomplish everything on your list, you may be expecting too much from yourself. Modify your list. Delete the least important task from each section from each day. "I cannot," you say, "I must do them all to succeed." If this is the case, your schedule is telling you something. Perhaps you:

+ Need help—hire someone, trade, or barter.
+ Need less rest or recreation and more self-discipline.
+ Are wasting time.
+ Can combine the most mindless tasks together to gather new time.
+ Are working at your low-energy periods.
+ Are ignoring priority tasks during high-energy periods.
+ Are permitting too many interruptions.

Set a Work Schedule and Stick to It

Effective schedules should represent realistic weekly goals. Modify them until the list is tailor-made for your energy level, lifestyle, and work requirements. Sticking to it will help you avoid leaving something undone at the end the week as you try to squeeze it all in. This creates only frustration—not saleable quilted products.

Here is a way to help you set up a work schedule and stick to it:

1. Divide a sheet of paper in half vertically.
2. List household and personal tasks on the left side of the paper in any order.
3. List quilting and professional chores on the right side.
4. Maintain the lists for a week until every activity that takes your time appears on one side or the other. Call this your first draft.
5. Next, divide another sheet of paper in half. Using your first draft, copy each household activity from the left side to the second draft in order of importance. Place the "must-dos" at the top. Continue adding tasks, ending with the mundane, least demanding jobs at the bottom. This list should account for every task, ranked in a sensible order. Repeat this process for your quilting and professional chores on the other side of the paper. You have before you a weekly schedule of tasks. Begin each day by tackling the chores that head each side of the lists.

Working on one week at a time keeps lists manageable. Check frequently to see if you are on schedule. If too many chores remain undone at the end of the week, either your list was unrealistically long, or you became waylaid or worked too slowly. Try eliminating the least important task from the bottom of each side and prepare a new work schedule for the following week.

Learn to study your work schedule week by week. Do you meet your deadlines? Do you spend too much time on trivialities? Do you procrastinate? If you find yourself behind schedule, consider letting go of something less important in favor of a highly profitable task or one that moves your business forward.

Distribute both personal and professional chores evenly throughout the week to avoid burnout. Balance slow, tedious tasks with those requiring more energy. Alternate sitting and standing jobs, and you may find you can work longer without tiring. Keep your eye on your schedule, making sure you do "first things first."

Post your finished work schedule on the refrigerator door for housemates to see. Post another copy in your work area. Educate friends and family who drop in unannounced because "you were home anyway." We need to state to others assertively that although we are at home, we are working at our livelihood. This will give you, too, a clearer picture of your own dual roles.

Work for pay during your prime time. Tell others and yourself, "I cannot watch TV now. I am at work." If you walk by a wilted plant on your way to the coffeepot, don't let it sabotage your schedule and cause you to fuss over all of your houseplants. Add a bit of water and say to your subconscious, "I am at work. Nothing short of emergencies will interrupt the life's work I have chosen." Then get back to your income-producing work.

Teach your children how to tell when you are working and when you are available to them. Preschoolers and young children can learn easily if you use a kitchen timer at first. When they interrupt, tell them firmly that you are working and set the timer. Explain that when the bell rings, you will be available.

Even a wait of ten minutes will begin to train children that you are there, but that instant gratification is not always possible. As they get older, you can stretch the time between bells.

Tell older children what your time may mean to the family unit. For example: "I know you want to tell me your news right now, but I am working on a deadline. When I finish this project, I will earn three hundred dollars for our family budget, which will mean new shoes for you. I care about you and can give you my undivided time at four thirty. Okay?"

Put a dollar value on your time. When tempted to stop work-for-pay to wander aimlessly in the house, ask yourself, "What is my time worth today? When I finish this quilt or write this pattern, I will have earned five hundred dollars. The next hour is worth fifty dollars to me. Do I want to trade fifty dollars for TV now?"

It is you who must communicate to housemates, "I am sorry, I cannot stop now, I am working." Answer the phone when it rings—but answering machines are better. When you are working, say so: "I am working on a deadline just now. May I call you back this afternoon, or is this evening better?"

Workaholics, note: You are the other extreme of this problem. If your family comes to resent your work, set definite "open" and "closed" hours for your business. Here are some ideas:

+ Buy a plastic clock with moveable hands, like the ones shop owners use. Start work on time and set the hands to closing time. Let your family know exactly when you will be available. Stop when you promised.
+ If a real emergency exists, you can make exceptions, but too many emergencies signal an unfocused or unrealistic work schedule. Work on weekends or late into the night only when needed to avoid burnout.
+ Set up a particular room in which to work, if possible. Assume the attitude that you are working for someone else when you enter this room. Allow no distractions; remove TVs and other diversions.
+ Many of us have a set of work clothes, whether they are overalls, a suit, or jeans. If possible, put on an apron or place a towel in your back pocket. This "uniform" will announce to the world and yourself that you are working. Take the uniform off when you leave the workplace. This is a sign that you are granting permission for your worker (you) to eat lunch, get coffee, or rest. Make sure you are clear and focused about it.
+ How long is lunch? Set a time and use it. This was a hard task for me to learn. I work from 8:00 AM to 9:30 PM. I can see the improvement in my stamina now that I take a whole hour for lunch. I leave my studio to eat. No more eating as I work. I watch the noon news and relax, but return to my studio at 1:00. As a workaholic, I have benefited from using self-discipline to rest, not to work more.
+ Set a few rooms in the house where work is not done or discussed. Start with your bedroom and dining room. Save these places for relaxation and family or personal activities.

✦ You may prefer to set a "quitting time," such as 6:00 PM, when work is no longer the main event. Then, be attentive to your own needs and those of your family.

✦ I work Saturdays in my studio or office, but quitting time comes earlier than on weekdays. Sunday work is out except for very pressing matters. Time to relax and enjoy life, family, church, and friends.

✦ Set a regular time for exercise and physical fitness. Do it days or evenings, but do it at least three times per week. We workaholics tend to neglect our body's needs in favor of working more.

✦ Set up a reward system for yourself. Remember, no employer will offer you incentives. If you finish earlier than expected one day, do not begin the next day's duties. Take the extra time for something pleasing and relaxing. Read a book. Work in your garden. When you earn playtime, then *play*, or your inner self will soon conclude there is no payoff in accomplishment and your self-motivation may suffer. Recreation is your reward. Enjoy being at home when you have finished your work-for-pay. Consciously tell yourself your work is over for the day and assume your "at-home" role.

Bear in mind that the ultimate goal of working from home is to lessen tensions and increase earnings. The best way to do this is through efficient work habits and a clear, well-maintained distinction between you the professional and you relaxing at home.

Managing a home while conducting an efficient business challenges everyone. Doing so when you *work* where you *live* magnifies that challenge. Distractions wait around every corner. Telephones, doorbells, pets, and neighbors may search you out, saying, "But you're home anyway." Frequent interruptions from small children and other housemates can undo even the most organized work schedule. Thus, the secret to success for home-based crafters is to keep professional and personal worlds organized and well managed, but separate.

Recently, professional quilt members belonging to a daily e-mail list, *QuiltDesigners@yahoogroups.com*, wrote in asking questions about organizing their time better when working from home, and even more shared their tips and ideas. The common problem among these busy quilters concerned what to do about interruptions from others when working from home.

Wheat Carr, a publisher of designer patterns and online list member, commented, "I believe that interruptions are not the problem; rather, they are the symptom. The problem is a lack of planned schedule and the discipline to stick to it. Once you have that in place, you can deal with interruptions with a 'Sorry, but I am up against a deadline, talk to you later.' The trick is to run your life on your schedule, not someone else's."

Some people prefer to work all day on their business two or three days a week, and attend to personal or household tasks on the remaining days. Others work on business tasks until lunchtime and tend to home-related jobs during the afternoons. Still others work at their business all week and save household responsibilities for the weekends. Choose the style that suits you, your energy level, and your family obligations.

The important thing is to create a manageable work schedule, prioritize your chores, and prevent yourself from becoming waylaid. If you think this sounds like it takes discipline, you are correct. Managing your life, home, and quiltmaking business must be taken seriously if you wish to succeed. Continue to modify your work schedule until it suits your personality, work style, and responsibilities. Sooner or later, you will find the perfect schedule. Make it your regular routine. The purpose of all this is to become the best worker you can possibly be for your favorite employer—yourself!

Defining and Achieving Your Goals

Defining your goals is the first step in achieving them. Take time to outline your goals, comparing them frequently with your day-to-day activities. Spend most of your time working on the tasks that lead directly to your goals.

Ask yourself why earning money from quilting is important to you. Do you want to contribute to your household income or start a savings account? Maybe you want to buy a new sewing machine or computer. Do you want money to buy unlimited quilting supplies?

Finding answers to these questions will help you define your long-term goals. If you don't know how much you want to earn or what an opportunity means to you, you may not become motivated enough to do your best. List your goals, being as specific as possible. Here are a few examples:

You want to earn $3,000 to buy a new electronic sewing machine.

You want to earn enough to buy all of the fabric and books you want.

You want to earn enough to pay all your expenses to a major quilting seminar each year.

Once you define your goals and are committed to them, post your goal list alongside your work schedule, where you can regularly check your progress. Each time you complete a goal, acknowledge it. Put a star beside it on your list or mark it with a highlighter pen.

Create incentives (other than food) to keep yourself moving forward. Buy a piece of equipment you have been wanting, or take time to read a new quilting book. Give yourself a pat on the back so your subconscious mind feels acknowledged. Since you do not have an employer to praise you, you must reward yourself.

Do some goals remain elusive? If so, avoid negative thinking. Determine the reason they are elusive. If the goal was too ambitious, simplify it. If you lacked motivation, ask yourself why. What got in your way? What can you do to improve next week?

Entrepreneurial Characteristics You Should Have

Working where you live, even part-time, becomes easier if you have or can develop a few special personality characteristics. According to the Small Business Administration (SBA), certain personality traits contribute more to success in business than the amount of money you invest.

Self-motivation heads the list. This refers to the ability to work on specific chores without anyone prodding you to get started or to keep working. You must have the drive to keep yourself moving forward.

Reliability comes next. Does procrastination derail you? Like Scarlett O'Hara, do you put off until tomorrow what you should do today? Do you only work when you feel like it? Do you often misplace things, only to find yourself searching for something you need but cannot find? If this describes you, step back and reconsider. Though procrastination may not disrupt your personal life, it contributes to the downfall of many entrepreneurs—part-time or full-time.

The ability to cope is also important. To profit from your quilting skills, your customers and students must be able to depend on you. Do you come through in a pinch? If a time crunch occurs, how well do you cope? Successful entrepreneurs have contingency plans. They prepare for the unexpected and have a plan of action ready when it happens. Do you?

The ability to prioritize is critical. Do you meet your deadlines? If you promise a finished quilt to a customer by the first of next month, do you stand behind your word? Meeting deadlines must take precedence over mundane matters such as organizing your fabric or designing your next project. If you develop the ability to rank tasks and deadlines in order of importance, you have won half the battle when working from home.

Time Management Skills

I have operated a home-based design and teaching studio for many years. The following tips help keep everything running smoothly. Students sometimes think I have a live-in maid or no family at all. Neither is the case. I owe my organizational thinking to a parochial school education, where orderly habits were part of the curriculum. It is never too late to implement better habits in your working life.

Know Your Goals

The purpose of using time more effectively is to gather what is wasted and put it to better use for something of value. What is important to you? Why is it important? Begin the organizing process by answering these two questions.

Imagine yourself needing to travel out of state to give a lecture. Your destination is the goal. Earning income and broadening your contacts are the reasons the trip is important. If you do not know where you are going or why you are going, you may not have the motivation needed to keep moving toward your goals. And, if you do not know how much you will earn or what the opportunity means to your career, you may not become inspired enough to do your best.

Serious quilters in the industry organize and plan an important business trip carefully. But how many of us give the same importance to planning our entire life's work? As professionals, we owe it to ourselves to plan our entire career with as much care as we would give to planning one automobile trip to deliver an important lecture.

Once you have defined your goals and committed to them, do monthly reviews. Check your progress. Have you reached some of your goals? If not, be sure of the reason. If the plan was too ambitious, modify it.

Set Your Priorities

If goals are like the destination of your trip, priorities are road markers to get you there. Once you know your goals and commit to them, you can set sensible, attainable priorities. Using the example of the long car trip, your priorities would be prearranged stops for rest, food, and fuel along the way. Priorities are planned events leading directly to clearly stated goals, which in turn manage your work and your life.

When you are clear about goals, setting priorities becomes even clearer. Whenever you are asked to take on something new, ask yourself this before answering: "Will this new activity lead me to my stated goals? If not, will I have time for it without sacrificing my goals and priorities?"

Become focused on where you are going and how you will get there. Maintaining a strong focus helps to eliminate unnecessary distractions and respond to unexpected requests for your time. Then, you can be more confident when you say "no." This is because you determined beforehand what particular activities would divert you from your planned goals and priorities.

Treat your quilting activities like a business as you make the transition from hobby to profitable enterprise. Remember that the IRS expects you to make every effort to earn a profit if you want to deduct expenses. This requires financial organization and bookkeeping skills.

Get It All Done with Action Boards and Monthly Action Lists

Do you keep talking about the wonderful ideas you have to help your quilting business grow? Do you post little notes everywhere in your studio to remind you of what you want to do—someday? Stop procrastinating! Stop wishing you had time to carry out your ideas. Make them happen now.

An effective technique to bring a new business to life, brainstorm for new ideas, or just problem-solve is the *action board*. Make your plans a reality with this simple, effective concept.

Action boards work well for one person or several. Participants can be employees, your spouse, grown children, good friends, or anyone else who cares about your business success. Give each person a three-inch-square tablet of Post-Its.

Begin by discussing exactly what you wish to achieve. Think specifics, not generalities. "Making more money" is too broad. Do you want to sell more products? Perhaps you want to increase foot traffic in your home-based shop. Do you want to see more of your quilting designs published in magazines? Do you want to teach more classes? Exactly what do you want to accomplish?

Whether you work with others or alone, set a time limit of one week for brainstorming. Instruct all participants to take their little notepad everywhere they go, day and night. Ideas can come anytime, so be ready. Agree not to exchange notes or share information during this period.

Each person should write down only *one* idea per piece of paper. Look for every possible solution or action that may contribute to the agreed-upon objective.

To be effective, do not dismiss any idea as too simple, obvious, or impractical. Set no limits on generating ideas. Do not listen to negative criticism from anyone.

Do not prioritize the notes; instead, make time for this later. Just search your mind for every idea that can potentially lead your business toward its goal. At the end of a week's time, the fun begins. Use a bulletin board, a wall, or a table. Have each person stick each little note face-up. Each participant should look over all the ideas. Eliminate any duplicate ideas, but nothing else!

Now, begin to put all ideas in priority order. Move the notes around, placing the most promising ideas and those to consider at the top of the board. The advantage of those gummed little notes now becomes apparent. You can rearrange them as often as necessary.

Look for the next-most useful idea and place it beneath the first. Continue in this way until all the ideas are in a rough priority order. Stand back and look them over. Take a few days to discuss all the possibilities offered by the group. If you work alone, use this time to consider all ideas. Rearrange the slips of paper into a new priority system as you think them through. It is surprising how many notions you can generate this way. Depending on the number of persons involved, creative energy can be doubled or tripled to benefit both the business and the owners.

When people feel free to draw from their creativity unhampered by judgments from others, more ideas and solutions can surface. Evaluate each one on its own merit. Respect each other's ideas and freely compliment the others on innovative thoughts and concepts you had never considered before.

Rearrange the notes into a permanent priority order that everyone involved agrees upon. Now, with a pencil in hand, assign a deadline to each action. Set a starting date to begin the entire new system.

Continue to date each slip of paper, allowing adequate time to complete each task. Erase and re-date as needed. Continue until everyone involved agrees with the new schedule and tasks are within practical reach.

If more than one person helps with tasks in your business, go back over each slip. Distribute the responsibilities fairly. Do this by encouraging each person to choose one chore from among all of them.

Bear in mind the areas in which each person is most competent. When each person has selected a task, begin round two. Allow each person to select again. Continue the process, alternating choices until all the tasks have been assigned. Have each person initial and date each chore for which he or she is responsible. When everyone is satisfied, transfer the information from the notes, in priority order, to a sheet of paper.

At the bottom of the sheet, agree upon a date when all the tasks are to be completed and the new system for growth and improvement is to be in place. Have each participant sign and date the document. Place it where everyone will see and refer to it often. Post copies on the refrigerator door, your office or studio door, on cupboards and bulletin boards. This will keep the ultimate goal of the business in the front of everyone's conscious mind. It encourages everyone, whether you are a single quilter working alone or part of a team effort, to keep fixed on the objective and to work at it steadily.

Cross off each task as it is completed, letting the person who brought it to completion initial and date the accomplished task. Compliment each other only on completed tasks. Avoid criticizing what remains undone. This will be obvious to everyone who looks at the list.

Your Action List provides a monthly "to do" schedule. Tasks and chores appearing on the list should lead to both short- and long-term goals. Refer to it often. See at a glance what you have accomplished and what remains. Remember to think of the list as a daily itinerary to keep you on track, leading to your ultimate destination: a successful part- or full-time quilting career.

Update your monthly list faithfully and you will never have the dilemma of remaining undecided about what to do next. Since your list ranks tasks by priority, you will always be able to decide immediately how to best spend your time and energy.

I store and update my monthly Action List on my computer. Each month, I delete completed chores. I carry those left undone into the new month and print out a new copy. It sits on my desk in plain sight. During the month, I date each task as I finish it to indicate "mission accomplished." Indeed, this type of self-awareness and recognition bolsters self-esteem. Think of each task you complete as a promise made and kept to the self, which results in self-assurance.

Procrastination means breaking promises made to the self. If we indulge in it regularly, the resulting disappointment damages our self-esteem. Regular procrastination makes us feel as though we have failed. We lose self-confidence. We begin to question our ability to conduct a successful business. We weaken our sense of self-reliance. Inside, we feel cheated. We become our own worst enemies.

Think of your Action List as an action plan that can become a marketing plan, a business plan, or simply a future growth plan for your teaching business. More about converting your Action List to a business plan can be found in chapter 2.

The important issue is for spouses, partners, employees, and/or owners to cooperate in the project. Achieving the goals will benefit the business, while cooperation between participants will enhance relationships. This, in turn, encourages everyone's resourcefulness and stimulates self-esteem. The business wins! The relationships win!

CHAPTER CONTRIBUTOR:
WHEAT CARR
e-mail: *wheat@craftwolf.com*

A Business Plan for Creative Quilters and Sewers

"You have such talent! Why continue giving away your lovely quilts when you can sell them? Go into business. Turn your skill into cash!"

Many professional quilters started their careers after being urged on by this familiar advice from friends and family. Affirmations and encouragement such as this are valuable. We treasure important people in our lives who sincerely praise and appreciate our skill. Yet, as you read in chapter 1, to succeed, you must clearly understand the difference between hobby and business. Entrepreneurs who believe that their quilting passion will substitute for business skills are in for a surprise. A quilter who opens a shop armed only with her love of fabric is heading for trouble. Enthusiasm matters, but it takes business skills to turn your hobby into a profitable business.

Can you make the transition to seeing quilting as an income-earning opportunity rather than as a pleasant hobby? Can you set aside your personal tastes and preferences while you observe industry trends objectively? And the most critical question: Will you make a sincere effort to learn business essentials like marketing, bookkeeping, customer service, and product information? A good business plan will provide answers for all these questions.

Business Plans Defined—Plan for Success

Alice in Wonderland asks the Cheshire Cat, "Would you please tell me which way I should go from here?" The cat replies, "That depends on where you want to go, otherwise it does not matter which way you go."

A definition I like is: *"The difference between a dream and a goal is a plan!"*

Often, when I ask students in my college classes if they have written a business plan, many assure me that they have. When I ask to see it, they tell me their business plan is in their head. Sorry, but *if your business plan is not in writing, you have no plan!* It shows you have not given your business top priority. My response to those wanting to start a business with no plan is to ask, "Without a plan, how will you measure success and recognize when you have met your goals?"

Another typical response I receive from students and clients when asking about their business plan is: "I am just too busy to write out a business plan." Here are some of my interpretations of the meanings behind that statement:

I do not *want* to take time from making money for unimportant paperwork. My business is small. Business plans do not benefit me.

Business plans require writing. I cannot write.
I am an artist, not a bookkeeper.
Organize my business on paper? Why?
I have no need for a loan, so why waste time writing? Who will read it anyway?

My reply? The most important reader of your plan, the one who must scrutinize it regularly, is you!

Three Reasons to Make a Business Plan

First, writing a plan provides the invaluable experience of imprinting a picture of your business on your brain. Researching, gathering, and organizing information, putting it into a logical sequence, and typing and editing are all steps that will remain in your conscious and subconscious mind.

Second, you will have an easier time making decisions when guided by the goals and priorities in your plan that you decided upon previously.

Third, if you need a loan to start your business or to buy equipment later, you *must* have a business plan to present to a loan officer. And the one in your head is not acceptable. Employers, clients, agencies, and others who want to help or hire you, or bring business your way, may ask to see a business plan. Your CPA will use it to set up your books and assess your business at tax time too.

A business plan is a detailed guide to plot the course of your business and to prepare for problems before they arise. A good plan provides goals and direction. Use it to measure the actual performance of your business when you compare what you planned with what actually happened. Business plans should:

+ Assess your ideas.
+ Develop your point of view and marketplace niche.
+ Help you set reachable goals in logical sequence.

A Road Map to Success

Imagine driving across the U.S. from coast to coast alone. Would you start your trip by merely backing your car out of the driveway on any random day? Do you find the destination so exciting that planning seems unnecessary?

What does cruise control mean to you? Does it mean your car will take you where you want to go, automatically? Do the terms "positive thinking" and "hope for the best" sound like appropriate travel guides to you? Should you lose your way during your journey, how confident do you feel that someone will come to the rescue? Will all Good Samaritans who offer help be experts on your needs? Would you begin a long auto trip such as this prepared only with these thoughts in mind?

Incredible as it sounds, many creative quilters start a new business with these concepts as their only tools. They begin their careers prepared only with a passion for their art and the wish to make a profit. They feel confident that their dedication will see them through any obstacle. They just cannot wait to begin! They can be rather like novice quilters attending their first workshop. They do not want to listen to the preparatory instructions the teacher offers. They just have to start sewing immediately.

Evaluating your business realistically and accurately, as I have already outlined, requires more thought than planning a cross-country trip. Driving from coast to coast will take only a few days or weeks out of your life, but a successful career can last a lifetime.

To succeed in any business, especially one that others perceive as recreational, you must take control. Choose your own route. Make your own decisions. Leave nothing to chance. Three wonderful, efficient tools will help point you toward success:

+ An Action Board. (You learned how to make one in chapter 1.)
+ A Business Plan.
+ A Marketing Plan. (See chapter 5.)

You have seen how the action board described at the end of the last chapter can help you gather and organize information. A marketing plan will help you aim your advertising and selling techniques by identifying your target market. A business plan becomes your customized road map to help assure your success. There is no magic, only hard work, dedication, and organization.

Let us go back to the analogy of the coast-to-coast auto trip in chapter 1 again. Suppose you plan to attend an important quilt convention in New York and you live in California. You have been asked to serve on a panel to speak about your quilting patterns upon arriving. You value the networking opportunity and the chance to promote yourself and your business. Are you armed only with a mental business plan? If so, you would begin your trip with no road maps or advance reservations—just a travel plan in your head. No sense wasting time and paper planning. No time for choosing routes or locating overnight lodging. Instinct will guide you. Merely point your car east. Not to worry, you will *feel* your way as you go. Allow yourself several days to travel leisurely. If your first scheduled appointment looms forward too suddenly, you can drive faster. You want to be flexible, right? Just cut back a little on sleep and motivate yourself to cover more miles for the last day or two. Things will take care of themselves!

"Attitude is the important thing," you tell yourself. "Expect the best and fly by the seat of your pants. There will be plenty of time to solve problems when they occur. Why worry in advance?"

Now, how many people would undertake a cross-country trip this way? Not I! How about you? Let's make a plan. In fact, let's dust off what we learned in junior high school about making formal outlines to organize ideas. You thought you would never need them in real life? Think again! The classic outline system is the perfect tool for creating a business plan for your new career.

I've heard the saying, "If timing is everything, planning is everything else." Many new business owners become intimidated when they first learn they should have a business plan. Think of it as a collection of notes, plans, and ideas to guide you in helping your business grow in the most profitable direction.

If you apply for a business loan, however small, your banker will request a business plan, but this is not the only reason you should have one. Financial advisors and your tax preparer may want to see it too. However, I repeat emphatically, you are the most important person who will read your plan.

Preparing the information and organizing and researching it provides you with practical direction in marketing, advertising, and bookkeeping. Theoretically, your plan will guide you as you make decisions, set policies, and make contingency plans. Think of it as a road map that will help you find your way through unfamiliar territory step by step.

Business plans need not take weeks to prepare. Use common, everyday language. Go back to that class you took in eighth grade about making an outline to organize information. Those Roman numerals and capital letters form an easy, sensible way to gather and organize your information. I have prepared dozens of business plans for those who do not type or do not have access to a computer, and I *always* use them.

Copy my business plan headings below and begin to fill in the blanks as you read this book. Complete each heading as thoroughly as possible. Do not assume every reader of your plan will know all the nuances of your business. Tell them concisely and precisely in your plan. Skip all sections that do not apply to you or for which you have no answers yet. Just begin.

Expand my outline as you add information into your computer. It is only an empty outline now, but will become a map you refer to as you plan your coast-to-coast auto trip. Think of it as a living document or business journal where you will make entries every day. You will learn more answers to round out your outline in the chapters to come. Don't worry about things you don't know now. Start with what you do know. I will be throwing a lot of information at you in this book. Use it! Organize it! Research what you don't know, and the first draft of *your* business plan will begin to emerge.

A Business Plan Outline for You

I. Title Page
Begin with a title page stating that the following contents are a "Business Plan" for: (name your business, e.g., Mary's Quilting Studio). Two inches from the bottom left, place your own name, address, phone, fax, and e-mail.

II. Table of Contents
When you have completed your plan, create a table of contents that lists in sequence all of the categories of information and their page numbers. Make sure to number each page of your plan.

III. Executive Summary

In one or two pages, present a brief overview of the entire plan. You may find it easier to do this after you have completed it, but nonetheless, it is the first section of a formal, written business plan. The executive summary of a business plan should not be a mere listing of topics contained in the body of the business plan. That describes the table of contents. The executive summary should emphasize the key issues presented in the plan. A critical point to communicate in the executive summary is your company's distinctive competence—the factors that will make your company successful in a competitive market.

IV. Mission Statement

Explain why you chose your business and how you feel about it. Express enthusiasm about your craft and why you believe it will suit you and lead to business success. One or possibly two pages are enough here.

V. Legal Structure

State whether you run your business as a sole proprietorship, a partnership, or a corporation. If you chose a fictitious name for your business, note it. You must use *both* your first and last name in your business name, or file a Fictitious Name form with the County Clerk's Office in the county you reside in. More about this in chapter 13.

VI. Owner Information

State who owns your business, with your address and phone number. If it is a partnership, include this information for each person involved, but not for employees. This information is required on all Fictitious Name forms to comply with full disclosure about your business.

VII. Personal History

List your qualifications and experience here. Include a copy of your résumé in this section. Include past business experiences you have had that qualify you to begin or expand your business. Include formal education and a synopsis of quilting workshops and education you bring to your business. If you have been published or had any articles written about you, include several (not an overwhelming number) here as well.

VIII. Type of Business

The terms "crafts" or even "quilting" are too general to describe your business. Explain whether you are manufacturing, wholesaling, retailing, exhibiting, designing, or writing about quilting. Describe the nature of your business completely. Quilting may be your passion, but readers of your plan need to know what quilters and craftspeople do. I identify myself as a fiber artist when introducing myself to new college classes. For many years, I have noted that no one really knows what this means until I explain it. Explain it in your business plan as if the reader knows nothing about it.

IX. Product Description
Describe your product. Include photographs, color ads, and fliers. Quilters who will perform services may conclude this section does not apply to them, but it does. Your service *is* your product. If you quilt, design, finish, bind, or restore quilts, explain!

X. Company Background
If you are starting a business from scratch, delete this section. However, if you are expanding or modifying an existing business, provide background information about the company, followed by the proposed changes.

XI. Business Objective
Do not be tempted to write "Make a profit" as your objective. Every business wants a profit. Perhaps your goal is to create a new fusible paper. Maybe you have a new system for writing instructions. Do you want to expand your teaching from local shops and schools to a national or international level? If so, state your purpose clearly.

XII. Product Benefits
Completing this section will be of tremendous importance when you begin to write advertising copy for your new business. State the benefits of your product or service from the point of view of consumers. Will learning become easier for them? Will your new textile paint dry faster? Are your patterns easier to follow than others?

XIII. Marketing Plan
Coming up in chapter 5.

XIV. Implementation Startup Timetable
Create a timeline of dates, proposing when each task will be completed.

XV. Budget Proposal, Funds Required, and Their Uses
List exactly how much money you need to begin and how you will use it.

XVI. Monthly Expenses
Make out a budget listing all expected expenses.

XVII. Cash Flow Statement
Show how much you expect to earn and how you will balance earnings with your business expenses.

XVIII. Prior Cash Flow Statement
Provide your actual Cash Flow Statement from the previous year, if you were already in business.

XIX. Proprietary Rights
Coming up in chapter 14.
   A. Copyrights
   B. Trademarks
   C. Patents

XX. Industry Data
Support the wisdom of starting your new business by offering an overview of the industry. I remember a client who asked me to prepare her business plan to sell beaded products for the sewing and quilting trade. I asked who else was making this specific bead item. She replied that no one else had thought of her idea (not true!), and that *everyone* would want to buy her product (far from true!).

The woman knew nothing about the industry she was entering. She was beginning a new business venture with only one thought in mind: how much *she* loved the product. Lack of knowledge leads to lack of preparation, which in turn leads to failure.

Prove your preparation and industry awareness by answering the following questions: How many people quilt in the U.S.? How many magazines are published? Perhaps you can find figures on how many quilters purchase their raw materials from mail-order catalogs as opposed to the Internet. Do many quilters in your field of expertise teach classes? How big is each portion of the industry? You don't know? Study the trade journals in your field and find out!

Include statistics and other relevant information about quilting, sewing, and the crafting business in general. You will find such information in quilt magazines and craft trade journals. Pretend that you must justify to someone else why you have chosen the quilting business. Support your choice by including copies of articles, reports, and surveys. Make sure you include information about the quilting industry survey as issued every third year. The most recent *The Quilting in America*™ *Survey*: Commissioned by: *Quilter's Newsletter Magazine* a Primedia Publication & International Quilt Market & Festival, a division of Quilts, Inc., Prepared by: NFO, Inc. and ABACUS Custom Research, Inc. See chapter 4 for survey details.

XXI. Other Supportive Data and Attachments
This is the last section in a business plan. It is the place in your business plan to insert photocopies of magazine articles about your industry. Choose a variety from business magazines, trade journals, and consumer publications, and make your case to support your decision as if you were an attorney!

Are you feeling a bit overstimulated? Good! Get started today to reach your dream of earning dollars in exchange for your quilting skills! I hope you take my advice and copy my basic outline for your business plan into your computer.

I have prepared business plans for many clients using this outline, expanding it to as many as fifty pages as I learned more about the client's business. I learned about importing shellfish, selling bicycles, and buying a music shop. If I learned about subjects I knew little to nothing about before I began, think of what *you* will learn about how to start up, operate, and profit from your quilting business when you *do* know something about it already. Now that you have seen the bare outline, other chapters in this book will provide you with the details you need to help you expand it until it becomes a plan you can proudly present to a bank or an investor.

Designing for the Quilting and Sewing Market

Q uilting today is BIG business! The latest Quilting in America study (2003, *www.quiltersvillage.com/qinamer03/*), says, "The market continues to grow, with 15 percent of U.S. households reporting quilting participation. Total quilters in the U.S. now exceed 21 million, a 50 percent increase from the 14 million quilters reported in 1997. With each quilter spending an average of $139.70, the estimated total dollar value of the quilting industry stands at $2.27 billion."

Travel to Houston every October to see the International Quilt Market—the largest trade show in the world for the quilting industry. Shop owners, teachers, writers, designers, and manufacturers come from all over the world to buy from more than six hundred merchant booths.

Quilters demand more tools, books, and patterns every year. Quilt addicts cannot seem to buy enough quilting patterns, which is why those who make patterns have a chapter in this book to themselves.

Defining Original Design

Webster's Dictionary defines "o•rig•i•nal" as:

1. Arising or proceeding independently; inventive.
2. Created, undertaken, presented for the first time.

From the same source, "de•sign":

1. To prepare preliminary plans to execute a work.
2. To plan and fashion artistically or skillfully.
3. To form or conceive in the mind; contrive; plan.

Manufacturers, magazine editors, and buyers eagerly seek designs from talented newcomers. However, submitted designs *must* be original. An item is *not* original if it is:

+ Made from a kit or variations
+ Made from a commercial pattern or variations
+ Made as a workshop project with input from a professional teacher
+ Made following instructions from a magazine

✦ Copied from a copyrighted design, pattern, or work of another
✦ Copied from an existing project
✦ Copied from a pattern, object, or instructions, but containing different colors, dimensions, or other changes

Originality means so much to editors who buy designs that, early in negotiations, they ask you to sign a document verifying that your work originated with you. Changing one or two elements of an existing design does not constitute "original" design.

Literature on copyright infringement defines this practice as "making derivative copies." Only the original copyright holder may profit from modifications of the original design. Copyright law prevents others from doing so. Penalties severely damage the career of quilters who violate these statutes. Look around you for ideas for original designs. Nature overflows with them. Start your next project from the very beginning, as defined by *Webster's*. Begin with your own drawings, charts, photos—not the work of others. More about copyright can be found in chapter 14.

Editors and manufacturers who buy your work may buy "all rights." This means you cannot sell an original design a second time without permission. When possible, try to sell only "first rights." This means you offer a magazine the right to publish the design for the first time, with all rights reverting to you after publication.

Selling a Design More than Once

Since you are the only person who can make derivative copies and variations based upon your designs, you may continue to profit from your original pattern—as long as you do not sell all rights. If you sell all rights, the person who will be able to make derivatives of the pattern and make a profit will be the buyer—not you. Below are twelve ways in which I profited from a pair of geometric designs embroidered on canvas. From the time I began work on these 12″ × 12″ projects, the reactions from others indicated they might become very popular.

"Warm as Gold" and "Cool as Silver" are both embroidered with silk floss and metallic threads. Both starburst designs feature an unworked background backed by foil paper so that a glow shows beneath the canvas holes. Both use identical stitching patterns and are exactly the same size.

"Warm as Gold" begins with gold thread in the center followed by the gradated, warm colors of the color wheel. "Cool as Silver," conversely, begins with silver thread followed by cool colors. This pair generated more income than any other work I have created before or since. Each piece cost $12 for threads and canvas, plus $8 for each frame. Revenues exceeded $4,000 in just one year. Note that I did not receive complimentary supplies or endorsement fees, as I was a relatively no-name teacher at the time. Here is how to extract all the profit potential from a solitary design.

1. Write a how-to article so readers can make the project. The magazine that purchased my designs "Warm as Gold" and "Cool as Silver" bought first rights. After publication, in a needlepoint magazine, rights reverted to me.
2. Write an article about an aspect of the design process. Many magazines feature in-depth articles about a single aspect in a work without publishing a complete set of instructions. I wrote an article about how I used a color wheel to select the careful gradations I chose to create special effects.
3. Place a classified ad in craft magazines and sell the item in a kit format by mail order. Many excellent crafters do not have an interest in or inclination to design their own projects, preferring work designed by others.
4. Sell the completed item by mail order to customers who do not craft. Home decor items appeal to a broad market, and many people buy ready-made crafts. If you have a surge of orders, enlist the help of people who can help you produce enough products to satisfy demand.
5. Rent a booth at craft shows, trade shows, or fairs. Sell completed projects or take orders to do custom work.
6. Give demonstrations to interested groups to generate interest in your work. Distribute brochures listing your line of goods and services. When I did this, I was hired to judge a show nearby.
7. Attend a street fair so others can observe you at work. I accepted an invitation to participate in an outdoor craft fair. The show featured local artists at work. I displayed my pair of matched designs as I worked on others. This resulted in teaching assignments and custom orders.
8. Give a workshop to help others make their own version of the item, teaching them basic skills. Teachers need appealing designs to inspire others wanting to learn specific techniques.
9. Write a project booklet giving complete instructions, drawings, and photos to recreate the item. Sell the booklet in shops, classes, or by mail order.
10. Enter exhibits and fairs where you can advertise your piece for sale.
11. When you feel a design has no more income-earning potential, give it as a deductible donation in a raffle or door prize. Such visibility becomes a profitable marketing tool.
12. Wait several years and do it again. In my example, the designs were first published in 1979, but in 1992, the magazine asked permission to reprint the original article and instructions for a slightly reduced price. I happily agreed.

Color and Design Trends

I love the coloring books published by Dover Publications and other publishers meant for doodling and coloring with felt pens. I have countless such books, showing flowers, birds, butterflies, and my favorites, stained-glass designs. Dover Books has a Pictorial Archive Series that is copyright-free, so you may use their designs in any way you like.

Add a color wheel, or preferably several, to your quilting supplies. They contribute the most to successful, original designs. Keep up with color trends by checking in with the Color Marketing Group and others on the Web (*www.colormarketing.org*). One of the joys of designing lies in choosing and playing with colors.

Consider the Color Association, which keeps you current with the latest color trends in their free e-bulletin, *Colorful*. You can sign up for a free subscription at *www.colorassociation.com/site/mailinglist.html*. Another site I check on often is Pantone, *www.pantone.com/pantone.asp*. Color and design books by international colorist Johannes Itten are simply the best resource for color theory. I cannot live without them.

Since color and design are such vast topics, you will find dozens of books and Web sites to research, but for the moment, let us return to our prime subject in this chapter—designing.

Should You Design Only What Is Highly Profitable?

Quilt hobbyists usually begin designing to please the self, while professionals spend their time designing items with the greatest profit potential. Sooner or later, both groups face a common dilemma.

Should a quilter make endless potholders, for example, because customers always snatch them up at craft fairs? How many can one manufacture before the definition of "handcrafted" becomes "handmade by assembly line?"

More questions arise. "Will I burn out by overproducing a particular item just because it pays the bills? Will buyers hesitate if they see too many identical products? Might they conclude that the uniqueness of such an item is compromised?"

On the other hand, the artist within us frequently demands self-expression. If we use all our energy to work and never "play," frustration follows. "I work so hard that I never have time to make what I want anymore," successful artisans lament. "I do not want to feel like a production machine."

It takes discipline to keep working on a product that bores you. Must we personally like everything we create for sale? Does quality suffer when we push ourselves to work with colors or textures that we no longer find pleasing? When do we get to have fun? While I do not presume to have all the answers, I have a few suggestions that may help you face this dilemma.

First, why must it be one way or the other? Crafters of all types often conclude that they must either mass-produce sure-to-sell pieces or earn less if they take time out to explore their medium. "How can I preserve my integrity as an artisan and maintain enthusiasm?" they wonder. Why not compromise and make room for both profit and nurturing the artist within?

Protect the Artist Within

If, like me, you are concerned with the possible burnout of your creativity by making too many identical products or spending 100 percent of your time producing, consider my solution. Determine how many hours per month you work at your craft. Set aside a portion of total work time to produce the items that pay the bills, say, 80 percent or 85 percent. Reserve the remaining time to nurture your creativity. Many argue, "How can I justify setting aside so much time that does not generate dollars?"

My answer? Look at the benefits you will reap by allocating time for research and experimentation. If you think of it as "wasting time," guilt and frustration may follow. Creative time spent developing my technique encourages artistic growth. It is not unproductive simply because it does not directly generate income. Creative time generates style, skill, expertise, proficiency, and facility. In short, it nourishes the artist within. Here are a few of the ideas I use during my "creative time."

- ✦ Visit museums and galleries.
- ✦ Go through every magazine you can. Tear out pages that inspire you. I used an ad in a motoring magazine for an interesting vanishing point, and the cover of a church hymnal inspired the colors and flowing shapes in a wall quilt.
- ✦ Manufacturers send me new products. I would never have had access to new products such as new bonding agents, textile paints, and embellishments without the generosity of manufacturers who send complimentary products to designers like me. I experiment to see how I might use them in future designs.
- ✦ Buy spools of thread in weights and colors you usually do not buy to see how they behave in your sewing machine with different stitch settings.
- ✦ I dye fabric scraps and old clothes to observe how the dyes mix or what new colors and variations I can achieve. Dyeing my own fabric scraps provides an endless supply of unusual colors over prints or solids, which in turn end up in my quilts.

The Importance of Playing with New Materials

Creative time provides an opportunity to explore new design concepts. It provides a chance to experiment with new materials—to familiarize yourself with the latest fibers, colors, styles, tools, and fabric, of course. Playing with fabric, color, and thread provides the opportunity for serendipity—a booster shot for your career. Time spent broadening one's skill results in improved quality for future sales.

End guilt by telling yourself that you assigned this time to develop and nourish your artistic integrity. Think of it as maintenance time for your most valued machine—yourself.

Professional quilters, at times, may encounter another problem. Sometimes we find that after creating "special pieces," it is too painful to part with them. Again, compromise. If the artist knows that not everything created from the heart will be sold for dollars, the inner self will feel satisfied. When we guarantee that we will occasionally make an item for ourselves, we feel better. We find it easier to sell most items if we know we can keep a few favorites.

Quilting for profit does not mean you must ignore your own creative needs. Both aspects can live in harmony if each receives respect and its own scheduled time. Moderation in the creative process provides balance. Thus, we can avoid feeling too commercial, frivolous, self-indulgent, or worse, and ultimately, we can fend off burnout.

Nourish Your Creativity

Do you believe creativity is learned or innate? Is one simply born with or without it? I believe strongly that not only can we learn it, but we must also study and develop our design ability. Creativity does not begin on paper, from a book, or with raw materials. It begins in the right side of the brain, which houses our creative self. Here is how I see the process:

First, relax your body so your mind can begin to visualize. The mind projects its ideas on a mental screen and begins the process of organizing images.

Next, begin to make choices. Drop some ideas in favor of others. For example, ask yourself, "What do I want my hands to make?" You may reject choices such as pottery, chocolate cakes, and floral arrangements if fascinated by fabric and thread.

Continue to narrow your choices. "What will satisfy the creative urge?" the mind asks. One more wall hanging, a bed quilt, a quilted garment?

The body may remain still while the brain races along. Creating a new project requires you to select from available design elements.

Once the brain chooses a project, it continues questioning. Do I want a contemporary or traditional design? Have I ever seen anything like it before? Can I capture the colors I see in my garden flowers? In a rainbow? In the bricks and stones of a building? Do I want a romantic mood full of curves and diagonal lines, or a classic design emphasizing vertical, horizontal, and geometric shapes?

What style will I express? Victorian, casual, elegant, country? In short, the next phase of creativity is refining your choices based on preferences and personal interpretation.

Finally, call upon your body. Hands need to feel textures and other materials you might use. Await just the right "feel" envisioned by the mind. Eyes examine color and proportion.

Quilters begin to gather fabric to bring to reality what began as an abstraction. Many fiber artists state that the raw materials, once in hand, can suggest the direction of the design.

Jokes about how much quilters love their fabric stash fill magazines, quilt shows, and Internet quilt digests. Quilters must have as comprehensive a stash as possible! At last, when they feel their fabric stash is as large and varied as possible, they begin to create, inspired and led by their fabric collection. The artist feels compelled to stretch the possible uses of available materials.

We may notice two colors that accidentally came to lie beside each other. Perhaps we never considered combining them, but there they are, right before our eyes!

Creative minds, always prowling for new impressions, record the textures, lines, and colors the eyes see. Our brains grab ideas from everywhere and file them for future use.

Hands and mind eventually begin to work together. The mind, with its idea in place, commands the hands to begin. We begin to choose, cut, and lay out patterns and shapes.

The selection process continues as hands check in with the real control—the creativity center in the brain. "Is this what I had in mind when I saw that garden, or was it this?" "Does this feel right, or should I try something else?"

Observe everything around you. Your mind will translate your experiences and impressions into your own art form. If you listen to your inner self, without fear of failure, creativity will come through. Not only that, but with each creation, the artist within improves and matures. Next time, you will have even more to draw from with additional self-confidence, thanks to your recently completed project.

As you add finishing touches, you begin to feel a sense of completion as you realize you have made something come into being that did not exist before. You have created a design!

How to Maintain a Stream of Ideas

"Designer's Block"—we fear the term. Magazine editors or customers may request a design idea, and you draw a blank. Other times, you may begin a project, only to bog down in the middle, unable to continue. What can you do? Plan for such eventualities, for they are sure to come.

Look for ideas that can serve as a springboard to stimulate and inspire original work. Magazines offer a plethora of ideas. Look for ads that combine colors in an unusual way. Look at models, but not only their clothing; examine their jewelry and accessories too. Home decor magazines offer a wealth of ideas. I once knit a coat inspired by floor tiles in a Middle Eastern mosque.

Comments from Professional Designers about Selling Patterns and Designs

Developing quilt patterns differs from making and selling quilts. "Labor intensive" is the term for the hard work required before actual production of patterns begins. Designers do not begin to make a profit until a given number of copies has been sold.

Many designers add up all overhead costs per month or per year and divide that by the number of copies they hope to sell in that period. Once they have a production price per copy plus overhead costs per copy, they can begin to compare the result with prices of competitive products to arrive at a profit margin.

Designers who sell their patterns independently have more than one market from which they can profit. Many designers sell both at wholesale to distributors, and to consumers at retail as well. A successful designer whose business is now full-time comments, "Since wholesale and distributors figure their cost on your suggested retail price, they must know what discounts wholesalers and distributors expect before designers can set a retail price for each pattern. Wholesalers expect a 50 percent discount on the retail price when they buy a minimum number of patterns. Distributors expect to pay less than required by wholesalers. They pay 50 percent less 30 percent (or 20 percent) from retail. This means most designers must work backward and at least double the actual cost of the pattern when selling to distributors."

Barbara Vlack, quilt teacher, designer, lecturer, and author, comments on the business of patterns and those who design them. "It takes lots of time and money on the production end. Many pattern designers I know do not act as their own publishers or distributors, thereby earning at least a percentage of a pattern's retail price. Pattern publishers, wholesalers, and retailers make the most per pattern—more than designers themselves who receive only royalties, even though they have overhead and other costs," she explains.

"When we buy shops or produce patterns, we cross the line from quiltmaking as a hobby to a professional level. Demand for our services exists, and we should all earn a fair price," says Barbara. "Quilting would not be the big business it is today if we all worked just because we loved quilting. The industry has grown because it supports those who choose as a profession teaching, designing, and producing quilt goods and tools."

Barbara asks, "What is fair compensation, minus production costs, to a designer for the anticipated sale of 500 patterns that have a successful run? Do not think of the cost of a pattern with the idea that it took ten cents per page to copy. After all, calico used to sell for fifty cents per yard and dress patterns cost thirty-five cents. We must advance our thinking in today's market terms."

Trudie Hughes, a well known and respected shop owner, buys paper piecing patterns for her shop. "I feel dismay with the quality of some patterns received in my shop," she says. "Recently, I picked up new pattern companies to sell in my shop, and I have been making models according to the pattern maker's directions. It amazes me how much new homegrown pattern companies want for their patterns. Yet when I read and follow the directions, I find many errors in patterns, whether or not they are typeset, improperly illustrated, or, worst of all, unsatisfying to customers," she declares.

"For example, I made up a paper piecing design that appeared attractive in the photograph, but the numbers were not in proper sequence, with some missing altogether. Though the pattern was printed in color on lightweight paper, which is usually an advantage, a customer could only use this design one time, as the layout sheet had to be cut up to make the pattern. The price? Twelve dollars for a tiny design.

"Another pattern company sent an attractive brochure requesting thirty-five dollars for shipping. We ship every day and know that forty-eight patterns do not cost that much to ship. This new company does not have a distributor, so if we want its patterns, we must pay inflated costs. For that price, we prefer to sell a book that looks more professional," she says.

Another shop owner offers advice for new pattern designers and writers. "Provide buyers with clear, step-by-step instructions to ensure success, encouraging repeat customers. Patterns should be written so novices can use them. Test your patterns in classes or among quilting friends. Make your instructions complete and accurate. Have your pattern reviewed or edited prior to publication to identify areas that need clarification. Taking these steps will help satisfy buyers that your pattern is worth the price they pay."

A designer with ten years of experience in selling her patterns says, "I researched patterns to learn how to price my patterns, so that I can price them competitively. I am concerned about poorly written patterns. Quality control should be the pattern writer's major concern. I have a kind friend who edits my patterns. She is so careful that I know when she has studied my pattern, it will work!

"Pattern writing is time-consuming, but when I look at a quilt that someone made using one of my patterns, I get a great feeling. Yet I still must cover production expenses and earn a profit for my work. Designers should not demand high prices for a simple appliqué block containing only a six-by-eight-inch piece of muslin. Perhaps quilt store owners should refuse those overpriced patterns and let pattern producers know that their patterns are too expensive."

Ann Anderson has been designing, publishing, and distributing patterns for six years, and also distributes a book on how to publish patterns. She says, "Shops mark up a pattern at least 100 percent, so if the retail is $8, the shop buys it for $4. The remaining $4 is split 30–70 between the distributor and the designer. This means $1.20 goes to the distributor, leaving the designer with $2.80 from an $8 pattern.

"Covers need color, and if you print your own, the cost can be 30 to 50 cents. Sending covers out to be printed reduces the cost per cover to 10 cents or less, but may have an up-front cost of several hundred dollars, as it does not make sense to print less than 1,000. Black-and-white pattern pages generally cost between 3 and 6 cents per sheet. Plastic hanging bags cost 2 to 3 cents. Folding and stuffing, another 5 to 10 cents. If a pattern contains 10 sheets, the total cost to produce the pattern could range from 50 cents to $1," Ann explains.

Ann advises designers to consider the labor it takes to produce patterns, including the final printing arrangements. Most designers use a computer and graphics software costing as much as $700, plus expensive color printers. Designers must amortize these costs and consider design time, time for making one or more samples, and hiring someone to proof the completed pattern. Designers incur costs for advertising, promotion, and marketing.

To answer the question, "How does a person determine the value of intellectual content in a design?" Ann replies, "From my experience, I know it takes a long time to work out a design, then write the pattern. It is tedious work, with much rechecking of figures and measurements." She reminds readers to consider the amortized cost of equipment, office costs, communications, advertising, show costs, and unsold inventory. Designers must sell a large number of copies of each pattern before seeing much profit," says Ann.

Jo Morton of *Prairie Hands Patterns in Nebraska* comments about minimum costs and shipping charges for her design patterns. "I have patterns handled by distributors, but after four years of adding new patterns, I found some shops do not carry my full line. I decided to implement changes with the shop owner in mind. After a shop opens an account with me (a total of twelve patterns in multiples of three), I no longer require minimums on reorders, and I do not charge for shipping. My minimum order is only nine patterns," Jo explains.

"I do not charge for shipping so that I do not have to give the distributor a discount, and that amount more than covers shipping charges," she adds. "If I were a shop owner, I would appreciate such cooperation. I considered both sides carefully before implementing this policy, and it has worked out very well, a win-win situation. We are all partners in this wonderful industry. My policy has not slowed distributor pattern orders. They keep growing."

Christine Tresch focuses on another aspect of pattern designing. "Quilting, pattern designing, and the Internet brought several of my interests together," she says. "I designed a pattern and placed it on my Web site. People liked my designs, so I made more. In 1996, I expanded my Web site to include my own domain name. Mine was one of the first quilting pattern sites on the Web.

"Deciding to sell quilt patterns is one of the best decisions I've ever made. Capturing the elusive idea and getting it on paper, followed by creating the design in cloth, excites me. I enjoy the work between the idea and the finished product. Some designs have taken years to bloom, and others have come in a flash and entered the market in just a few months. Designing patterns may have many tedious steps, but they are all part of the job, and very worthwhile for me."

Alice Lynch designed and published her first pattern, "Collector's Christmas Tree," in 1990. "I have creative freedom publishing my own designs, and can work at my convenience from home," she says. "I began my design business by printing my patterns at a local copy shop. I traded the shop owner a custom wall quilt for copy services—a good move for me at the time.

"My first covers were photographs stuck with double-sided tape to card stock," she explains. "I shot my own photos and still do. Later, I had them commercially printed as four-color glossies, but ran into problems when my address changed. Reasonably priced color printers and better photo software brought me to the point where I am today, printing my own covers as needed. I use bright white heavy ink-jet paper and get very good results.

"I advise new designers to follow their own instincts, not just market trends. I sold my banner patterns before the current trend in stained glass appliqué, but did not sell well until Clover came out with fusible bias rolls."

Alice vends at one retail show a year—the Houston Quilt Festival. She has worked this show every year since 1995, until this year, when she missed the deadline to rent a booth. "I attended the market and walked through the show. I made connections for design work that I would not have made had I been cooped up in a booth, so I guess I am established enough that I do not need to depend solely on shows," she says.

"An important point to remember is to refer to other patterns in a series inside your pattern envelope," Alice advises. "People will call you directly for other patterns if your information is included, and shops order from you too. Many times, customers take a design they bought from me into a shop. The owner often calls for a brochure or places an order for a class! This is my best method of advertising, and does not cost me anything!"

Ruth Blanchet designed her first pattern in 2001 in New Zealand. "The great thing about designing your own patterns and selling them is that you do not need a lot of capital to start. It was a great way to become self-employed," says Ruth. "It takes hard work and may need to be supplemented by another form of income, but I look forward to the day when it can stand alone as my sole income. I like the freedom to design and produce patterns, and found that teaching supports pattern designing and pattern designing enhances teaching, so they work together nicely. I can do what I love and make a living from it," she explains.

"Designing has always interested me so much that I planned to write a book, but did not have the time," she explains. "I decided that designing patterns would be quicker and make much more money, so I spent time in research. I learned all I could about business practices and teaching. The online group for pattern designers (*quiltdesigners@yahoogroups.com*) is a valuable source of information. It is important to talk to others in the same business.

"My advice is to talk to as many other designers as possible, read, and learn about all aspects of business and designing. Get ideas and advice. Make the best of all available help. The best thing about this business is that you are not the first designer in the world; therefore, you can learn from those who have gone before you and learn from their mistakes and achievements and become more successful sooner."

Susanne Wegert (Sue) is a new designer who spent a year researching how to operate a quilt design business and how to create designs for patterns. As a complete novice, she recommends three wonderful resources she says helped her: the online QuiltDesigners List, Nancy Restuccia's book *Publish Your Patterns*, and the business course at Quilt University, "Making Money with Quilting."

Sue benefited from using the mentoring services provided by the Small Business Development Center (SBDC). Through SBDC, she worked with a group of college students in an entrepreneurial program. The student team performed a feasibility study of her planned business and helped her decide which design areas to emphasize first.

Her business research included market analysis, review of equipment needed to self-publish patterns, and the preparation of a business plan under the guidance of my classes at Quilt University. Sue also researched software programs she would eventually need to create and publish the designs. Additionally, she created a five-year plan of goals, as well as the equipment and training needed to reach them. She strongly recommends taking the time for research in order to avoid pitfalls or investing too much time and/or money in an unproductive area destined to fail without research.

"My first step was to network so that I could develop contacts in quilt designing, quilt magazine publishing, and fabric manufacturing," Sue says. "I plan to sell patterns through one or more distributors and at quilt shows, and to set up a Web site to sell my designs at retail."

"Target a specific group of consumers with your choice of designs," Sue advises. "My target consumers are parents, grandparents, and church educators looking for a way to illustrate Judeo-Christian values through the Biblical designs I create. Join quilting guilds and attend quilt shows as often as possible to see what is selling. Show your samples to guild members and local quilt shops to see if there is interest in your designs before expending too much time and money in publishing. Most important of all, enjoy what you are doing, because in the beginning you will be spending a lot of time and effort for a small return while you are getting established."

Ruth Sparrow Gendron, currently president of the prestigious INRG (International Needlearts Retailers Guild) promotes shops and feels strongly about wholesalers trying to be retailers. "I have a retail needle art shop in Cincinnati, Ohio—traditional brick-and-mortar style," she says. "But my wholesale design company is in St. Louis. When a stitcher wants to buy directly, I point her to their nearest needle art shop. If they do not have one nearby, I give her the toll-free number at my retail shop."

"Freelancers must answer a critical question," she says. "Do they want to sell hundreds of a design, or thousands? Do designers who sell directly to consumers make a living selling designs one at a time? I believe that paperwork and shipping details would consume most of their time. If their designs have merit, they will find at least four to six distributors in this country. Exhibiting at trade shows may bring in two to ten international distributors more. Distributors can help designers sell thousands of charts of a single design for many, many years," she says.

"If a person is serious about starting a design business, she must remember that it may require capital, hard work, and promotion. Go to trade shows, promote your designs on a Web site, send postcards, connect with distributors, and work hard to succeed," she concludes.

Contributors to this chapter:
Barbara Vlack
Sweet Memories Publishing Company
36 W 556 Wild Rose Road
St. Charles, IL 60174-1149
cptrdeo@inil.com

Trudie Hughes
Patched Works
13330 Watertown Plank Road
Elm Grove, WI 53122
trudiehughes@msn.com

Ann Anderson
QuiltWoman.com/Make It Easy® Sewing & Crafts
3822 Patricks Point Drive
Trinidad, CA 95570
(707) 677-0105, Toll-free: (877) 454-7967, Fax: (707) 677-9162
ann@quiltwoman.com
www.quiltwoman.com

Jo Morton
Prairie Hands Patterns
1801 Central Avenue
Nebraska City, NE 68410
(402) 873-3846, Fax: (402) 873-3848
jomorton@alltel.net
www.jomortonquilts.com

Alice W. Lynch
Owner/Designer
Woodside Country Store
4203 Tealwood Drive
Jonesboro, AR 72401
(870) 931-0935
www.woodsidecountrystore.com

Ruth Blanchet
Arbee Originals
Nelson, NZ
http://ArbeeDesigns.co.nz

Susanne Wegert
17 EMS B61G Lane
Warsaw, IN 46582
(574) 834-2096
swegert@bnin.net
www.lilypondquiltdesigns.com

Ruth Sparrow Gendron
Twisted Threads
The Trilogy
ruth@twistedthreads.com
www.twistedthreads.com

Your Marketing Plan

Marketing does *not* mean selling. Marketing *precedes* both advertising *and* selling. Successful selling can only take place *after* researching the current market, which in turn helps you identify and find your most likely customers.

Marketing is a never-ending business process of evaluating what works and what does not, what is wanted and what is not. This is what I call "learning about the external marketplace." You must develop a sensitivity toward producing what customers want to buy, rather than what you want to sell. Avoid the common notion many new business owners often have about marketing: that customers are as enthused about buying your product as you are about selling it to them.

Marketing reality begins by realizing that no single product appeals to everyone. If your business offers a service rather than a product, do not assume marketing does not apply to you. Service *is* your product! Since not every potential buyer of quilt products and services will buy from you, begin your research by answering the question, "What segment of the market will buy?" Defining your target market means identifying the group of available buyers most likely to show an interest in what you have to offer. Decide what is special about your work. Where in the quilting marketplace do you hope to see yourself? Where do you and your specialty fit in?

What Is Special about Your Work?

What can you do that no one else or very few others are doing? Have you heard about successful quilting-related services in other parts of the country that do not exist in your community? Do they appeal to you? What do you do best? Many quilters do not like to design a quilt or piece it together. Others love this process. Would you prefer to make the quilt top and have someone else quilt it for you, or would you prefer to quilt the tops made by others? I prefer hand appliqué. Others will only do appliqué by machine.

Quilting superstar Linda Schmidt has an uncanny way of recreating bodies and faces of both humans and animals. She does it so well that many people seeing her work for the first time assume her quilts are oil paintings. When she displays her art quilts, she never fails to win ribbons and sell the pieces she wishes to sell.

Judy Simmons, another quilting superstar, prefers flowers. Her garden flowers are so real that fading petals seem to drift away from the flowers, even to "fall" out of her quilts and onto the borders. She makes individual petals, shapes them with wire, and attaches them where she pleases. Looking at Judy's work leaves no doubt about her love and skill for floral design.

Yvonne Porcella, superstar and quilting colorist, specializes in art-to-wear garments in bold, bright colors combined with black and white. Her unique garments have become recognizable at a glance. A former nurse who declares she will never again dress in all-white clothes, she edged into her specialty gradually. Today, readers snatch up her latest books and gasp when they see her clothing in fashion shows.

After reading about three of today's quilting superstars, where do you see yourself in the quilt industry? What do you want others to note about your work? To begin earning money in the quilting field, begin with what you already know. You can expand later, when you have a plan in place and have acquired some experience. For now, determine your area of expertise. Here is a list to get you thinking about the possibilities. Please add to it.

+ Accessories
+ Appliqué
+ Appraiser
+ Art quilts
+ Author
+ Columnist
+ Consultant
+ Contemporary quilter
+ Designing patterns
+ Designing for magazines
+ Fabric printing, dyeing, marbling
+ Freelance writer
+ Internet quilting Web management
+ Judge
+ Mail-order retailer
+ Manufacturer
+ Publisher
+ Quilt restoration expert
+ Quilt seminar producer
+ Services for others (finishing, basting, quilting)
+ Shop owner
+ Software designer
+ Speaker
+ Teacher
+ Television quilting
+ Traditional pieced quilter
+ Wearable art designer

Turn Your Specialty into a Niche in the Marketplace

Choosing which aspects of quilting appeal to you will help you determine your specialty. Once you have singled out one or more specialties, do your home-work. Study and compare the major quilting magazines. Analyze current trends. Read letters and questions to the editor by readers who want to learn more. Request copies of quilt catalogs to see what they offer. Catalogs are expensive to produce, so most are market-driven, meaning they contain what consumers want to buy as opposed to what the seller wants to sell. More about market-driven products later.

Attend local, regional, and national quilting seminars and conventions. Note which classes fill to overflowing and which attract only small numbers of students. Learn what topics popular teachers offer and which lectures keep the audience's attention. After completing your market research, you will be in a better position to create a market-driven product or service yourself—one that satisfies a recognized need.

In an earlier book, I interviewed Millie Becker, a disabled quilter. She explained how she targeted a very specific market. Knowing that no one can reach every American consumer, she found excellent ways to reach likely buyers of her products—those confined to wheelchairs. She does not advertise in quilt magazines, but rather in publications for the disabled. She identified her market accurately and now works steadily, making and quilting tote bags and other accessories for wheelchair-bound people. She understood marketing principles very well and is successfully working at her business full-time today.

Once you have defined your niche in the marketplace, you too will be better able to:

+ Locate the most likely customers for your product or service
+ Advertise and promote your business where it will do the most good
+ Learn what to read and where to find help and information
+ Focus your effort and energy in the direction most likely to be profitable
+ Avoid becoming too scattered and diversified, which minimizes success

Your Target Market: Who Will Buy?

Good marketing techniques require you to have an accurate picture of your likely customers. You need to identify, describe, locate, and eventually reach them. You cannot aim your advertising dollars at your targeted customers if you do not understand who they are, what they read, what they need, and why they need it. Target marketing contributes greatly to the success of any business, large or small. Creating a profile of your most likely customers is a vital step in your marketing efforts.

Describe your potential customers on paper to get started. Who are they? Where do they live? What advertising and promotions methods will reach them? What do they read? Find out by requesting writers' guidelines from prominent craft, quilting, and sewing magazines. Guidelines describe the magazine's readership and offer demographic data.

Ask yourself if people of all age groups will be drawn to your product, or if it will appeal primarily to a particular group. For example, hand-quilted baby items and toys will interest new parents and grandparents, but fashionable vests will attract more clothes-conscious younger women. If people of a certain age will be those most interested in buying your product, the language of your advertising, color selection, and style must suit their tastes to encourage them to buy. For example, to target seniors specifically, your literature might contain conservative language written on traditionally colored papers. However, if your market reaches out to teenagers, you might use more contemporary or "cool" terms and neon and other bright, modern color schemes that appeal to them.

Perhaps a certain educational level is required for buyers to appreciate your product. For example, only computer-literate consumers would be interested in your new quilting software, but educational level is immaterial if you specialize in quilted items for the kitchen.

Economic buying power of your likely customers may be a consideration if you offer primarily high-end art quilts for sale. Buyers must have greater discretionary income and more expressed appreciation of art than, say, those who want only washable, practical bed quilts. Though the latter group still must have dollars, these buyers may more likely be families with children and limited income.

Where Do Your Customers Shop?

Once you have a profile of the type of people most likely to show an interest in your product, you need to find out how to reach them. Ask yourself where your customers would most likely shop. Where would they go to find items like yours? Some places to consider include:

+ Quilt shops
+ Consignment and gift shops
+ Exclusive boutiques
+ Quilt shows and exhibits
+ Art shows
+ Street fairs
+ Tourist shopping areas
+ County and state fairs
+ Online Web sites

Street fairs may be the ideal place to offer quilted wallets and potholders, but art shows would not be the best choice for these. Consider art galleries for large art quilts. Perhaps your customers would respond better to reading about your product. You must decide which magazines they would most likely read. If you plan to finish quilts for others, advertising in the classified sections of quilt magazines may be a good idea. Readers are primarily quilters, some of whom may prefer to have their quilts finished for them.

If you plan to design and make quilts for consumers, consider leaving flyers and brochures at local sewing centers. Customers who admire such items but cannot or do not have the time to quilt often seek referrals from shops where fabric is available for sale.

Perhaps your target buyers might be more apt to find you on the Internet. You will find quilt-related malls, Web sites, and online quilting information in the last chapter of this book. In my opinion, Caryl Bryer Fallert's Web site for serious quilters is the most outstanding, comprehensive, and beautiful site of its kind on the Internet. Look her up and see if you agree at *www.bryerpatch.com*.

What Do They Want and Why Do They Want It?

Determine whether gender affects the purchase of your product. Generally, quilted items, supplies, books, and patterns are bought by women, but perhaps you can produce an item to appeal to men buying quilt-related gifts for their wives.

Must your buyers have sufficient discretionary income to afford your product, such as a long-arm quilting machine?

Does their social or educational level matter?

How will potential customers learn about your product/service? Why should they buy your product? How do you know they want or need your product/service? Will they pay your price? How do you know? Find out the answers to these questions. They will be important to your marketing plan.

What About Your Competition?

Once you decide exactly what you are going to sell and whom you will be selling to, you must learn all you can about your competitors, including their strengths and weaknesses. Begin your research by writing answers to the following questions. Think of this as the rough draft of your marketing plan. Begin by scanning classified ads in local newspapers. Have you found anyone doing what you plan to do?

Where are your competitors located? What makes your product/service better than theirs? Read your competition's advertisements. Can you determine the benefit of their products or services for the customer?

How do your prices compare with the competition's? What products do they carry? What services do they offer? Who are their vendors, distributors, wholesalers? Visiting their locations and scrutinizing their sales literature and catalogs will help you determine the answers to the last three questions.

Check the yellow pages in your local phone directory and call the competition. What other quilting products and services appear in their ads? What can you offer that they do not? If no one in your community machine quilts for others, for example, you might fill this need. Conversely, if many other professional quilters in your area specialize in machine quilting, perhaps you can consider specializing in heritage hand quilting, or reach out of your city or state for customers.

A designer I know makes only contemporary quilts on commission, but a nearby competitor limits herself to making quilts based on old, traditional patterns using Depression-era fabric styles being remanufactured today.

By assessing your strengths and weaknesses and comparing them to your closest competitor's, you too may find success developing a complementary specialty with your competitors, rather than vying for the same customers.

Why You Need a Written Marketing Plan

Full-time or part-time business owners who want to succeed know the wisdom of drafting a marketing plan to outline and organize marketing and advertising strategies. Saying that your marketing plan is "in your head" reveals that you have not taken its value seriously. Like a business plan, a marketing plan must be in writing. Without a plan, you will have little direction, no stated goals, and no way to measure and recognize your success.

Your marketing plan should:

+ Be in writing
+ Be updated annually
+ Always consider the changeability of the external marketplace
+ Have defined objectives
+ Include an implementation timetable
+ Be easy to understand, precise, and clear
+ Be practical and realistic
+ Be flexible and adaptable to change
+ Be as complete as you can make it

Creating Your Plan

Start by answering the following questions: What business are you in? What do you want to sell? Be specific. For example, do not just say, "quilts." Say whether you plan to design, make, teach, restore, or sell quilts. Others who need to see your plan may not be as familiar with the market as you are, so start your plan with good, strong sentences answering these two questions.

Does a demand exist for your product or service? How do you know? Read the major craft, quilting, and trade journals. Why will your product or service sell? Can you describe at least three of its principal benefits to the consumer?

Before probing into the questions listed above, consider one more point. Will your product or service be market-driven or product-driven? Market-driven products are aimed at satisfying an established and desired need in the market. A current example in the quilting world centers on batting. Customers (the market) have increased their demand for batts made of natural fibers, such as cotton and wool. Producing these in greater quantities, sizes, and styles would fit the definition of "market-driven."

Product-driven items usually do not fare as well in the marketplace. Product-driven companies often insist upon selling what they *want* to produce, as opposed to producing what the market wants. Using our batting example again, a product-driven company may decide that polyester is cheaper to manufacture and weighs less than natural fibers. To ignore the growing market demand for natural fibers would undoubtedly lead to lower sales of polyester batts, as buyers today favor natural fibers.

Let's say you plan to design and make quilts to sell. If your line is product-driven, you would stress product benefits in your advertising. For example, you might underscore that you use the most economical batts available. You might also assure customers that you guarantee that your quilts are colorfast and shrink-resistant. Perhaps you could point out that you will make quilts to fit any bed size, and that your wall quilts can be custom-ordered to any measurement. Note that all of the above stress the benefits of the product. If this is what customers are buying, you may do well.

However, if you decide on a market-driven quilt business, you would stress how your products and services relate to current trends and preferences. For example, referring to the batts on the market, your advertising might mention that you have added a line of cotton batts in various thicknesses and sizes from which customers may choose.

Color choices you choose would reflect today's current jewel tones, as opposed to the earth tones so popular a generation ago. Market-driven quilt-makers must constantly observe trends and remain flexible enough to respond to them to satisfy consumer demand.

Remember the Color Marketing Group, which I mentioned earlier in this book? It is a nonprofit international association of 1,200 design and color professionals dedicated to forecasting and tracking color/design trends in the U.S., and meets twice yearly. It analyzes current consumer color preferences and predicts color trends two years in advance. Studying this information allows you to get a head start on choosing color schemes that are coming up in the market, rather than those that are passé. Do you see how this idea helps prepare you for the market—specifically, to choose colors that are market-driven? Many craft and quilt seminars offer annual lectures and presentations by a Color Marketing Group representative, or you can call (703) 528-7666 for more information.

Marketing Strategies

Answer the questions below to create your own marketing strategy guidelines:

+ How does your product/service fit into the present market?
+ What system did you use to arrive at your prices?
+ Is there risk in trying your product?
+ Will consumers require training to use the product?
+ Are there government regulations relevant to using the product?
+ What follow-up customer service method will you use?
+ What sales strategy will reach your target market?

Market Research Techniques

You can pay a professional who charges high fees to do marketing research on your business, but you can also do it yourself by doing the following:

+ Interview your customers. Ask them about the strengths and weaknesses of competitors.
+ Listen to reactions from others.
+ Talk to other business owners with related interests.

+ Read and talk with others in the industry.
+ Interview others who belong to pertinent trade associations.
+ Try to visit with direct competitors. (This is more easily said than done.)

Paying to Get the Word Out

Once you identify your target customer, think about what advertising style will be most suitable to them. Marketing and advertising experts often reduce an advertising style to three basic choices. Will your product/service appear to be the best, fastest, or cheapest?

Take the idea of selling quilting fabric by mail order as an example. To be the best, your advertising should provide details about the high-end brands of your fabrics and promise to offer the latest popular styles, colors, and prints. However, if your niche is to offer the quickest service, you might stress that you always ship on the same day you receive an order. Impatient customers in the midst of a project or those far from a quilt shop would become your most likely market.

If you prefer to offer the lowest prices, you may want to become known for regular discount pricing. Your literature should stress low prices, and you might even consider offering discontinued or imperfect fabric samples.

Once you have identified your target market, the next question to answer is, "How will I reach my customer?" Your choices fall into two basic categories: paid advertising and low-cost promotion. You have many choices when you pay to advertise. You can place ads in magazines, telephone books, trade journals, newsletters, and local newspapers.

Advertising in Magazines

Generally, advertising offers two alternatives: classified ads where you pay by the word, and display ads where you pay by the size of the space where your information appears. Classified ads accept words only, while display ads may include words, your logo, line drawings, sketches, and photos.

Classified Ads Compared to Display Ads

Classified ads will cost less and generate more sales if you write them as professional writers do in what is called "tight writing." This means using the fewest, strongest words that say the most. Practice writing your ad. Include the essentials: *what* you have to sell, *where* the customer can reach you, *how* they can pay you, and *what* they will pay.

Next, write the ad again, eliminating any unnecessary words. Write it a third time. Try to combine words if possible. Why say "black-and-white" if you can say "b/w", for example? Write it a fourth time and eliminate prepositions and adverbs. Write it a fifth time using strong, imperative language. Some examples: "Buy now!" "Don't wait!" "Order today!" Teach yourself this important skill by reading the book *Write Tight* by William Brohaugh.

Though you may think that consumer magazines such as *Better Homes & Gardens* or *Sunset* offer the ideal place to advertise, think again. Magazines that focus on home issues and activities are too general for one-person quilting businesses. You may also be shocked when you learn that they charge thousands of dollars for color display ads.

Narrow your search instead. Look for magazines that have a smaller readership but that are focused on your market. They charge less than large, glossy publications while addressing likely buyers more closely.

Writer's Market (F&W Publications) is an annual directory for writers listing hundreds of magazines, many of which could be suitable for you as an advertiser. Identify one or two whose readership matches your target market, and you have won half the battle of successful marketing.

A quilting expert in marketing quilts and other crafts throughout the United States offers this wise advice: "When a quilter decides to start advertising, she needs to plan a minimum of four ads a year in the same publication. She needs startup funds and should not expect her mailbox to be stuffed with orders when the first ad appears. The ad needs to reflect the product and should always be simple and to the point. A new businessperson can consider the first ad successful if it only recoups the ad cost. Usually, it is the publication of the second or third ad that begins to generate profit."

Telephone Book Display Ads

Once you have a business telephone number, your phone company will automatically list your number in both the white and yellow pages in your local phone directory. However, you may broaden this coverage by placing a display ad in the yellow section. You must pay an extra monthly charge, so check your phone directory to learn the costs of different-sized boxes of information. Remember, unlike classified ads, display ads permit you to include your logo, line drawings, and sketches, in addition to text. Unquestionably, display ads enhance your credibility as a professional, but you will have to weigh this against the monthly charge.

Trade Journals and Newsletters

Browse through the *Encyclopedia of Associations*, available in your public library, to find lists of groups, clubs, and trade associations that publish trade journals or newsletters. Target a specific group devoted to your specialty. Placing ads in these smaller but highly specialized publications costs much less than advertising in consumer magazines and reaches your target consumer more directly.

Newspaper Advertising

Consider newspaper advertising if your quilting business offers service over product. Since coverage is local, you will reach residents in your own community. Teachers and those who offer longarm quilting services to others find newspaper advertising beneficial. Newspapers also offer both classified and display ads, so before proceeding, check to see how your local competition uses this valuable tool.

Defining Your Product's Benefits

Whatever marketing and advertising methods you choose, your buyers must be able to perceive the benefits of your product or service to justify buying. When customers buy a frozen dinner, for example, they settle for lower-quality food than they would in a home-cooked meal. Convenience is what they are really buying.

Using the same theory, let's say you sell small quilted items such as place mats, tote bags, and wall hangings. Point out, for example, how much time customers will save when they buy from you and how distinctive handmade gifts can be.

If you hand quilt tops for others, consider stressing a benefit to encourage buyers. For example, "Do you love to appliqué but dislike hand quilting the background? Let me do it for you, freeing you to do what you enjoy most."

Quilting teachers can gain from marketing this way as well. Your literature could say: "Do you admire beautiful handmade quilts? Do you wish you could make one yourself? Don't wait any longer. Sign up for our basic quilting class and have a lovely quilt finished by Christmas."

Compare the quoted material above to this: "I have always admired beautiful, handmade quilts. I want to show you how to make one. Sign up for my quilting class and I will teach you to make a quilt."

The first quote, written in the second person, addresses prospective customers and points out a clearly stated benefit: ". . . a lovely quilt finished by Christmas." The second quote, written in the first person, has too many uses of "I" and does not stress a benefit for the consumer.

To sum up, before spending hard-earned advertising dollars, study the results of your marketing research. Make sure you have determined exactly what you have to offer in very clear terms. Create and write out a comprehensive profile of your target customers. Find out how to reach them as effectively as possible. Identify your product's benefits.

Your Professional Image

Announce to the world that you take your business seriously by creating an image on paper of who you are and what you do. Make it easy for potential buyers to find you. Start with a business card. It immediately identifies you as a professional.

Business Cards

Unless you want to continually explain what "Mary's Handmade Treasures" are, make sure the name you choose states what your business is clearly. "Mary's Quilts" on the first line of your business card immediately tells us what Mary does. Add a subtitle, such as, "Each a handmade treasure," beneath the name in a smaller font. This describes the business and states a marketing benefit; "handmade" followed by the word "treasure" indicates something that is of high quality and is precious enough to keep for a long time. Avoid cute cards, which are rarely taken seriously by editors, manufacturers, and other professionals.

Letterhead Stationery

Manufacturers from whom you want to buy wholesale will not consider you a serious professional if you request a catalog written on personal stationery or binder paper. Letterhead stationery announces that you are in business. If you have unlimited funds, you can pay a graphic artist to design both your business cards and your letterhead. If you have a tight budget, access to a computer, and an understanding of graphics, you can do it yourself.

Computer software today allows you to design your own letterhead, brochures, business cards, and even catalogs with the help of a laser printer for a "professionally printed" look. Software today makes the task easier than ever. If you do not have a computer or software, go to a neighborhood printing company and rent them, or ask the company to run as few as a dozen sheets on a letter-quality photocopy machine.

Brochures

Consider a brochure as your next investment. Here, you can tell a more complete story about you and your business than what appears on your business cards and letterhead. When designing your brochure, choose paper heavier than standard 20 lb. bond. If you write your own brochure text, here are a few points to keep in mind:

Use an economy of words. Verbs and nouns shout a strong, easy-to-understand message. Too many adjectives and adverbs clutter your message. Use forceful but simple language stressing the benefits of your service or product.

Here is a suggested arrangement for your information, but feel free to design your own: Fold a sheet of paper in thirds horizontally. Open it again. Notice that you have six vertical panels in which to place your information. Brochures like this are called "tri-fold brochures."

- ✦ Panel #1: The front cover should contain only your business name, your name, address, and phone numbers including fax. If you have a logo, include it here.
- ✦ Panel #2: Use the left inside panel to describe your product or service.
- ✦ Panel #3: Use the center inside panel to include a brief biographical (bio) sketch. Consider a photo of yourself at the top of this section.
- ✦ Panel #4: Use the right inside panel to describe the typical customers you serve—your target market.
- ✦ Panel #5: Use the center outside panel for a mission statement, or leave it blank if you want to address the brochure for mailing.
- ✦ Panel #6: Use the right outside panel to list endorsements and testimonials from satisfied customers.

Never attend professional functions, conferences, and seminars without a handful of business cards and brochures. Hand them to those who ask questions about your business. Let your brochure tell your story to the recipients when they have more time to study it.

Your Résumé

Do not forget a résumé. It speaks for you. Experts suggest that you limit a résumé to one page. If you have extensive experience and references, you can go up to two pages, tops.

Your Portfolio: Do Not Make It a Scrapbook!

Buyers, editors, and publishers peruse portfolios at shows, seminars, and conferences. Shop owners, teaching centers, and others interested in hiring or buying from you can also receive a professional, pictorial story about you and your business from a well arranged, compelling portfolio.

Quilters sometimes confuse a scrapbook for a professional portfolio. Padding the cover of a binder and adding a patchwork design framed by a ruffle shouts "scrapbook." A proper, zippered portfolio portrays your business image far more professionally. Portfolios, which are available in stationery or art supply shops, contain non-slippery plastic pages and conveniently protect and display photographs and tear sheets from magazines featuring your designs and copies of published articles you have written. Take care not to crowd the pages of your portfolio by placing too many small items on one page, collage-style.

What to Put in Your Portfolio

+ Your *business card*, placed in the small window on the inside cover.
+ Your *brochure*.
+ A *short biography*. Typed on letterhead stationery, your bio should be a well written statement about yourself. Provide answers to questions others often ask, such as when, where, and why you began quilting. State when and where you became a professional and close with recent achievements.
+ Your *résumé*. Many new quilters worry that they do not have much professional experience to list. If you are just starting out, list your education and past work experience, especially if it relates to your present professional quilting activity. For instance, you should list a degree in art or experience in a sewing shop.
+ A *photograph* of yourself. Polaroids and fuzzy snapshots do not project the image you want. Strive for professional quality in your photos, or hire a photographer.
+ A *mission statement*. This describes what you do, how you do it, and why you care about it. Let your passion for your work shine through in just a few paragraphs written on your letterhead stationery.
+ *Tear sheets* from magazines. When the designs of established quilt designers appear in magazines, the publisher sends them one or more complimentary issues in which the work appeared. Tear the page from the magazine. (Thus the term "tear sheets.") Trim ragged edges and ads or other text not related to your work. Place one tear sheet per portfolio page. Type the name, date, and issue of the publication on a label and paste it neatly above the tear sheet. If your work has not yet been published, do not despair. Try writing a letter to

the editor of a magazine or newspaper, offering your opinion on a pertinent quilt-related issue. You might also write articles for newsletters of local craft groups or fraternal organizations. Even though you receive no payment for these, their appearance in your portfolio will project professional credibility.

✦ *Magazine covers* that feature your work. If you are fortunate enough to have your quilts appear on the cover of a magazine, position it prominently in your portfolio.

✦ *Articles* written about you by others have great value. Include the article, labeled with the date and issue number of the magazine or newspaper, in your portfolio. Writing about yourself and your work is not as effective as when someone else writes about you. The publicity adds credibility to your professional status.

✦ *Photos of completed quilts* and related items. Group photographs of quilts for sale. A label stating "Available Designs" will separate these from those items no longer available. Color photos of completed projects form the heart of your portfolio, so make them as professional as possible. These can range from 3″ × 5″ snapshots to full-page 8″ × 10″ professional photos.

✦ *A series of color photos* showing a project in progress always catches the viewer's eye. Include several photos showing:

  ✦ A collection of fabrics for a quilt
  ✦ A shot of the quilt top before assembling the quilt sandwich
  ✦ The basted quilt
  ✦ The completed quilt on a bed or hanging on a wall

✦ *Photographs of your quilts displayed during shows and exhibits* create credibility. Label each to show where your work appeared, with the place, date, and name of the show.

✦ *Photographs of awards, ribbons, and recognitions.* Treasure your awards, ribbons, and recognitions. Do not include the actual ribbon itself, for it creates too much bulk. Instead, take a close-up photo of the quilt with the ribbon attached. Add the program booklet issued at the show that details winning entries, and write down the name of the event, place, and date.

✦ *Copies of class schedules* describing your classes if you teach. Make sure the name of the school, shop, or event appears at the top of the class description sheet.

✦ *Photographs of yourself teaching, exhibiting, and demonstrating.*

Arranging Your Portfolio

Place promotional documents like your résumé, brochure, bio, and mission statement in the front pages of your portfolio. Many craft designers, artists, and quilters arrange remaining portfolio items in one of the three ways listed below:

Chronological. Show photos, articles, and tear sheets in sequence from front to back, starting with your earliest designs. Some people reverse the process, adding new designs to the front while keeping older work in the back.

Style. If you make traditional as well as contemporary quilts, for example, have a section for each group, placing photos of similar styles together.

Technique. If you make quilts as well as wearables, group these in separate sections. For example, you can show your quilts in one section, wearables in another, and stuffed patchwork toys in a third. Take care to update your portfolio regularly. A well prepared, organized portfolio presents a pictorial documentation and history of your quilting business. Treasure it and share it at every opportunity.

Little-to-No-Cost Promotional Ideas

Unlike advertising, where you pay dearly to get the word out, promotion costs little to nothing while letting your potential customers know what you have to offer. Here are a few suggestions to get you started. Add to this list as your business grows.

+ Join non-quilt-specific organizations such as art groups or business and civic groups. Let members of your community know what you do.
+ Give fliers and brochures to your Chamber of Commerce, which is where new residents go to learn about local products and services. Get a business phone and make sure it is listed in the yellow pages. Send newsletters or fliers to nearby guilds and fabric stores. Place posters or fliers in shops or places where people gather. Check first to see if you need permission to do this.
+ Write a press release for your local newspaper. Make it interesting. Newspapers do not find it worthwhile to publish mundane information, which should be in their classified section. Give your release a special twist that attracts attention.
+ Offer to give demonstrations for local civic, craft, and other interested groups at every opportunity. Participate in fairs and exhibits in your community. Join local and regional quilt and craft groups and start networking.
+ Expand your personal network of business contacts. It is critical to your success. Though you may prefer to work in solitude, you cannot succeed in business alone. Quilters keep busy, but doesn't everyone? Artisans sometimes avoid social contacts saying that it takes too much time, energy, and effort. Fresh business contacts, however, become valuable sources of new ideas and contacts.

Many quilters recognize the importance of developing a network, but do not overlook other opportunities. Connect with non-quilters and other small business owners to refresh yourself and your ideas. Becoming visible in your community bolsters confidence, increases market potential, and provides continuing stimulation. Here are a few ideas:

Visit your Chamber of Commerce and obtain a list of local organizations. Check off at least five that sound interesting. Attend a meeting or two of each group. Select one or two favorites and join! Participate! Always attend events with a pocketful of your business cards. Promote yourself, but be attentive to others. Ask questions. Share your expertise by giving short talks, giving demonstrations, or displaying your work. Above all, listen.

After a time, begin the process again. Choose another organization and become involved with its activities and members. Does this sound as if you are creating your own little world? You are. We call it "networking."

The Importance of Networking and How to Do It

Questioning what you already know keeps you vital and interesting. New information stimulates your brain and creativity. Remaining informed becomes even more important when you want to profit from your knowledge. Quilt professionals must continually broaden their technical skills while keeping up with what goes on in the field. Try not to limit yourself by settling for only quilt-specific information. You also must keep in touch with crafts in general, economic issues, and the external marketplace. "But how?" you ask. Network!

Networking means the informal sharing of information among individuals or groups who are linked by a common interest. Today, it has become a buzzword critical to everyone who wants to get ahead in any business, large or small, part-time or full-time.

Quilt hobbyists enjoy getting together to share techniques and to admire each other's work. After all, this is the primary function of quilt guilds. Quilt professionals, however, must go beyond quilting on a social level. Networking with others in the field develops professional contacts and encourages sharing manufacturer and product information such as wholesale sources, marketing trends, teaching opportunities, and upcoming trade shows. How do you participate?

Networking can take place at guild meetings, shops, classes, and conventions. At first it may sound like conversation. But, listen carefully. Rather than hearing small talk shifting from one subject to another, you will find that networking remains focused on business topics.

Participate by asking questions and listening attentively. When someone needs information you have, share. Networking at conferences and conventions invites an even more avid discussion of common goals, ideas, and problems.

Participants introduce themselves and then respond to previously agreed-upon issues common to them. Think of networking as playing two roles simultaneously—that of teacher and student. Take pains to avoid a common networking pitfall. It is not fair to drain others of information and provide none yourself. Exchanging freely and equally characterizes good networking. But where do you start?

Join local, regional, and national organizations where quilters and other crafters gather. Quilting organizations address quilting issues and provide continuing education in the field. There are two large primary organizations for quilters, the National Quilting Association (NQA) and the American Quilting Society (AQS). Both groups publish quarterly magazines to keep serious quilters up to date on the status of quilting. NQA maintains a teachers' directory of members they have certified, and AQS maintains a directory of appraisers they have certified, but these activities are only a very small part of what these two invaluable organizations have to offer.

Both quilting associations feature annual quilting seminars with an array of classes taught by today's best national and international designers and teachers. These are the places to go to see hundreds of quilts, attend classes and lectures, see fashion shows of wearable quilts, and best of all, visit the mall where hundreds of companies specializing in quilt-related goods have booths. These are retail shows; therefore, unlike trade shows, you can buy directly at these shows. Demonstrations of the latest products go on continually, and you are free to try new gadgets and notions yourself before you buy. Join one or both of these organizations to further your business.

The Value of Trade Associations

Next, consider joining a non-quilt-specific craft organization. Their seminars and publications will help keep you informed about the entire craft market, of which quilting is a part. You must know how quilting fits into the crafts world—needlework and sewing in particular. A list of these organizations and their addresses appears in the last chapter.

Let us take an in-depth look at two national organizations I find very valuable. Membership in both propelled my quilting business forward. These are the Hobby Industry Association (HIA) and the Society of Craft Designers (SCD). Membership will help you see the business of quilting in craft context. Most of the editors, publishers, and suppliers I work with today were introduced to me at one or the other of these associations. They, along with many others, provide regular conferences and seminars giving professionals the opportunity to exchange ideas and to meet others in their field to discuss common concerns. These associations also give professionals the chance to actually try new products and take them home to experiment with them.

The Society of Craft Designers

The Society of Craft Designers (SCD) provides an annual seminar at different locations throughout the U.S. where members meet and network with magazine editors from most of the craft magazines. Editors scrutinize the latest craft designs, including quilting, to become familiar with the work of designers and to buy their latest creations. Designers may meet up to twenty editors during the seminar, with each meeting offering a potential sale or design assignment. I sold quilt designs to the editors of *Crafts Magazine, Crafts 'N Things, Quilt Craft*, and *Lady's Circle Patchwork Quilts* while attending SCD seminars.

During seminars, editors from different craft magazines explain what they need to fill the pages of their magazines. They describe what is *not* selling and what colors, products, and styles to avoid. Color and trend experts share their expertise and forecast colors for the upcoming season. Manufacturers fill meeting rooms with the latest supplies. Tables arrayed with countless complimentary products invite exploration by designers for their future designing.

What does this mean to the average quilt designer? Opportunity! Many designers receive enough assignments to keep them producing all year. Editors find exactly the designs they want to publish. Designers gain the security of knowing that completed projects have a ready buyer.

SCD publishes a bimonthly newsletter for its members, and also maintains a directory of members, cross-referenced by specialty and state. Manufacturers, editors, and publishers who are looking for quilters or other craft specialties refer to this directory when they need new, fresh designs.

For example, one company introducing a line of quilting thread contacted me and other quilt designers. They generously sent spools of all their colors and invited us to experiment. Each participant who submitted quilting samples using this product received a lovely sewing basket filled with even more samples.

The Hobby Industry Association

HIA, the Hobby Industry Association, has been the largest national and international craft organization in the world—and I mean the whole world, with members, manufacturers, and craft seminars abroad. However, as I write this book in early 2004, big changes are underfoot. The boards of HIA and ACCI, the Association of Craft and Creative Industries, announced an upcoming merger. The new, combined association will better serve member organizations with two annual shows and more intense leadership. This will be a critical organization to watch. The combined membership list will include:

+ Manufacturers
+ Wholesalers, including fabric, thread, sewing, and quilting supply companies
+ Manufacturer representatives, who can create new markets for your quilted items
+ Trade and consumer publishers
+ Professional craft producers. Those of you who mass-produce quilts and related items for sale will find a strong, growing network of talented quilters who make a career selling what they make
+ Service suppliers, includes quilting teachers and designers

Professional training programs will continue to be a prime HIA service after the merger. See chapter 12 for details about HIA's Certified Teacher Training and Certified Professional Demonstrator programs.

Here is another HIA benefit for quilters. Manufacturers offer dozens of hands-on workshops to HIA's members during conventions. From brief "make it, take it" experiences to in-depth classes, members learn how to use the latest products. Manufacturers and their staffs, experts in developing products, show you how to use them.

Do not expect HIA to offer in-depth, all-day quilting workshops for beginners. Choose national or regional quilting conventions and seminars for quilt-specific classes. Attending HIA's convention, however, does permit you to see the latest fabrics, notions, threads, and tools for quilting and how quilting fits in with other crafts. Why not design your next quilt for sale based upon the latest trends in color, subject matter, or style? Here are other HIA benefits:

+ Receive a head start on design and color trends. Attend panel discussions. Listen to editors of prime magazines tell you what they need for publication. Each year, editors from the major quilting magazines inform participants of industry trends.
+ If you already quilt professionally, HIA's annual survey will help you decide how and where to advertise effectively.
+ If you sell quilting items or literature, you learn what consumers want and what they are currently buying.
+ As a teacher, you can plan classes around consumers' preferences and promote timely techniques.

Expand your personal network of business contacts and organizations if you want to profit from your quilting. Though quilters generally work in solitude, you cannot succeed in this business alone. Networking offers continual sources of information, ideas, and additional contacts that help keep you profitable.

As you can see from this book, countless opportunities exist to support, advise, and educate hard-working quilters and other crafters to succeed.

Networking experiences are critical to professional quilters. Never underestimate their value. Question everyone around you and be generous with your own information. Join both quilting and non-quilt-specific craft organizations. Membership provides continuous fresh, updated information and helps you get ahead. The groups mentioned in this chapter are but a few of the many excellent choices you have.

Most quilters who profit from their skill agree that at least one visit to the International Quilt Festival/Market in Houston is a must. The exposure, stimulation, and opportunities are absolutely overwhelming. Before starting a quilting business of any kind, you owe it to yourself to see your ideas in perspective. Go!

Remember to establish and remain focused on your niche in the marketplace. When considering adding a new activity to your business time, ask yourself if it fits in with the goals outlined in your marketing plan.

Now you know what a marketing plan is and why it belongs within the pages of your business plan. Attend quilting events frequently to remain as informed as possible. Marketing, a never-ending process, is critical to the success of your business.

Marketing Comments and Advice from Quilt Professionals

Betty Alofs of San Diego, California, started her business to make just enough money to buy supplies. "Quilting is not inexpensive," Betty says, but she wanted to see if she could make a quilt business work. Handling all the chores herself was important to Betty.

She did the research by visiting with shop owners and students in her classes. She noticed interest in her patterns and, with support from her husband, invested in startup purchases such as duplicating and printing supplies.

Marketing came next. Betty first invested in business cards, letterhead stationery, and envelopes. Armed with these, she visited quilt shops and fabric stores with samples in hand. "I learned how to step up and introduce myself, and then I went on to let them know my product would interest their customers," she explains.

"My pictorial patterns portray scenes in particular cities, so I visited gift shops in each geographical area with samples of what I could do," Betty says. "For example, one of my patterns was for the Mission San Diego de Alcala. Their mission gift shop now carries my patterns and has a sample to show how it will look when finished," she says.

Next, Betty sent letters to quilt shops further from her home using the same approach as she did with local shops. Following that marketing technique, she prepared a trunk show, had copies made of all of her classes, including explanations of her methods, and sent letters to quilt guilds.

During this time, Betty also took online classes on marketing for entrepreneurs. She took another class to learn to create her own Web site. These marketing activities started Betty on the right path. She adds, "I generated enough business to keep me going, traveling, teaching, and creating for a long time."

I asked Betty to describe her ideal customer or specific market. "I determined which particular quilters and needleworkers would be interested in my style," she says. "Then I listed where to find these potential customers. Quilt and fabric shops, guilds, hobby and gift shops, tourist-oriented shops, and events such as trade and quilt shows came first. I included retirement homes, assisted living facilities, and other spots that have activities for residents. I talked to school teachers and scout leaders."

Describing how she measures her marketing success, Betty said, "I study surveys, cash flow statements, increased customer lists, and increased yearly income. I measure my success by asking myself if I am in the black, increasing my income and customer base. I need to know if my work is paying for itself. I do not want a big business—just enough to keep me in the loop and involved with other quilters. I measure my success in terms of my own satisfaction and happiness. I am meeting people, finding great friends, participating in many wonderful events, and keeping busy at my 'little hobby,' as my children call it."

Susan Purney-Mark and **Daphne Greig** are partners in their quilt business in Canada, Patchworks Studio. They did very little market research when they began their business, encouraged by a local shop owner who thought their patterns had potential. In eighteen months, they recognized the need for a marketing plan and included it in their formal business plan when they applied for a line of credit through a local bank.

Describing their current marketing techniques, the partners are active members of several online groups such as FabShop Network, Quiltbiz, QuiltDesigners, and QuiltTeach. They agree that this keeps them current with topics and trends in the quilting industry. "We have an online *Studio Snips* newsletter for retail customers, and send an update/marketing note out at least once a month," Susan says. "We also write articles for *McCall's, McCall's Quick Quilts, Canadian Quilter,* and *The American Quilter.*"

Susan and Daphne's marketing arm is sizeable. They advertise in industry and trade publications such as *McCall's, American Quilt Retailer,* and *Canadian Quilter* magazines. They also advertise in Quilt Guild newsletters and write articles for their local guild newsletter. They contacted fabric companies offering to use their fabrics for articles and patterns. They have done so well that today, many manufacturers contact them, asking if the partners will use their company's fabric in their designs. They maintain a large mailing list of wholesale customers and send an updated catalog to them twice a year. They present lectures and workshops at retail shows to educate quilters and promote their products.

Susan and Daphne also have a rather unusual position in the quilting industry. Together, they started an Electric Quilt Software User Group to provide their software customers with tips and information in exchange for the opportunity to show them new products.

"Our marketing techniques work if they are repetitive," says Susan. "We generally do not see a lot of results from a single promotion, but once an ad has run a few times, we always see results. We hired a marketing specialist to help us develop a 'sell sheet' for our most recent line of patterns, and to create a news release for us. We worked with FabShop Network to distribute the sell sheet to shops, which resulted in a very good response to our new designs," Susan says.

The partners agreed to remain fairly selective when choosing marketing opportunities where they receive solicitations for products or articles. They always ask each other, "What is in this for us?" before accepting. They give gift certificates to guilds that ask for donations, and they write articles for publications that will promote them and their products if they believe their story fits the particular publication.

The partners relied on the IQA/Primedia survey to inform them about the quilting marketplace. They often ask, "Who is our prime customer?" for particular products, or, "Who will this appeal to?" when designing patterns, selecting fabrics, putting together kits, and preparing classes.

Susan and Daphne created the Canadian QuiltDesigners list to provide a forum for Canadian designers to interact with one another. They believe in spending time in competitors' booths at retail shows where they also vend, which lets them know what customers find exciting.

"We constantly ask, 'What's next in the industry?' Every October, Quilt Market gives us accurate and immediate feedback. We receive orders from customers there and for months afterward. We measure how successful our marketing is by seeing increasing numbers of customers and increased annual income. Our growth has increased since we began print and industry marketing and advertising," they say. Advising others wanting to succeed in the industry, Daphne and Susan say, "Always ask new wholesale customers where they heard about you to get an indication of what marketing technique works best."

Contributors to this chapter:
Betty Alofs
Lakeside, CA
msbtybp@cox.net
www.bettyalofs.com

Susan Purney-Mark and Daphne Greig
Patchworks Studio
2552 Eastdowne Road
Victoria, BC
V8R 5P9
Canada
(250) 595-4411
patchworkstudio@shaw.ca
www.patchworkstudio.com

5 *Selling Your Quilts*

Quilting has grown so much that several spinoff industries have evolved responding to demand from quilters. There are manufacturers who do little else but produce specialty tools for quilters. Some national book publishers issue quilting books exclusively. Others make a living supporting and offering services to the quilting industry.

During a three-hour pledge drive by a Public Broadcasting Station in Redding, California, to raise money for programming, quilters, speakers, and teachers kept the telephone ringing and pledges coming. Management acknowledged that only *The Three Tenors* and *Riverdance* produced more revenue.

So what is it about quilting that generates all this interest and industry growth? I believe there are several causes. Quilting in America is tied in with the country's history. Quilt history buffs unearth information about pioneer women making quilts as they trekked across the country. Black slave quilters have left behind a rich legacy in the colors, fabrics, and stories attached to their quilts. So avid are quilters to know the story behind every quilt at a show that today, the storyboards of the quilt's history are what they read first. Memorial quilts made of the clothing left behind from a loved one always move viewers. Art quilts such as the September 11, 2001, quilts tell a sad story in cloth, capturing the pain and detail of a terrible event.

Marriage and baby quilts memorialize happy family events, which become the history of the future. Quilts made for a special person utilizing photos, awards, embellishments, and more have become treasured gifts, and yes— quilters still make quilts for beds.

The Quality of Your Work

If you want to maintain quilting as a hobby, you can continue to make whatever pleases you or the family and friends to whom you give your quilted gifts. To turn your hobby into cash, though, you *must* produce a high-quality product that people want to buy. Before you can begin to sell, assure yourself that your work measures up in quality.

Your quilting must pass muster as professional work. You must produce a well-made product, exhibit good workmanship, and make good use of color, design, and finishing details. If you are not sure that your skills have reached a professional level, consider entering a quilt show or two. Quilting judges not only award ribbons to winners, but we also provide *written* notes for entries that do not win, commenting on what we found lacking.

Judges I work with agree that to determine whether we will grant an award or provide written suggestions for improvement, we consider the following:

+ Use of color
+ Use of design elements
+ Quality of hand or machine work
+ Consistency in workmanship
+ Finishing, which includes framing, lining, binding, and borders on quilts and quilted items.

Exhibiting your work will help you evaluate your skills and determine whether or not your work will stand up to public scrutiny. Winning one or more ribbons can indicate your readiness to enter the quilting marketplace, but failing to win should not discourage you. Where else can you find a qualified, objective critique of what you need to practice and perfect? Keep and study judges' comments after you have entered a show. Follow up on their suggestions by studying quilting books and magazines. Polish up your skills and try again.

Selling at Retail

When you sell at retail, whether in person or at a distance, you charge and collect the full price, plus tax when applicable, from your customer(s). Direct selling like this involves no middleman like those often involved when selling at wholesale.

Commission

Quilters agree that selling on commission is the best of all methods. Quilting on commission means you have a sure sale before you begin a new project— a happy arrangement. You do not have to worry about finding a buyer or marketing the product because in commission work, a buyer awaits. You create a project made to order, following the customer's preferences. "Customer" includes not just individuals who pay you to make something for them, but also magazine publishers, manufacturers, and organizations who commission you to make specific projects to order. People who order from you must feel confident that you produce good work and do it on time.

What could be better? No wonder quilters and freelancers prefer to sell by commission whenever possible. Desirable as it is, design commissions can also create problems—primarily for the quilter.

Occasionally, customers change their mind *after* you have begun a project, or perhaps when you're nearly finished with it. Many people who hire others to make things for them do not know how complicated it is to "make a few changes before you are done," as they usually put it.

Recently, a quilter asked others on an online quilting group for suggestions about a problem she experienced. A customer commissioned her to make a quilt, and when it was nearly completed, she called the quilter, asking her to

make "minor" changes and adding many hours to the work as described originally. The quilter wondered if she should add on to the original price or take
a loss on her labor.

A helpful quilter responded, "Sorry, but I advise you to take the loss and
stick to the original estimate unless when you quoted your price, you specifically mentioned that should the job take longer, you would bill extra.

"I learned an important lesson when this first happened to me. Today, I get
all the particulars of a job in advance and in writing. I list everything as specifically as possible. Make a checklist of all the variables that could happen and
include this information on your order form. Below, I've listed a few possibilities to think about.

"Assign each task a specific price per hour for your time. Remember
Murphy's Law and add on at least 25 percent to the hourly time you expect it to
take. There should be extra charges for the following special needs:

+ Sewing on the bias.
+ If the customer supplies fabric, who supplies extra for errors or miscal-
  culations?
+ Buttons, cording, and embellishments requiring hand sewing or basting.
+ Hand quilting, by the hour only.
+ Hand washing.
+ Ironing and preparing fabric.
+ Using challenging fabric with special patterns such as stripes, checks, plaids.
+ Fabric requiring special handling such as silks, organza, and fine materials
  that may not work easily by machine and need hand sewing instead.
+ Patterns supplied by the customer that need altering due to inconsistencies.
+ Will the customer layer and baste the quilt sandwich?
+ Has the customer provided a low-quality batting? If so, explain that you do
  not guarantee the finished project if the product is inferior."

This quilter now lists these charges on the back of a laser-printed order form
and includes basic prices added up on the front. "Have the customers sign it,"
she says. "Go over it with them. Make sure they read it and know what they are
signing. This way you and can add to it if needed."

Ending on a personal note, our quilter says, "I receive many advantages
from my home-based business. I am home with my children, and love the control of running my own show! If I do not get what I feel is fair, I prefer not to
make a particular item rather than undercut myself. To feel good about my
work, I will refuse an order rather than feel someone has taken advantage of
me. Better to give such items as outright gifts than to give myself the message
that my work is not worth much."

Make time to formulate a contract to guard against misunderstandings
between you and your clients when designing and/or making quilts and related
items on commission. Outline the conditions under which you will work. More
about contracts in chapter 8.

A frequent problem with quilting on commission occurs when clients change their minds or back out of an oral arrangement after you have begun their project. Avoid getting stuck with supplies ordered for a customer by requesting a down payment to cover initial purchases of raw materials before you shop. This prevents you from investing your money rather than the customer's.

If you have a client change her mind or try to back out of an oral arrangement after you have begun the project, there are solutions. Jane, a textile artist, shared one of her commission experiences. Most crafters, at one time or other, have faced a similar situation.

Jane received a call from her neighborhood bank. The manager explained that the branch planned to remodel. Jane's large, contemporary hangings, which hung in various locations around town, had received rave reviews. The bank manager wanted to hire Jane to design an 8' × 10' hanging for the bank. "I felt elated to have my work displayed in my own neighborhood," Jane admitted. Both artist and manager agreed on a completion date. Jane presented her preliminary drawings of the project to the bank redecorating committee.

Management approved the dimensions, colors, style, and design of the hanging. Jane rushed out to buy supplies so she could begin work immediately on the project, estimated to take three months.

After two months of work, Jane moved her piece into the bank. She needed to complete the project while considering the surroundings and available light. She continued the construction process on the premises.

Immediately, Jane had a volunteer audience making suggestions as the work progressed. The bank manager asked her to modify the design in-progress by altering the colors and changing design lines. Jane complied patiently, replacing some materials.

When management suggested more changes, Jane balked. She explained she would need more time to replace the section in question and begin anew. The manager reminded her of their agreed-upon completion date and total cost of materials.

Designers working on commission can avoid such problems with a simple contract outlining their terms. In my classes and books, I suggest, the "1/3, 1/3, 1/3" commission contract. Here is how it works.

Make sure the buyer has seen samples and completed photos of your work, and that the final price satisfies both parties. After preliminary discussions with the client, draw up your contract.

The First 1/3

State the final price in the first paragraph of the contract. In the next sentence, make it clear you will begin the work upon receipt of one-third of the total cost as a down payment. Explain that you will use these funds to buy raw materials.

This protects you in two ways. First, you will not be using your personal funds to buy raw materials for someone else. Second, should the buyer default, disappear, or lose interest in the project, you have not lost your own money.

Buyers who sign a written contract must understand that breaching the contract will cost them one-third of the total price.

The Second 1/3

I call the second paragraph the "review/final approval" section. Invite the buyer to view the project in-progress once or twice, and once more for the last time before you complete the project. Make it clear that after that date, you can no longer make changes or alterations. After the last review, the second one-third installment becomes due and payable *before* the work continues.

The Last 1/3

When you complete the work, *never* release it to the buyer without receiving the final one-third payment. Surrendering the completed item before receiving final payment causes you to lose a valuable negotiating position. Pleading for money you have already earned is unpleasant and damages your self-esteem.

Allow me to say a few words in defense of buyers. Though a few deliberately prey on inexperienced crafters, most disagreements occur because buyers do not understand the work process, rather than because of deliberate efforts to cheat.

Sandra, a quilter, experienced such a situation. A couple commissioned Sandra to design and produce an elaborate quilt for their parents' twenty-fifth wedding anniversary. Both parties agreed quickly on the design, color, layout, and style of the quilt.

Sandra drew up a contract featuring the 1/3, 1/3, 1/3 system to protect herself. The first third went smoothly. However, during the final review, problems arose.

Though they expressed satisfaction with Sandra's work, her clients had second thoughts about elements in the design. They wanted her to include details not previously discussed and not in the contract. "Just move this section over and add this in," they suggested. They were sincere in their belief that Sandra could accommodate their wish for last-minute changes.

However, Sandra took the time to educate her buyers—both non-quilters. She told them how long it would take to replace portions of the work to make room for other, unplanned design elements. She showed them how their idea would disturb the symmetry of the overall design.

She voiced her concern that it might be difficult to match the additional materials required with the original purchases. Finally, Sandra gently explained that the alteration would probably affect the promised completion date.

The buyers expressed surprise. They had no idea what their "small suggestion" would mean to a work-in-progress. Because they did not understand the quilting process, they did not realize how much they had asked of Sandra. The couple honored the original contract and design and expressed delight with the finished quilt.

Because Sandra had a *written* contract and conducted herself professionally in educating her customers, she averted hard feelings and misunderstandings.

Importantly, she also fostered good will for her business by creating satisfied customers.

Use promotional methods to find commission clients. Write on letterhead stationery to fabric and craft shops and quilting magazines. Many keep a file of dressmakers and quilters who will work on commission.

Place want ads in the "Services Available" section of your local newspaper or in the classified sections of quilting magazines. Contact local community groups offering to give programs, exhibits, or demonstrations about what you do. Show your work at exhibits and fairs so others can see you at work. Onlookers at fairs or those who attend programs you present can become potential clients, so engage them in conversation. Educate them about the value of handwork, and distribute flyers and brochures describing your services whenever possible.

Consignment

Unlike commission work, you design and complete an item, then look for a buyer hoping to find one. Visit local consignment shops, malls, and galleries to begin your research before you decide upon this venue. Survey the shop carefully to answer the following questions: What fills the shop? Does your work fit in? Does your style fit the shop's mood, theme, and price range? Does the staff respect the work of its consignors, protecting it from handling? Do you find most items tastefully displayed?

Once you find a shop or craft mall you would like to deal with, express interest and ask to see their consignment contract. Shop owners always protect their own interests in their contracts, but the contracts do not always protect the interests of the individual consignor—you! Here are a few key areas to investigate:

How will they display your work? If you submit a full-sized quilt, for example, will it hang on a wall or rest on a bed? If it is to be the latter, will customers be able to sit on the quilt or handle it? Does the shop allow customers to bring food and drinks in the shop? Quilts fade in direct sunlight. Request that your work be protected from this, as well as over-handling by many caressing hands.

What percentage of the retail price goes to the shop owner and to you? Though amounts vary from one shop to another, the last few years show that 50/50 is becoming the normal percentage, though you will still find some that pay 60/40 or even 70/30, with the larger amount going to the consignor. Absolutely *never* settle for an oral agreement here—get it in writing.

Does the shop owner have the right to lower your retail price if the quilt does not sell in a given time? If you do not want this to happen, say so in writing. At times, experienced shop owners realize a quilt is underpriced and would bring in more money if the price were higher than the one you set. If you disapprove of this, again, say so in your contract. But if you are just starting out in consigning, take time to listen to an experienced shop or gallery owner. If you find you continually undervalue your work, your pricing schedule needs immediate attention.

How long will it take the shop owner to notify you that you have a buyer for your quilt? Disappointment and frustration ensue if you find a quilt sold immediately upon display, but you did not know it for three additional months. Do not let shop owners operate on your money interest-free indefinitely. Frequently visit the shop unannounced. If the shop contract does not set a limit on when to notify you of a sale, and the shop owner did not feel obligated to call you immediately, receiving payment for your item could take several weeks.

Make sure to ask if the shop has insurance that will cover your quilt while it is in their possession. Ask to see the policy and request the name of the insurance carrier and agent. Fire, theft, or other damage to handmade quilts may be infrequent, but when it occurs, it is always tragic. Protect yourself from this possibility by making sure that the shop owner's coverage protects your items.

Talk to your insurance agent before problems arise. Fortunately, my agent introduced me to the nuances of "fine-art floaters" added to a basic home-owner's or renter's policy. He also recommended umbrella policy coverage under certain circumstances. Either of these arrangements provides coverage if your handmade items are lost or damaged while on display, in transit to another location, or in your vehicle.

Check the consignee's contract for details about all of the consignment issues discussed above. As consignor, if you find that your interests are not covered to your satisfaction, either ask the consignee to amend her contract or submit your own as you negotiate further.

Once your quilts or other handmade items saturate nearby consignment stores and are selling well, it may be time to expand. *The Crafts Report*, among other trade journals, provides monthly lists of consignment shops throughout the U.S. that seek textiles and quilted items. They usually describe what they are looking for and what they do not want. For example, in a recent issue of *The Crafts Report*, two shops on the East Coast wanted Victorian quilted items, while saying they were not interested in country-style designs.

Contact this magazine and others with persuasive cover letters and quality photos of your work. Good relationships with a few consignment shops across the country can keep you in business for years.

Craft Malls

Craft malls are another consignment method of retail selling. Crafters' malls seem to be declining in the face of Internet selling, but there are still some around. Some require you to sell your wares in person and to be physically in the location. Others have a co-op system where someone else sells your items directly to the consumer.

If you cannot find a local crafters' mall, check the malls across the country that appear in trade journals and the Internet. Write to ask if you can deal with them at a distance as you do with out-of-state consignment shops. Check the popular Coomer's Craft Malls, listed in the last chapter. As with commission and other consignment venues, a *written* contract is a must.

Direct Mail, Also Known as "Mail Order"

Direct mail selling, also known simply as "mail order," enables you to offer goods and services directly to customers. Selling this way continues to attract new entrepreneurs who believe that selling by mail guarantees a million-dollar income for minimum, easy work. Unfortunately, such hyperbole does not present a realistic picture. Selling by mail may not earn you millions, but it does provide extra income if you are detail-minded and willing to work diligently.

Items not readily available in retail stores sell best, such as one-of-a-kind pieces, hand-embellished wearables, or unusual, original, and unique designs. Choosing to sell items easily found in discount chain and "big lot" stores is not a good idea. Custom and handmade goods cannot possibly compete with the merchandise such stores offer. However, although you cannot compete with the prices of mass-produced goods sold in chain stores, you can sell items not available at those giant retailers. Quilters can sell not only handmade quilted items, but also patterns, kits, raw materials, notions, fabric, books, and booklets.

As you think about mail order, realize that you will order raw materials at wholesale prices, create the product, and sell finished items to consumers at retail prices. Even if you already have a profitable quilting business, you can consider mail-order selling as an adjunct to retail sales.

Avoid wasting time and money. Research meticulously before you begin. Start by writing a detailed profile of your typical buyer. When you have defined your target mail-order customer, you are ready to research the advantages and challenges of selling by direct mail.

Find your typical consumers by choosing several consumer publications you believe they read. *Quilter's Newsletter Magazine* offers a large, general classified listing of fabrics, patterns, books and notions. However *Piecework Magazine* might be more suitable if you wish to sell antique tools, books, or patterns, as it specializes in the historical aspects of quilting.

Write to magazines to request press or media kits. Magazine addresses appear on the masthead. The publications will send you everything you need to know about advertising within their pages. Media kits also describe their typical readers for you. When you receive the material, determine whether their demographics match your customer profile. If not, contact a few other publications until your target customer coincides with the profile of the magazine's typical reader.

Next, ask yourself if your product matches what you have learned about its readership. Do this by scanning the magazine's classified ads in several issues. Do you find items similar to yours listed?

Choose either a one- or two-step advertising process when you are ready to place your ad. One-step advertising means you sell your item directly to the buyer from an ad. The consumer reads your ad and sends you a check. You send the ordered product. Each of you had to take one step to complete the sale.

Two-step advertising may be needed if your product description requires more than what you can express in a classified ad. If you prefer to offer potential customers a catalog or brochure providing more details, you have set up two-step advertising. The customer responds to your ad by requesting more information. You send a direct-mail package including a catalog, persuasive sales letter, order form, and complete, detailed descriptions of the products. The customer sends you a check and orders the items. You fill and send the order. In this case, both of you had two steps to follow to complete the sale.

Contact the Federal Trade Commission (FTC) and request their free booklet explaining the Mail-Order Rule. The FTC regulates what you may and may not sell via mail order. The booklet will help you learn how to abide by the law while satisfying your mail-order buyers.

Direct-mail advertising differs slightly from general mail-order selling, in which potential customers read your ad and send you a check for their purchase. Direct-mail advertising means that you make your offer to consumers by sending them a catalog and other information whether they requested it or not. Success in mail order comes from repeat sales and satisfied customers. Make time to study direct-mail methods, since they require much preparation to target consumers wisely.

Begin a direct-mail program by formulating a "house list." This means that you make a list of potential customers by using the names of your friends, neighbors, and business associates. Take care to use current addresses, avoid duplications, and organize the list by zip code. Continue to expand your house list by adding the name and address of everyone who sends you an order or makes an inquiry by mail. Consider trading customer lists with other quilt-related business contacts you may have to expand your house list.

Mailing list brokers found in the yellow pages can help to expand your list. Brokers can create a larger list for you guided by the description of your target customer. When dealing with list brokers, you must keep in mind that they only rent you their list—they do not sell it to you. This means you may send mailings from a list provided by a broker only *once*.

Though you may add any buyers or inquirers to your house list, you may not mail to the broker's list again without paying another rental fee. List brokers make sure that those who rent their list use it only once by including a "dummy" name in the list. When your literature reaches this name a second time, you will hear from the broker that you have violated their one-time use only rental agreement. You may rent such lists from a list broker in groups of one thousand names at a time. Expect to pay more if you request specific demographics, such as a list of names of those who purchased quilts before or are of a certain age or income. Consider placing your items in established catalogs too. Study many craft, sewing, and quilting catalogs before choosing the one most suited to your products and style.

Contact catalog companies whose product lines align with your products. Write to them expressing your interest in having them carry your products. Make sure to send photos of professional quality. Include brochures and other literature describing your items.

When you hear from interested catalogers, prepare to negotiate. State your terms to the buyer. Let the buyer know how much profit you need to earn to compete in the marketplace. Make it clear you are willing to compromise but not surrender wholly to the catalog buyer's business preferences. You must also make your production schedule clear. No established cataloger will want to continue working with you if they advertise and receive orders for your product, only to find you cannot meet their customers' demands. If you can only make two dozen patchwork pillows per month, for example, explain this to the catalog buyer early. Later, if your pillows sell well, they have the opportunity to ask for a greater quantity while giving you sufficient time to find someone to help you produce more in less time.

Many excellent craft catalogs have editorial boards that jury potential merchandise from freelance crafters. This assures the buying public that they will receive the highest quality in handcrafted items. Consider small, specialized catalogs too. They advertise in trade journals and in various arts and crafts publications.

Learn about the mail-order company you want to work with. Many new business owners assume that mail-order catalog companies will undertake the preparation details of your item. But do not expect them to take the time to create, lay out, and write your sales copy, for example. Make it easy for them to work with you by doing a good job of this yourself. Send high-quality sketches or photographs that clearly illustrate your item and include details about prices, sizes, and colors.

Creative people often have introverted personalities and dislike asserting themselves. However, you must learn assertive marketing and sales techniques and must speak and write in a confident manner if you want to expand your business via mail order in established catalogs.

Producing a catalog alone can be expensive when you consider photography, production, printing, binding, and postage, to mention a few prime expenses. Perhaps you have friends who wish to sell by mail order with whom you can share expenses and work. Do you belong to a quilt guild where several members have something to sell by mail order? Consider a co-op catalog featuring the work of each person. Several quilters pooling resources make this idea practical.

Consider placing a small ad in a networking publication and offer to trade your house mailing list of customers with another craft professional. Choose a complementary market, not a competitive one. Trading lists name for name works well if you check to make sure the business you are considering has a list as current as yours.

Defray your own expenses by offering to include literature and brochures from colleagues in your own mailings. Suggest they do the same for you. All of you will increase the size of your in-house mailing list for little cost, reaching consumers directly.

Technological advances today make it necessary for even home-based entrepreneurs to have a computer. Selling by mail order requires most of the basic components of computer technology. You will need a word processing program to write ad copy, deal with correspondence, and write instructions. Select a spreadsheet program to show income and expenses and to help prepare your federal income tax returns each year. Choose a database to maintain customer and mailing lists, and software enabling you to print labels, although you can postpone this until your mail-order business increases. Plan to update your programs, and to protect your computer from "malware" such as viruses and Trojan horses. Good, thorough, and regular backing-up of all your programs and records is a must once you rely on your computer to be the backbone of your business.

Consider using direct mail to follow up when interested customers request information about your products. Always have a printed brochure or catalog available to mail promptly upon request. Charge for a small brochure or catalog to defray costs. This will sift out people who love to get anything free by mail but never intend to buy.

Each time you fill an order, practice the "stuffing" technique used in direct mail. This means that when you have completed packaging an order, you "stuff" further brochures, flyers, sale notices, percent-off-of-next-order coupons, and other promotional materials into the package. Since such packages will already reach customers with an interest in your products, make sure they know about the additional items you offer. In direct mail, repeat customers become the most valuable of all, so do not miss a chance to reach out to them in every way you can.

Selling by direct mail requires extensive research, thorough preparation, and comprehension of mail-order techniques, advertising, and postal regulations. Do not overlook the critical need for educational information in this area before proceeding. See the final chapter for books about selling by mail order.

Selling from Your Web Site

Workers leaving corporate America to work from home are responsible for a great increase in online buying and selling, which was nearly unheard of just a few years ago. Home-based entrepreneurship requires organization, research, and priority-setting skills. If you have these skills, selling directly to the consumer via your own Web site may be for you.

Working to sell online from a home office requires basic equipment, including:

+ A computer
+ Knowledge of how to create Web sites and manage graphics
+ An Internet Service Provider (ISP) to allow you to access the Internet. Choose from DSL lines, T-lines, cable, or the least expensive (and slowest) option, dial-up services
+ A modem. Get nothing less than 56K, and decide whether you want an internal or external modem
+ Phones and fax lines

Many comprehensive books have been written about the Internet, so I will be brief as I outline a few thoughts for you to consider:

Create a "Presence" on the Internet
The best way to let the world know about you and your product is to subscribe to online e-mail lists and user groups (also known as Usenet). Join in the discussions with others who share the same interests as you do. You will find a list of these groups in the last chapter. At first, just read the postings (which is known as "lurking"); then, begin to contribute when you are sure that the information you are sharing will benefit others on the list. Avoid blatantly advertising your business in this venue.

Choosing a Name and Signature Line
Take care when you choose a name. Will you use your own name, or do you prefer to use a fictitious name? (See chapter 11 for business names and trademarks.) Scour the Web for information about creating and registering a domain name for your Web site.

Creating Your Web Site
Surf the Web to see how others present products and services like yours. What features, bells, and whistles would you like or not like to include on your site? Get ready for e-commerce *before* you begin building your site. Consider the following:

+ What types of quilt products and services will you offer?
+ Will your prices be higher or lower than those of local retail stores?
+ How will you handle order fulfillment and shipping?
+ How will you handle sales calls and customer service?
+ How will you guarantee satisfaction?
+ Will you have a return policy?
+ How will you handle international orders, if at all?
+ What about security issues? Make network security a top priority *before* your e-commerce site goes live. Look into programs that provide virus protection and firewalls to keep your computer free from corruption and invasion.
+ Decide how you want customers to contact you. Make it easy for them. Do you prefer e-mail, phone, fax, or snail mail?

Products that sell well in retail stores do not necessarily sell well online, so start simple. Avoid creating a Web site that is too complex or that offers too many products at first.

Yahoo, Internet Explorer, Netscape, Tech TV, e-Bay, and many more will help you design your site yourself. Read about FrontPage software. It features ready-made templates to make creating Web sites easier. However, if you already have extensive computer skill, you may prefer to go it alone. At the very least, you must learn how to combine graphics and text to make your site flow easily, smoothly, and quickly for those who want to know more about you and your work.

How fast does your page load? If you use too many or large graphics, visitors can become discouraged waiting for your site to load and may look elsewhere for what they wanted. Animated images and moving graphics load very slowly. Do you need help? You may need to hire writers, computer consultants, or Web site creators to get your site up and running if you are new to managing one.

Financial Considerations When Selling from Your Web Site

Will you accept credit cards from your customers? Watch out—it is not as easy as you may think. Escrow companies have sprung up to act as a conduit between you and your buyer, to lessen the chances of your getting an out-dated or stolen card or a bad check. Look for such companies on the Internet itself. I have had very good experiences using PayPal, but there are many others.

Visit your local post office for free rate charts, envelopes, and boxes. Look over their special "flat rate" envelopes. You may stuff anything you want, regardless of weight, into these special, sturdy envelopes. Since I primarily sell my own books, I find it costs me less than half the price to ship my books when I use flat rate instead of ordinary mail.

One last tip as you consider whether or not to create and sell from your own Web site: Get yourself a copy of *Internet Marketing Secrets for Dummies* and *FrontPage for Dummies*, both wonderful resources.

Selling at Wholesale

Selling at wholesale is indirect in that you do not deal with the ultimate consumer; someone else does. This person you sell to may be a shop or gallery owner, a sales representative, or even the staff of a catalog house, but in this case, there is a middleman.

Selling to Shops

Approach small shops and boutiques if you want to sell your goods at wholesale. Visit potential businesses. Observe and browse carefully while answering the following questions: Do your items fit in with the existing merchandise? What type of shoppers do you see in the store? Do they show a likely interest in your products? Do you find the store clean, professionally arranged, and appealing?

If you answer "yes" to these questions, do not approach the owner or manager yet. Go home and prepare. Make sure your portfolio showcases your line to your advantage. Select a sampling of your wares, grouped and packaged attractively. Look over the quality of your brochure and business card. They convey your professional status.

Though many crafters barge into shops unannounced, most managers appreciate hearing from you first. Call ahead to get the name of the contact person in charge of buying. Ask if he or she would like to see your work. Inquire about the best time to visit to avoid catching the person when he feels rushed.

Dress professionally, armed with your materials. *Never* be late for this appointment. Remember, you have come to sell yourself as well as your products. Establishing regular accounts with a few shops in your geographical area is ideal. Treasure such relationships.

Sales Representatives Can Create Markets for You

Sales representatives offer another possibility for selling your quilts and related items. They advertise in craft trade journals when they wish to take on new artisans to expand their line. Hardworking reps take your items on the road for you. They find new markets at further distances than you might travel. They visit boutiques, shops, and retail outlets, representing you and your work. Since they usually represent several crafters, make sure your rep does not carry a competing line. For a percentage of the retail price, averaging 15 to 20 percent, reps sell your goods outright or take custom orders on your behalf.

Carefully choose and then nurture successful business relationships once you find them. Competent reps can expand your market and enlarge your customer base. They can pass valuable marketing information along to you, such as color and style preferences, new product ideas, or price changes. Before hiring a rep, ask for a generous sampling of present clients, then call them. Inquire about the rep's effectiveness in finding new business, and his promptness with paperwork. Most importantly, ask about the condition of unsold merchandise that is returned to the client. Is it still fit to resell? If you can maintain regular contact with a sales rep and learn to work together, the rep can increase your income.

Fairs, Exhibits, and Trade Shows

Quilters wanting to sell their work directly to the consumer have many alternatives from which to choose. *Webster's Dictionary* defines a "craft fair" as "an exposition in which exhibitors participate, with the purpose of buying or selling or familiarizing the public with products." Who can say it better?

Consumer Craft Fairs

Craft fairs are the most traditional way to sell your quilted items directly to consumers. Do you enjoy meeting the public? Craft shows, boutiques, fairs, and flea markets may be a good choice for you if you have an outgoing personality and can express enthusiasm for your products to buyers. If you enjoy talking to potential buyers personally and love explaining your creative process, you may enjoy working a craft fair, where many types of crafts are represented.

Start with small, local fairs in your community. Many experienced artisans who travel across the country to sell their wares began by selling from a card table at a community sponsored fundraiser and craft fair. This way, you will learn the system and gather experience before attempting larger fairs.

Finished products such as bed quilts, wall hangings, toys, clothing, and accessories appeal to the buying public shopping at local, county, and state fairs. You may be surprised to learn that while customers prefer exclusive, one-of-a-kind, handmade items, they often expect to pay the same prices that they pay for ready-made items found in chain department stores. Educate your buyers and explain the differences between handmade and mass-produced items or imitation imports from outside the U.S.

Photos of you at work, and those that show works-in-progress, tell potential buyers your story. Smile warmly while you explain the benefits of your products. Be ready to answer customers' questions about raw materials used and product care. Prepare to answer the question, "How long does it take you to make this?" many times. Finally, consider whether or not you want to be able to process credit-card purchases, as fairgoers typically make impulse sales.

Regardless of which type of consumer show you choose, start small and work up to larger events, for you will need to gather practical experience. Look for neighborhood shows that will rent a space for a small fee to learn if the fair circuit is for you. Travel expenses are low, and table and booth fees are minimal.

Church fundraisers, craft fairs, and other nonprofit events are easy to find in your community too. Look for event names, places, and dates in your local newspaper and at Chamber of Commerce offices. After you work a few shows, you will have a realistic picture of the market for your products.

Think twice about going to any fair or show, however small, by yourself. You will need someone else to help with errands, making change, purchasing food, providing you with rests and breaks, and, critically, keeping any eye out for the ever-present shoplifters. Just unloading and reloading supplies from car to craft table can be a problem if one or the other is left unattended. Engage a friend or family member, but do not consider doing this alone. Neighborhood, county, regional, and state fairs are a good choice if you offer quilted items with broad, general appeal. For listings of most craft shows across the country, look to *The Crafts Report*, or the quarterly *Crafts Fair Guide* published by Lee Spiegel. Also, check out the book *How to Sell What You Make: The Business of Marketing Crafts at Fairs, Boutiques, and Exhibits* by Paul Gerards (Stackpole Books).

Check with your community and state as you prepare to make sales directly to your customers, the ultimate consumers. The franchise tax board in most states requires sellers to collect sales taxes from consumers. You must add the tax to each item sold. State franchise tax boards across the country differ in minor details. Check with the office in your county to learn more. Not only will you collect the taxes, you must set the money aside to make annual or quarterly payments to your state franchise tax board. More on this topic in chapter 11.

Home Boutiques

Home boutiques provide another entry to selling directly to consumers, though you will need quite a bit of time to prepare. Two sisters in Northern California illustrate how simple, yet effective, home craft boutiques can be.

Both sisters work all year making quilts, sweaters, wreaths, floral arrangements, dolls, and home decor crafts. During the first weekend of December, they decorate one of their homes with their collection.

They advertise simply by placing ads in local newspapers and distributing colorful flyers at nearby schools and churches. Shoppers looking for one-of-a-kind hand-crafted items for gift-giving come to buy.

The sisters spend a week before the event arranging an appealing display and pricing each item. In one weekend, they generate enough income to buy craft supplies to make new items for the following year, pay expenses, and add to their bank accounts during the holiday season.

If you decide to sell this way, plan ahead. Collect names and addresses of customers who visit your home show or boutique. Make a signup sheet readily available. Each year, you can mail invitations to those who have supported you in the past.

Once you gather experience at small fairs, flea markets, and home boutiques, look to larger events. Spend time developing a dynamic display to showcase your products for larger shows, where you will compete with seasoned crafters. Attractive displays are critical to lure fairgoers to your booth.

Quilt Shows

Quilt shows are more specific than general craft fairs, where many types of crafts are for sale, including quilted items. Quilt shows, fairs, and exhibits differ from general craft shows because buyers have already expressed a specific interest in your product—quilts—by merely attending a show. Recognize people who attend these shows as your target market. Quilt shows attract quilters at all levels and can be wonderful if you have products specifically directed toward them, such as tools, books, and patterns, in addition to quilts. Quilt shows allow you to make direct sales to dedicated, quilt-oriented consumers.

Competition may be stiff, as most booth vendors will have products similar to yours, unlike craft fairs, where competitors may be few in number. Presenting yourself as a professional in your field counts even more when dealing with quilt-knowledgeable buyers. Answer questions completely, because show attendees come to learn about new materials, tools, and techniques. Information and displays about your products and how to use them are vital.

Successful vendors at quilt shows are often those who attract attention with interesting activities such as speed-cutting fabric, making templates, using tools, and demonstrating the latest fusibles. Quilt shows are more targeted and sophisticated than general craft fairs and require more preparation and experience.

Choose the best display equipment you can afford, as you will be competing with established quilt professionals who are on a higher level than you would usually find at local and neighborhood events. Manufacturers of show display equipment advertise in craft trade journals, especially *The Crafts Report*. This publication also runs frequent articles about how to prepare and set up show displays of all sizes, and advertises where to buy display equipment such as tents, lighting, shelves, and tables. You must learn to:

+ Set up appealing displays to showcase your products
+ Greet the public
+ Have a large quantity of informational literature, business cards, and brochures on hand
+ Explain your wares
+ Answer unexpected questions
+ Set prices appropriately for your geographical area
+ Devise a security system to protect your goods during the show
+ Build up an adequate inventory of goods available for sale well before an event

QuiltDesigners@yahoo.com is the most helpful source of information I have found to help quilters prepare to sell their goods at quilt shows. New and experienced quilt designers ask questions and receive answers as upcoming quilt shows approach. Discussed are tips on how to select tables and booths, how to book into a show, how to set up and decorate your booth, and shipping, pricing, and marketing details. Anyone planning to vend at a quilt show will learn much from this free online newsletter about preparing for every facet of an upcoming show. The debriefing comments and summaries that appear online after quilters return home are fascinating, too.

Finding quilt shows is easy. Nearly all quilt magazines provide monthly listings of shows throughout the U.S. *Quilter's Newsletter Magazine* provides the most comprehensive list, state by state. If you belong to quilt and craft guilds, you will receive advance notice about upcoming quilt shows. Each time you attend a quilt show, you will find flyers about upcoming shows readily available.

Trade Shows

Trade shows—so named because they offer products directed at a specific trade—require more preparation and professional status than the consumer shows or craft fairs that were described previously. Here you will sell to professionals who own shops, boutiques, catalogs, and other retail connections. They will create new markets for your products.

Trade shows, also known as wholesale shows, require more preparation and professional status than selling any other way, but this is the best way if you want to sell your quilted products in quantity. Prepare thoroughly to deal with experienced professionals who are already experts in some aspect of the quilting market. Trade shows are fewer in number than retail, consumer-oriented shows.

Since shop owners sell your products for you, realize when selling to them that you will charge them wholesale prices—not retail. Customers who patronize shops and catalogs will pay the retail price for your products and the shop owner or catalog owner, not you, will collect sales taxes.

Though you charge them less, remember that when you act as a wholesaler, you can require minimum orders to encourage larger sales. Keep in mind that unlike consumer sales, payment is not immediate. You may wait for up to sixty or even ninety days for payment from retailers.

Since trade shows do not admit consumers, professionals must prove they qualify by producing any or all of the items listed below. Expect to prove you are part of the sewing or quilting trade when applying to attend or participate in these shows. You may need to show a business license, copies of your Seller's Permit, letters requesting show information on letterhead stationery, a voided business check, and business cards.

Before considering selling wholesale, make sure you can manufacture your product in sufficient quantity. Retailers who buy to resell expect a reduced price in exchange for buying large amounts of merchandise from manufacturers and distributors—which include you.

Selling at wholesale trade shows is not for beginners. Wait until you are well established in your business. Make sure the quality of your products is consistent. You must have experience setting prices to ensure that the discounts you offer retailers still provide you with adequate profit. Attend smaller, then medium-sized, retail shows before considering renting exhibit space at your first wholesale show. Remember, retailers do not pay at the time of purchase as consumers do. Your budgeting must allow lag times between shipping your product and receiving payment.

Preparation and quality displays become more important than ever, for your customers are experienced craft business people themselves. They immediately recognize quality and performance. They expect service and readily available information about your products so they can profit as they resell them. Trade shows bring fewer buyers than retail shows, but your reward is volume selling.

Some shows are juried. This means that a group of qualified people working for an event will meet to select the crafters who will participate in a particular show. They screen participants by requesting slides of each crafter's work. Thus, merely applying for entrance does not mean automatic acceptance. Expect to pay "booth" or entry fees if accepted. Successful shows often fill so quickly with regulars that newer artisans must be diligent in applying and returning completed paperwork.

Trade Show Benefits

Consider attending non-quilt-specific trade shows. The Hobby Industry Association (HIA) sponsors the largest of all the annual craft trade shows in the country. In fact, they have grown so much that they now sponsor international shows in Mexico and Europe as well.

Quilt vendors sell at this show, along with hundreds of other craft professionals. HIA shows are held each January, alternating sites in Las Vegas, California, and Texas. See their Web site or newsletter for dates and locations of international shows.

Selling at Both Retail and Wholesale

Every August, in San Francisco, the American Craft Council provides an opportunity for quilters to sell at both retail and wholesale. During the first two days, this comprehensive show serves the trade only. Buyers from all over the West Coast come to select merchandise to fill their shops.

During the last three days of the show, sellers prepare for consumers. Overnight, they switch price tags on merchandise from wholesale to retail, and prepare for a fresh new onslaught of eager buyers.

Quilt industry trade shows such as those in Houston every fall also offer both ways of buying and selling. When you, as a vendor of quilting supplies, attend a show where you sell at retail to consumers for a day or two, then to other quilt professionals and shop owners a day or two later, you must shift your thinking as you identify each group. Quilt professionals who buy from you do so with the intention of reselling your product to the ultimate consumer. They will pay your wholesale price. They collect and pay the sales tax—not you. This is a different process from when you sell directly to the ultimate consumer, who buys from you at your full retail price directly. You are the one who must collect and pay sales tax.

Wholesale and Retail: Two Different Pricing Schedules

Selling at wholesale means a retailer will *sell* your item at the same price that you do, but expects to *buy* your merchandise for less—usually 50 percent less. This 100 percent markup, also known as "keystoning," covers the retailers' costs of operation and contributes to their profit. Many seasoned quilters decide to sell their products not only to consumers at full retail prices, but also at wholesale to shop owners, distributors, and catalogers, who in turn sell their products for them.

Quilters may feel confused as they set up two different pricing schedules—one price when selling an item at retail, another to sell it at wholesale. Some, in fact, choose to sell only at retail just to avoid this dilemma. However, it need not be so daunting. The fundamental process when preparing to sell a craft product at both retail and wholesale is to create a basic price that can be at least doubled or tripled.

When you plan to sell at wholesale to shop owners, you must at least double the total costs of your product so you can still make a profit. Triple it or more when you sell directly to the consumer. Sharing in your profit allows stores to pay for rent, salaries, and advertising.

Deciding whether or not to sell at both retail and wholesale requires research, but note the advantage of wholesale selling. Retail customers do not necessarily become frequent, repeat customers. Wholesale customers, when happy with your product, generally order frequently and will usually increase their orders from you if your items sell well.

Ask yourself three questions before you undertake selling at both retail and wholesale:

1. Can you make money selling your work for half of what you sell it for at retail shows? If so, wholesaling is an option. In most crafts, including quilting, the difference between retail and wholesale is 50 percent, but recognize that you have to sell in quantity to profit when selling wholesale.
2. Does a seller who wants to sell for you sell at the same fair or show as you? If so, it may be hard to avoid undercutting your retail clients. Most become hostile if they feel they are competing with their own wholesaler in the same arena. Before attempting this, check with your retail customers (shop owners) and make sure you can work something out from which you can all benefit.
3. Wholesaling means you do not have to bear the expense, time, money, and energy of attending shows yourself or opening your own shop. But don't forget to review your costs of operation in view of selling at 50 percent of retail, to determine if it can become profitable for you.

Important Annual Quilt Shows

The annual Fall International Quilt Festival and Quilt Market (the name used by the corporation that runs this show), held every October in Houston, Texas, is the largest trade show in the United States devoted exclusively to quilting, but it is not the only one.

The National Quilting Association (NQA) holds a major quilt show every June, plus exhibits, workshops, lectures, and a fashion show, as well as running a large vendor mall. Unlike the Houston event, NQA moves from one state to another each year. NQA offers correspondence courses and certification for quilters wanting to become teachers.

Paducah, Kentucky, hosts another important annual quilt show, exhibit, and contest. Held in the spring of each year, this event is sponsored by the American Quilter's Society. This organization publishes excellent quilting books each year and offers an important certification program for those wanting to learn to become quilt appraisers.

In person, by mail, or via the Internet, opportunities abound to sell well-made, appealing quilt products. Explore each outlet to decide which is best for you.

6 *Negotiating Contracts*

To "negotiate" means "to confer with another in order to reach an agreement." It also means "to make an agreement between two or more parties, especially one that is written and enforceable by law."

These definitions all matter considerably to quilters if they want to avoid disagreements and misunderstandings and head off unpleasant, acrimonious relationships, potentially spoiling a partnership beneficial to both parties. If you never considered the possibility that quilting business matters can benefit from contractual agreements, take note. There are actually four major books written for those who work in the creative arena:

+ *The Law* (*in Plain English*)® *for Crafts*, 5th Edition, Leonard D. DuBoff, Allworth Press (Allworth Press is the publisher of this book and many others about small business.)
+ *Simple Contracts for Personal Use*, Stephen Elias & Marcia Stewart, Nolo Press Self-Help Law Books
+ *Business & Legal Forms for Authors & Self-Publishers* and *Business and Legal Forms for Crafts*, both by Tad Crawford, Allworth Press

The Importance of Contracts

Smiles and handshakes over coffee may feel good. Exchanging pleasantries feels even better. However, neither comes close to the excellent relationships between professionals that contracts can provide.

Take the time to formulate a contract to guard against misunderstandings between you and your clients when designing and/or making quilts and related items on commission. Outline the conditions under which you will work. See my 1/3, 1/3, 1/3 contract in the previous chapter.

Magazine publishers and editors will send you a publishing contract telling you what rights they wish to buy in order to publish your design in their magazine. This contract tells you the deadline when you must submit your work and when they will pay you—on acceptance or publication. If you hire an agent, not only will you sign the agent's contract, but all agents also have a responsibility to negotiate other contracts for you.

Before delving further into contract negotiations, I want to introduce you to two professional quilting teachers I interviewed. I asked them about their experiences in dealing with contracts and how using them affected their businesses.

Interview with Kathleen Bissett

Kathleen Bissett, a quilting teacher, has had many experiences with teaching contracts. They range from having only verbal agreements to making multi-page detailed contracts between her and the guilds, shops, and conferences where she teaches.

"The most frustrating experiences come from guilds," Kathleen says. "The likely cause is that from year to year, guild representatives change, and many guilds do not have standard contracts.

"This week I had to write a contract myself and sent it to a guild. I did not mind, but customarily, teachers receive a signed contract from the hiring group. I do not commit to a guild until I see their offer in writing with a signature. I wrote the contract and sent it to the guild representative to complete, requesting that a copy be sent back to me, signed. At least I have a signature."

How long have you been in business?

"I have been teaching quiltmaking for about twenty years and have published patterns since 1995. I focus on teaching/lecturing but my pattern business has resulted from my successful classes."

Have you negotiated with a third party for contracts?

"Four different distributors sell my patterns—two in the U.S. and two in Canada, my home. Three of them approached me first, but I approached the fourth. I made the same arrangement with all four companies and it has worked well. None are on consignment. A couple of the distributing companies have sales reps, but I do not deal with reps directly."

Have you written up your own contract in the event you do not agree with one presented to you?

"When I approach shops requesting a contract, they often say they use only verbal arrangements. When that happens, I write them a letter outlining what our conversation was. In closing my letter, I state that unless I hear differently from them, I assume I have outlined it correctly. This makes them feel that they did not have to sign a contract when I explain that all they did was sign a letter clarifying the agreement."

What action do you take if the other party does not abide by the contract?

"I remind them about the contract's details and initiate a discussion. Usually it works out, but on two occasions where I was teaching at shops, I simply stopped teaching there, preferring to work at other shops where conditions were made clear."

Have you requested and received changes to an established contract?

"I have requested and received changes to an established contract when I felt the details were not clear enough—changes when I asked for more adequate space for students or accommodation conditions (clean and quiet). After a few uncomfortable situations when staying at a guild member's or shop owner's home, I found they expected me to entertain them during the time I needed rest. I now spell out that I require 'down time' in my contract."

Please offer your advice on contracts to others just starting out.

"Do not be afraid of clearly stating what you expect in all areas concerning the arrangements of an upcoming event. If you receive a contract that does not outline the arrangement in enough detail, make sure the contract is clarified in writing. Be sure to have more than one contact person and more than one method of contacting them."

Interview with Ann Anastasio

Ann Anastasio has given lectures, workshops, and a play to guilds for over twenty years—at first alone, and for the last eight years with her quilting partner, Lani Longshore. Together, as *Broken Dishes Repertory Theatre*, they present a highly successful quilting musical comedy program to guilds.

"I am the one who deals with contracts," Ann says, "but since we are partners, guilds seem unsure about how to work with us as a team. I am specific when speaking with guild program chairs by saying that we will accept sleeping accommodations together, but want separate beds. They usually put us up in a motel because it is easier than finding someone to house us both. We prefer motels."

"Guild contracts often do not spell out everything that we find necessary. Some shops have no contracts, which becomes very difficult. We have had no problems with our contracts, but at times, we have experienced a lack of planning on the program chair's part. Sometimes, we find no motel reservations, a locked program location, no materials list given out, and misplacement of sample quilts we sent ahead of our presentation. Contracts help tremendously to resolve these issues."

Have you written up your own contract when you do not agree with one presented to you?

"No, but I cross out things I disagree with, such as the high percentage some guilds want from sales of our patterns or of hand-dyed fabrics following our presentations."

Have you requested and received changes to an established contract?

"I have had to negotiate about: the number of guild members I can expect to manage in a class, the exact location of program, the time I was expected to arrive, when they wanted me to speak, the location of member's home or motel and the phone number, meals provided, when I should send sample(s) and/or materials list(s) to promote the program, and where they are to be sent and to whom."

What do you do if the other party does not abide by the contract?

"As the current program chair of my own guild, I have come up against problems when hiring others with contracts, involving missing sample quilts, unmentioned fees, miscalculated mileage, unfilled workshops, whether or not to pay airfare in advance, and more. All such disputes were settled to both parties' satisfaction, which was helped along by the existing contract. For a program I presented at a quilt council a few years ago, I prepared a guide for guilds and their program and workshop chairs describing how they should work with visiting teachers."

Please offer your advice on contracts to others just starting out.

"Keep your own list of information you find necessary. Keep it near the phone for reference when guild representatives call. If an issue that you need is not in the contract, discuss it with the program chair, then add it to the contract, if necessary. Ask whether sponsors will take you out for a meal just before or after the program. What is the exact name and address of the restaurant? At what point will they pay you? We prefer to receive a check at the end of the programs, but it is better to know. We ask if it is not offered. You should have your own invoice, on which you list mileage, fees, and any other expenses en route (bridge tolls, meals), to give to the program chair."

Interview with BrendaLou Scott, Shop Owner

To get a balanced view of contracts used in the quilting industry, I asked BrendaLou Scott to share with readers the document she has drawn up as a shop owner to present to the teachers she invites to her shop to conduct classes.

BrendaLou Scott owns a successful shop in Northern California. She hires dozens of teachers to come to her shop each year. Brenda is also a welcome contributor to the daily quilting digests, often sharing her expertise and experience from a shop owner's point of view.

Two years ago, she generously posted the details of the contract she drew up for her shop. I thought it so complete that I asked her permission to post it on the copyright page of my Web site. Response was so positive that once again, I asked her to share her outstanding and comprehensive contract with readers of this book.

Guidelines for Class Instructors

Scottie Dog Quilts 301 W. Harris Street Eureka, CA 95503 (707) 444-9662

We at Scottie Dog Quilts realize that classes are one of the most important services that a quilt shop can offer. We are committed to offering classes by committed, talented, well-prepared, caring teachers. We expect our classes to be an enjoyable experience for both teacher and student. If you, as an independent instructor, ever feel a need to discuss any problem about the shop, the class, the students, or advertising, we hope that you would speak with us sooner rather than later. BrendaLou Scott is owner of the shop and all classes, scheduling, policy decisions are up to her.

All instructors are independent contractors and will provide Scottie Dog Quilts with a completed W-9 form. In January of each year you will receive a 1099 IRS form. Your income will be reported to the IRS. There are absolutely no exceptions. We follow the letter of the law and you would do well to be professional in your teaching career.

Class Times:
Whole Day: 10 AM–4 PM
Half Day: 10 AM–1 PM OR 1–4 PM OR 6–9 PM

On occasion there is a two-hour class scheduled.

Lunch breaks are up to the instructor (although if no lunch break has been taken by 1 PM, we usually remind you to take one). We encourage sack lunches or takeout. There are several restaurants nearby that allow takeout, and we will offer the menus around 11 AM.

Teachers are expected to arrive fifteen to twenty minutes early and to be ready to teach at appointed times. Class will end at the ending time. Do not clean up a half hour early. You are a professional and are expected to teach your students for the fully allotted time.

Class fees are set by the individual instructor. Understand that SDQ will collect the fees up front and pay the instructor according to the following schedule within forty-eight hours of the class.

Any fee under $10: less $1 per-student fee
1–5 students: less 10% per-student fee
6–14 students: less 20% per-student fee

Our cut from the class fees helps (but in no way covers) to pay the added costs of the room, electricity, equipment (mats, rulers, irons, design walls, ironing boards, etc.), liability insurance, cleaning, advertising, promoting, and bookkeeping that we incur for these classes.

Teacher Discount: All teachers will receive a 25 percent discount (excluding consignment items and Featherweight Sewing Machines) for all regularly priced items they buy at Scottie Dog Quilts during the quarters they are teaching.

Class Size: Class minimums will be set by the teacher (usually three students). Our classroom can comfortably accommodate up to twelve students. We have seats for sixteen people and will discuss larger classes. One week before a class is to run, we check the class list. We will confirm that the class has enough students. You will be responsible for calling and reminding your students about the class and offering to answer any questions regarding class list, equipment needed, and other details. This nice touch is to your benefit. Students who feel valued by their instructors will repeat again and again with that particular teacher.

Scheduling: Classes are scheduled six weeks before the beginning of the next quarter. Note that the quarters overlap.

January-April: November 15
April-July: February 15
July-October: May 15
October-January: September 15

Please be prepared ahead of time. I will call you, but if you can save me time by contacting me with a presentation, your classes will get better preference.

Advertising: Scottie Dog Quilts will advertise your classes in the following ways: Putting a notice in the Quarterly Newsletter, mailed to over 1,000 quilters. Hanging your sample in the shop with pertinent information posted with it. Promoting your class with customers who drop by the shop. Passing out class lists to interested quilters who drop by the shop. When possible, mentioning our ad in guild newsletters. Having class lists available at guild meetings. If you would like to do additional advertising, you are welcome to do so.

Samples: Teachers are required to submit samples in a timely fashion at the beginning of the teaching quarter. Classes without samples do not sell. We appreciate but do not require samples made out of our fabrics. Samples should be fresh-looking and not outdated, dirty, or worn.

Material Lists: Material lists are required for all classes when the newsletter goes out. It is a good idea to put the date of the class on the list or to provide a blank for us to write that on. It would be nice, though not required, if you also put Scottie Dog Quilts and the address and phone on it.

Room Setup and Take-down: Scottie Dog Quilts will have the tables, chairs, ironing boards, and cutting mats set up, trash bags in place, and floors vacuumed before your class. We will also vacuum the room and empty the trash after you leave. We will clean the bathroom. If you have additional setup and cleanup, it will be your responsibility. There is running hot and cold water in the classroom, a microwave, and small refrigerator. The refrigerator is stocked with water and sodas for a small fee.

Exclusivity: Scottie Dog Quilts in no way wants to limit your teaching opportunities at other shops and venues. We do ask, however, that you DO NOT teach the same class at another local venue in any given quarter. We ask that you don't promote classes in other shops while in our building.

Private Business: We at Scottie Dog Quilts do not discuss private business with anyone else. If you are privy to any private business, please don't spread it around like common gossip. We do not discuss other shops and their problems, their employees or owners, or our opinions of them in the store. We attempt to foster good will and encouragement in the quilting world, and feel there is no place for gossip or backbiting. This is very important to us.

Copyright Issues: At Scottie Dog Quilts, we take copyright very seriously. All students and teachers MUST buy any pattern or book from which a class project is taken.

Class Materials: Any books, patterns, notions, or specialty fabrics needed for a class should be discussed with us up front to make it possible for us to order them. Sometimes suppliers may be out of stock. We do not require fabrics, books, notions to be purchased at our shop, but obviously we can only offer classes if we stay in business. You are not required to do a sales job on your students, but we ask you not to send students to other shops. In addition, please don't discuss super sales at other stores while at our shop. "I buy all my batting half-price at J_____'s" is a good example. It is hard enough to compete in this marketplace.

We at Scottie Dog Quilts strive to create an atmosphere for our customers, students, and teachers in which they feel comfortable, creative, and welcome. We hope that you will be willing to help foster that atmosphere by being thoughtful, friendly, and approachable. We value you very much. If you have any concerns or problems, please bring them to BrendaLou's attention ASAP.

—BrendaLou Scott

Letter of Agreement

Caryl Bryer Fallert, perhaps the most respected and sought-after textile artist in the world today, graciously gave her permission for me to include much of her letter of agreement in this book. Visit her site to study the complete detailed document at *www.bryerpatch.com*.

Letter of Agreement and Contract for Workshops and Lectures by Caryl Bryer Fallert

A signed copy of this document must be part of any agreement between Caryl Bryer Fallert and your group. All requested information must be filled out, signed by you, and returned to Caryl Bryer Fallert no later than 90 days prior to Caryl's departure for your venue (120 days for international venues). Please read this entire contract before requesting that Caryl reserve time in her schedule for your group. If your group has its own contract, this contract will also be needed, in addition to your own contract. Please cross out and initial any clauses in your contract that are in conflict with the requirements spelled out in this contract. If you would like to reserve dates before you know the exact locations of your events or the exact workshops your group wants to book, you can send the preliminary agreement on dates to reserve your spot in Caryl's schedule, and send this full contract later.

This is to confirm our verbal agreement that Caryl Bryer Fallert will present workshop(s) and/or lecture(s) for:

CONFERENCE/GUILD NAME: _____

CONTACT PERSON: _____

ADDRESS: _____

PHONE: HOME _____WORK _____CELL _____ E-MAIL: _____

WEB SITE: _____

TO BE HELD ON DATE(S): _____

Fees are as follows:

Lectures: $400 with workshop/$425 for lecture alone.

Six-Hour Classes and Multi-Day Classes: $700 per day for up to 20 students. ($750 after January 1, 2005). Additional students may be added for an additional fee of $15 per student, per day, up to a maximum of 25 students, providing the classroom is adequate. (See "classroom requirements" link at bottom of each class description)

Two- and Three-Hour Workshops & Seminars: $450 for each class, for up to 20 students. Three-hour classes must be combined with other classes and/or lectures to equal a minimum of $850 per day.

Note: Two three-hour classes and an evening lecture may be scheduled in a single day; however, three 3-hour classes may NOT be scheduled in a single day. If Caryl flies to your location, there may be an additional handout fee in some workshops. This is due to the high cost of shipping, and the new 50-pound limit on the airlines. If you prefer, a master copy of the handout can be sent ahead of time, which you can print and collate for the group members. In this case you will be responsible for collecting the cost of the handout from the students.

Sales: In Caryl's workshops and lectures, a number of items will be available for sale to interested students. The guild/conference will not expect to collect any commission on these sales. Caryl will not promote these items during the class, nor will she spend class time selling them. They are simply available for sale to interested students. These items may include:

+ Books, patterns, and CDs by Caryl
+ Hand-dyed or other fabrics designed by Caryl
+ Posters and postcards of Caryl's work
+ Fabric printing products
+ Items needed by students to complete the workshop projects

Fabric dyed in color and value gradations will be available for sale in classes that require graduated colors for completion of the project. Prices vary, depending on the number of colors in the packets and the size of the individual pieces. Students are not required to use this fabric, but may bring fabric from home as specified on the supply list.

GENERAL REQUIREMENTS FOR CLASSROOMS AND LECTURE HALLS

Specific requirements for each class and lecture can be found by clicking on the links located in the individual workshop descriptions. Links to individual workshop descriptions and supply lists can be found on the Workshops Menu Page: *http://www.bryerpatch.com/wkshops/workshops_menu.htm*

EQUIPMENT NEEDED FOR LECTURES

I use a digital projector and computer. If a digital projector is available at your facility, please let me know. Otherwise, I will bring my own projector. You will need to provide:

- Room that can be darkened. Projected images will not show up well in a light room.
- Projector stand
- Podium or professional music stand for reading notes.
- Small table near podium for computer
- Screen which is large enough to see clearly from the back of the room. If more than 30 people will be in the audience, please have a large screen or a large blank, white wall available. Slides shown on a home movie screen cannot be seen from the back of the room. Screens can be rented from camera stores, libraries, and schools. If you meet in a church that has not been used for slide lectures in the past, please check the setup ahead of time. Many churches now use screens that are set up for a computer projection system which hangs from the ceiling. Please check to see whether we can plug our computer into this system. If not, we will need a screen that can be used by a projector sitting on a table or stand.
- Public address system (preferably with lavalier microphone) for audiences of more than thirty people.
- Two or more tables for display of work
- Quilt stand(s) for hanging quilts (if available)

GENERAL WORKSHOP CLASSROOM REQUIREMENTS

- Room that can be dimmed. Projected images will not show up in a light room.
- Projector stand
- At least two tables for display and one additional table for demonstration.
- Table space with enough room for each student to work at a sewing machine, with a large cutting board and iron next to it (ideally, one table per student).
- Outlets and electrical capacity to support sewing machines and at least one iron for every four students. Access to the circuit breaker box is very important. (DO NOT IGNORE THIS REQUIREMENT.)

+ Room must have adequate lighting and ventilation
+ For 3–5 day workshops: Work wall that can be pinned into, or movable design boards, such as 40" × 60" foam core, or insulation board. 40"/1 meter (minimum) per student.

Additional equipment requested if available:

+ Quilt stands
+ Overhead projector (selected workshops only). See individual room setup requirements

Important: Please fill in ALL of the requested information below, including: date, name of venue, street address, city, zip code, phone number, and time. I will be driving to a place I have never been before, and need print maps and directions from the Internet before leaving home. I also need to leave contact information with my family when I'm on the road.

LECTURE(S) REQUESTED

TITLE OF LECTURE: _____

DATE: _____ TIME: _____

TITLE OF LECTURE: _____

DATE: _____ TIME: _____

LOCATION (*please include name of venue*): _____

STREET ADDRESS, CITY, STATE, ZIP _____

PHONE NUMBER: _____

WORKSHOPS REQUESTED

1. TITLE OF WORKSHOP: _____

DATE: _____ TIME: _____

LOCATION (*please include name of venue*): _____

STREET ADDRESS, CITY, STATE, ZIP _____

PHONE NUMBER: _____

Supply lists are available by clicking on the name of the workshop on the Workshops Menu Page: *http://www.bryerpatch.com/wkshops/workshops_menu.htm*.

Visuals to promote workshops and lectures can be sent upon request. Biographical material and pictures for brochures, newsletters, and introductions available at: *http://www.bryerpatch.com/about/shortbio.htm*. Images from the workshop pages on Caryl's Web site may be used in brochures and other publicity materials to promote her workshops and lectures. If you need a picture of Caryl for your brochure, you will find it at: *http://www.bryerpatch.com/about/publicity_pictures.htm*.

Travel arrangements will be made by Caryl Bryer Fallert or the travel agent of the conference/guild, with Caryl's agreement on dates of travel, routes, airline, etc. (United Airlines is preferred whenever possible. If you are making the reservations, my Mileage Plus number is 00000000001. No seating on aisles or bulkheads, please.) In order to secure the most economical air transportation, Caryl must be provided with all necessary information about exact dates and times of workshops and other events at least 90 days prior to the first scheduled event on the trip, which includes your events. Please keep in mind that you may not be the first group on her itinerary, and you may be required to provide this information more than 90 days prior to your events. If your failure to provide this information results in increased travel expenses, your group will be solely responsible for paying the difference in cost.

Expenses: All travel expenses will be borne by the guild/conference. These include:

TRANSPORTATION
Driving: When driving to workshops, Caryl will expect the group or groups to pay or share

1. Mileage (35¢ per mile) or the economy airfare to your location(s), whichever is less.
2. Highway tolls

Flying:

1. Round-trip airfare
2. Ground transportation to and from airport

+ Mileage to O'Hare Airport or Midway Airport (90 miles RT) plus parking ($13 per day, subject to change at the whim of the Chicago City Council), and/or
+ Shuttle service to and from Caryl's home: approximately $75 each way (also subject to change), and/or
+ Mileage and tolls (if Caryl's husband or assistant are able to drive her in her personal vehicle).

Flat rate for 90 miles round trip, plus tolls: $30 each way, $60 for beginning and end of trip.

At Workshop Location: Ground Transportation: Arrangements will be made by the guild/conference to meet Caryl Bryer Fallert at airport locations with a vehicle adequate to handle three large (50–70 pound/23–30 kilo) suitcases. Remember, we will be lifting them in and out. Please do not bring a little sports car. Your new BMW with the white leather upholstery is probably not the best choice either. Please be sure the person providing the transportation is able to help lift suitcases into the vehicle. If airport shuttle or taxi service is used, Caryl will be provided with transportation to and from the shuttle terminal, and the guild/conference will be responsible for the cost of this service.

Lodging in a private room in a hotel, motel, or dormitory (if held on a university campus); no private homes. Sleeping rooms must be free of pet hair, cigarette smoke, mold, mildew, cloying floral scents, and feather products (down comforters, feather pillows, etc.).

Food must be available in or near the hotel (walking distance if Caryl will not have a car).

Cancellations: The guild may cancel a workshop due to insufficient enrollment at any time prior to the purchase of non-refundable airline tickets, or any other expenses incurred by Caryl Bryer Fallert. If a workshop is canceled due to insufficient enrollment, Caryl Bryer Fallert must be notified before incurring any expenses. If a workshop is canceled after the purchase of airline tickets, the guild will be responsible for paying for the tickets. If a workshop is canceled, and coming to your group for fewer workshops or lectures than originally agreed upon in this contract will cause economic hardship for Caryl Bryer Fallert, she reserves the right to cancel the remainder of the contracted workshops/lectures. If your workshop cancels in the middle of a multi-venue tour, your group will be responsible for covering Caryl's daily minimum fee of $750.

See Caryl's Web site for details about meals, traveling to another workshop in your area, and international workshops.

When the time comes for you to enter into a contract, keep the basics in mind. Does the contract:

+ Reflect a meeting of the minds?
+ Make a clear statement of intent?
+ Include a timetable for performance, deadlines, penalties, and schedules?
+ Use clear, easy-to-understand language?
+ Offer appropriate warranties?
+ Include provision for mediation/arbitration?

Gregg Levoy, in his book *This Business of Writing*, says, "If you win at somebody else's expense, they will resent it, and this will come back to haunt you. Also, the more you enter into negotiations in the spirit of cooperation and mutual benefit, the more you will enjoy those relationships." I could not agree more.

Contributors to this chapter:
Kathleen Bissett
109 Thorndale Place
Waterloo, Ontario
N2L 5Y8
Canada
(519) 747-1275
info@kathleenbissett.com
www.kathleenbissett.com

Ann Anastasio
(925) 455-5677
aanastasio@comcast.net
www.annanastasio.com
www.brokendishesrepertorytheatre.com

BrendaLou Scott
Scottie Dog Quilts
301 W. Harris Street
Eureka, CA 95503
(707) 444-9662, fax (707) 443-6649
ScottieDogQuilts@aol.com
www.scottiedogquilts.com

Caryl Bryer Fallert
P.O. Box 945
Oswego, IL 60543
(630) 554-1177
caryl@bryerpatch.com
www.bryerpatch.com

Pricing Quilts, Products, and Services

Published designers who receive phone calls from editors interested in buying their work stutter when asked, "What do you want for your design?" Creative people responding to calls from publishers, shops, manufacturers, or consumers often feel unprepared and insecure about establishing a fair yet profitable price for their goods.

As a professional designer and small business teacher/writer since the mid-sixties, I hear these questions often. Attending professional conferences and listening to my students, I find that the topic that bedevils every artisan is: *pricing!*

Magazines that target consumers who craft from home also find readers asking pricing questions. Trade journals, relied upon by craft and quilting professionals, deal constantly with questions and suggestions surrounding pricing issues. Letters to the editor in these publications feature questions from readers about what they should charge for their products. Online mailing lists for professional quilters continue to proliferate on the Internet, and the most frequent topic is pricing.

Experienced quilters and those just beginning to sell their work always need information about pricing structures. They want to know what price range the market will bear for particular items. Listening to them at national craft shows and conferences each year, I find this paradox: Each artisan wants to know what others earn from publishers, wholesalers, catalogers, and even retail customers, but this is the very information they hold back themselves while networking.

Heard at conferences for professionals is: "What did this magazine pay you to publish your design?" Answers vary from "The usual" or "Between fifty and two hundred dollars" to "I can't remember." Why is this so?

Do we fear we will appear underpaid when compared to others?
Do we fear that if we earn more than others, they will rush to crowd our markets?
Do we want to know where to stop negotiation with a publisher, manufacturer, or each other?
Do we all want to know more about pricing strategies without revealing our own?

This chapter brings you the inside story from my own experience as a professional quilt designer, plus interviews with several quilters.

Pricing Basics

Before you can think about pricing your products and services, you must understand and define the elements one must consider in pricing anything.

Value is how your customers perceive your product in relation to what they want and how much they are willing to spend. If a particular item is welcomed by a buyer, she may accept whatever price you set. If buyers perceive your product as poorly constructed or made of inferior materials, they may not accept the lower quality, no matter how low your price may be compared to competitors. Marketing experts say that consumers *will* spend more for a product if they clearly recognize it as one of higher quality. Products described as "fade-proof," "shrink-proof," "100 percent cotton," and the all-important "handmade in America" are examples of products boasting increased quality for which consumers will pay.

Labor costs should include not only how long it takes *you* to make a single quilt for sale, but must also consider what you would have to pay an employee to duplicate it when you need help. You may be happy to charge $4 per hour to craft your item because you work from home, eliminating childcare expenses. But what will you do if you become ill or need to pay someone to help if you receive an order too large to fill by yourself? Will you find others willing to work for this amount? Consider this question when you build labor costs into your price structure, as it is critical in today's market.

Raw materials include all the supplies required to manufacture your product. Fabric, thread, and beads seem obvious. But do not overlook small items such as glue, pins, fusible interfacing, and textile paints.

Overhead refers to the non-productive, incidental expenses too small to calculate individually. Examples: rent, utilities, postage, insurance, wear and tear on your equipment, travel, repairs and maintenance, telephone, packaging and shipping supplies, delivery and freight charges, cleaning, office supplies, show fees.

Wholesale prices are those at which you sell your quilts to someone else who, in turn, will resell them to the ultimate consumer. Shop owners, consignment shops, and catalogs are some examples.

Retail price refers to the price paid by the person who buys your quilt and takes it home, also referred to as the "ultimate consumer." People who buy handmade items rarely concern themselves with how much time it took to make them. This is why the final price you choose for each item you sell must conform to what the market will bear where you live. Do not be surprised if you rent booth space at a show, only to find that buyers want to negotiate and dicker over your prices as if they were visiting a flea market. Once you settle on a price, stick to it during a show or boutique, unless you've had the item for awhile and want to get rid of it to recover material expenses.

Wages refer to the sum you pay someone else who works for you. This expense is often confused with "owner's draw," which means when you—the owner of your business—write yourself a check from your account to pay yourself.

Profit refers to the money that remains after you sell merchandise for more than it cost you to manufacture it, including your labor. Profit is why we work. New business owners often fail to add profit into their price structure. They merely consider both wholesale and retail prices based on the cost of materials, labor, and overhead—an expensive mistake. After all I've said, you really don't *want* to give away your work, do you? If not, let us talk about setting prices.

Pricing Methods

The easy part of pricing your quilts, products, and services is calculating realistic prices that include profit margins. The *art* is in adjusting them so they appeal to customers and stimulate them to buy. A perfect formula to set prices for all quilting products and services for every person does not exist. You must assess the popularity and trends in your particular field, the geographical area in which you live, and whether or not your products are high-ticket items. When you have researched all of this, you will know that you have several methods to choose from to set a price for a specific project, whether you sell only one or dozens.

Begin your price-setting efforts by checking with competitors in your community. Learn what other teachers, designers, and quilters charge for their services. Read their classified ads in local newspapers and call for information. Visit quilt shops and learn what they charge for services and products comparable to yours. Consult the phone directory to call other quilt professionals and request price quotes.

Below is a list of pricing strategies I offer my students. Perhaps one of them will be perfect for you.

Direct Labor

This method focuses on labor for projects that are labor-intensive but require very few or no raw materials. Suppose you also make beaded earrings in addition to quilted items. Seed beads and earring findings are inexpensive, but what if it takes three hours to make a pair? You might charge $8 per hour ($24) and add $4 to the total to cover supplies for each pair. The final price would be $28 per pair using this method.

Mark-Up Pricing

Mark-up pricing works when the cost to manufacture a product is fairly consistent. For example, if a single item (a baby shirt, for example) cost $6.50 to buy and consumers will pay $10 for it after you machine-embroider a flower to alter it, the dollar markup is $3.50 ($10 – $6.50), or 35 percent. Ask yourself whether a general markup of 35 percent would be consistently profitable to you for other objects you produce, whether they're larger or smaller. Wholesale price of goods is the basis for mark-up pricing.

Break-Even Point

Finding the break-even point is an excellent pricing method to arrive at a set price per project if items are similar or identical. It happens when total income equals total expenses for a specific quantity of products you make. Suppose you have made 100 small, machine-quilted potholders to sell at a local show. Total all raw materials you will use to make them. Let's say the total comes to $200, including freight charges to ship raw materials directly to your studio. Selling each for $20, you will break even after you sell the tenth. The remaining 90 percent would be profit plus labor. The other expenses would have been included in the original $200 investment for materials.

Labor + Materials + Cost + Profit = Price

Use a simple profit system when pricing a single large job. Add up the actual costs: labor, raw materials, and overhead. To this, add 15 percent for profit. Quilters who make objects requiring costly materials can make this system work to their advantage. Simply tack on 15 percent more to the total of your labor, raw materials, and overhead to arrive at your final selling price.

A quilter who makes many small, miscellaneous craft objects to sell exclusively at craft fairs explains that she uses this idea to price each item she makes, even though they vary in size, intricacy of workmanship, and cost. She adjusts prices based on the local market where she is vending. She establishes a minimum wage, adds the cost of raw materials, then adds 10 to 25 percent to offset the costs of booth space, price tags, advertising, business cards, and distance traveled to the show.

Patchwork tree ornaments, her top-selling item, provide an example. If it takes one hour (at $6 per hour of labor) and $4 in raw materials to make one ornament, method number 1 looks like this: Labor: $6 + Raw materials, $4 = $10. Cost: Covering show expenses @ 25 percent ($2.50). Final price to the customer is $12.50 + $1.50 per item profit, or $14.

Shortcut Method

A shortcut pricing method used by many crafters and quilters is to double the total cost of the raw materials to arrive at the wholesale price and to triple them to arrive at retail; $4 × 2 = $8 for wholesale price; $4 × 3 = $12 for retail price.

Pricing by the Hour

Charging by the hour works well. Set your minimum hourly fee and multiply by the units needed. For example, if it takes you three hours to cut, piece, stitch, and baste one 14" block and you charge $6 per hour, you would charge $18 per block. If your customer ordered the same block on a king-sized quilt composed of 24 blocks, you would charge $432 for everything except the quilting ($18 × 24 = $432 for 72 hours of work). For quilting, you can negotiate whether the buyer wants it done by hand or by machine and charge accordingly.

Setting a price based on an hour's labor works well when you set a fee primarily based upon performing a service rather than selling a product. Suppose you mend and restore quilts for your customers. You need no raw materials other than thread and fabric. Time yourself to determine an hourly rate that compensates you fairly for your labor, then multiply by total hours spent.

Pricing by the Square Inch/Foot/Yard

Bakers often charge a given price for a single donut or cookie rather than by a dozen. Why not quilters? You may find it easier and practical to charge by each specific element consumed in producing your product or service. For example, needle-pointers and cross-stitchers base their fee on covering a single square inch of fabric. When they set a fee per square inch, they merely determine the total number of square inches in an individual piece and multiply by their square-inch price. Try this system with quilts as well.

One quilter determines the square-foot measurement of quilts she makes and multiplies it by $20 for easy design work, $25 for medium design work, and $30 for complex designs.

I sold a quilt to a magazine and neither the publisher nor I itemized how we determined the price. I tested this quilter's method to compare the actual amount I received to the amount I would have received using her approach. My quilt measured 36" × 42" or 1,512 square inches. I divided this by 144 inches (the equivalent of 1 square foot), which equals 10.5 feet. Since my quilt featured intricate appliqué and hand quilting, I multiplied $30 (complex design) by 10.5 and arrived at the price of $315 to do the work, plus raw materials. The design featured fabric painting, piecing, and quilting all by hand. The publisher of the magazine had paid me $310 for my work. Since publishers customarily return quilts and other projects after photography, I had the option of keeping or reselling my quilt. Though I had not heard of the system presented by the quilter above, using her formula proved that my publisher had paid me a fair price and that the quilter's pricing system was valid.

Pricing Based on Spools of Thread

Quilters often charge by the spool of quilting thread. Thus, when a client wants a quilt top hand-quilted, the price depends on the amount of thread consumed. Large quilts with scant hand quilting may cost the same as small wall hangings bearing rows of profuse, close quilting. The concept is simple. It takes the same amount of time to make so many stitches, widely spaced or close together.

Pricing by Yardage Consumed

Have you thought about charging by the yardage consumed in your labor? For example, if a quilt consumes 8 total yards of fabric for the top alone, and you base your fee on $7 per yard, you would charge a total of $56 for each yard, which would equal $448 to make the quilt.

A quilter in my guild says, "I sell quilted wall hangings, and I charge what the fabric costs multiplied by three to find my direct cost. I arrive at my selling price by allowing 1/3 of the price for actual fabric costs, 1/3 for labor, and 1/3 for profit. When hand quilting a piece made by someone else, I charge by the square foot depending on the design, but marking and basting are always separate charges. A set price for the overall quilt doesn't work, as some quilts have intricate hand quilting, while others are not heavily quilted." Perhaps some of you readers may want to try this simple pricing strategy.

Devising a Pricing Range

Making quilts for sale is the sole occupation of a quilter I spoke to recently. She sets her prices based on finished size. Each price bracket includes a range based on whether the design is simple, medium, or intricate. Here is her system, based on the quilt sizes that follow, considering her labor only. Customers purchase all materials and notions.

Miniatures up to 2 feet: $125–$150 (Simple: $125, Medium: $135, Intricate: $150)

Wall quilts up to 4 feet: $100–$175 (Simple: $100, Medium: $125, Intricate: $175)

Full-size bed quilts up to king-size: $350–$500

Establishing a Pricing Template

A "pricing template" is a system that you can use to determine the selling price of a particular item or items. Once you calculate labor, raw materials, overhead, and the profit you wish to earn each time you make a specific item, you no longer have to calculate each item individually. Simply apply your pricing template to a group of items even if they are somewhat dissimilar. Such a system benefits all artisans as they struggle to price in a way that is fair to both artisan and customer.

Interviewing many quilters for this book, I asked each person to present her pricing ideas using my pricing template below. You will find variations in pricing templates, but they all have one element in common: a predetermined system to price different items in their line.

To invite their objective ideas, as a professional knitter as well as a quilter, I based my pricing template on knitting a single skein of worsted-weight yarn, any fiber, so each quilter would have to substitute all her own information and not be tempted to use my exact figures.

3½–4 oz. Skeins
Simple Patterns: $12
Intermediate Patterns: $14
Advanced Patterns: $16

For a woman's simple sweater requiring eight skeins, I charge $96 ($12 × 8 skeins = $96). If the customer requests a sweater made up of intermediate patterns such as easy cables, small repeat laces, easy textured patterns, etc., I charge $14 per hour, as this technique requires more time and skill ($14 × 8 = $112). Had the garment been very intricate, I would have increased my labor cost to $16 per hour × 8 and charged $128.

What about customers who want a complex sweater in knitted lace or dozens of colors, which requires a high skill level and takes more time? A garment like this would consume more yarn, so I move to 9 skeins × $16 and charge $144 for the labor alone.

Many years ago, a client came to see me after seeing sweaters I had made for a friend who wore size 12 garments. She already knew the price I had charged my friend and expected the same. However, the new customer weighed 300 pounds and wore a size 24! She felt that a sweater was, well, a sweater. Fortunately, I had my chart ready (my future pricing template). I showed her that knitting the identical garment for her would take not seven skeins, but eleven or twelve. She agreed this would take more time and involve more stitches and effort. My price chart helped her understand that it was fair to raise my price based upon the materials consumed in making the project. Everyone came away satisfied. My pricing template idea was born!

A student said she had been selling beaded jewelry and wanted to expand her activities into full-time work. She said she priced her pieces by doubling what the raw materials cost. Beading does not require expensive raw materials, but it is very labor intensive. When I asked her how much she charged for a pair of Bedouin earrings she was wearing, she explained the supplies cost about $6. She had been selling them for $12, though making one pair took her four to six hours. She was surprised when I pointed out that at this price, she had been paying herself $2 per hour for her labor—less than half of our state's minimum wage!

Had she created a pricing template for herself, she could have avoided undervaluing her time. Women working from home often undervalue their labor until they gain more experience in the market as sellers. If you convey the attitude that "This is just a little something I do in my spare time," or "I keep my prices low because I work from home," your pricing structure will probably be too low.

Ignorance about current market trends and checking out competition may cause you to charge too much. Do not let personal friends and family tell you what you should charge. Remember, they may not be thinking objectively, but subjectively, based upon their relationship with you. You must learn all you can about the market and how your product fits in objectively.

When to Adjust Your Prices

Learning what the market will bear requires research and time. Visit galleries, shops, shows, malls, boutiques, and even online catalogs to help you set your prices competitively in the area in which you plan to sell them. Consider cutting your total retail prices by 5 to 10 percent when selling in a rural or low-income geographical area, and raising them by the same amount from the original price when selling in a top-selling market in an urban area.

How Will I Know When to Raise My Prices?

Learn if a price you are considering is acceptable to your target consumers. Some shoppers consider price first when choosing to buy. Others consider quality, variety, service, or convenience first. You must know about your customers' desires in relation to your products when setting prices. What matters most to *your* customers?

Next, find out what your competitors charge. How does your product differ from theirs? Attend quilt shows and study the trade journals to learn this information. Visit malls and shops in your area. Listen while customers chat as they are buying.

Consider a marketing technique called "penetration strategy" when you offer a product for the first time. This means you will keep price to a minimum during an introduction phase in order to gain market share or presence as you jump into the competition. For example, your preliminary advertising may say "Special Introductory Price" or "For a Limited Time Only." Take care not to continue your introductory prices for too long. Once you have credibility and market share, you can begin to raise prices with careful timing.

Residents of large cities may be willing to pay more for an object than those in small, rural towns where more people are crafters themselves. People will also pay more for an item when they recognize an element of increased value. (Cotton over blends, for example, or glass instead of plastic beads on your wearables.)

It makes no difference *how* you arrive at your asking price if it is too high or too low for your market. The market itself, not your costs, labor, or overhead, determines the price at which you can sell your goods.

How Can I Compete with Others with Similar Products Who Charge Less?

A student told me she was unhappy with the profit she was earning for her handmade doll clothes. She explained that the only other person selling similar doll fashions at craft shows she attended sold them for $30, while my student sold hers for $10. She boasted about how many more outfits she sold than her competitor.

Unfortunately, she did not recognize that the other person not only charged more per outfit while selling fewer items, but she earned more, which covered all her expenses, plus profit. My student sold more units, but did not earn enough to cover booth expenses at this particular show. She learned too late that cheaper is not always better.

How Can I Increase My Profits?

There are only two ways to increase your profits while competing in the marketplace. One is to lower your expenses, and the other is to raise your prices. If you have a good product and your customers correctly perceive its benefits, make sure your advertising and literature describes why they may pay more (e.g., handmade rather than machine-made, all-natural materials). Some will consider it.

What Do I Say if Buyers Say My Item Costs Too Much?

When you set prices higher than your competitors, consider justifying the difference to your customers when you speak to them personally and in the wording in your brochures, sales letters, and Web site. For example, if they state that your price is too high, consider explaining how you choose higher quality materials, have better or faster service, or offer an unconditional guarantee.

When customers say your price is too low, you can explain that your company has acquired more production methods or has lower overhead and thus can pass the savings on to the customer. "Not likely," you say? Consider today's quilters. For many years, people who quilted for others had no option other than doing the work by hand. Technology has provided more options with the advent of longarmed quilting machines that can do the same work in less than a tenth of the time it took for hand quilting. Thus, machine quilters generally charge less than their counterparts who quilt by hand.

Consider demand-oriented pricing when trying to decide if you are charging too much, making customers hesitant to buy. Demand-oriented pricing answers the question, "What is your consumer willing to pay?" Study your competitors and the market in general. Evaluate your pricing structure continually as material costs increase or inflation rises.

A Pricing Example

Let's say that you have been commissioned to design and make a quilted wall hanging. How would you calculate the fee? Your customer wants a wall hanging that measures three feet square. The client does not know about the time or skill required, but has specifically asked for a floral design in appliqué with a hand-quilted, all-over grid pattern for the background.

Raw materials:	2 yards of fabric for a quilt top in several colors	$14.00
	1½ yards of fabric for backing @ $6 per yard	$9.00
	1 bag of batting, crib-size	$2.49
	1 spool of quilting thread	$2.00
	3 spools of sewing threads	$4.00
	New pencil to mark design	$1.29
	Stencil chosen by customer	$2.99
	Total cost for materials	$35.77

Suppose you charge $8 per hour. To make the quilt top, calculations show that it will take you about eighteen hours to make an easy appliqué design with a few large shapes, twenty-two hours to make one a little more complex, and twenty-five hours for more intricate appliqué shapes. Rounding off fractions, your fee schedule could look like this:

	Simple design	Medium design	Intricate design
Labor:	$150	$175	$200
Hand quilting:	Lines at least 1" apart $50	Lines ½" apart $85	Stippling (¼" apart) $125
Drafting original design:	$25	$40	$60

Add up the appropriate totals based on the medium design, and you will find that the final price to make the quilt would be $300. Factor in the cost of materials and overhead expenses and the time needed to draft the design.

Study the price schedule above and compare it with what the market will bear in your area. If you live near an artists' colony where handwork is prized and highly valued, you may have no trouble charging this amount. But suppose you live in a small farming community where many people quilt and there are frequent shows with quilts for sale. You may need to drop your price to compete with the current local market. Note that prices vary from one geographical area to another.

Yet another well-known quilter tells me she sticks by a basic hourly formula that works well for her. She charges $50 per square foot, plus materials. To find a price-setting formula perfect for you, try this. Choose a quilt project you might undertake in your business. Price fabrics and other needed materials in your area. Set up a mock materials cost list like the one shown earlier.

Now, price this quilt project using each system described above. Take the resulting price from each system and add them together. Divide by the number of systems you used and you will have an average of all the systems. Then, visit quilting events and shops in your community. How does the resulting price fit in your geographical area? Is it higher or lower than the market will bear? Is it competitive with other quilters nearby? Perhaps it will provide you with a practical fee schedule you can live with for quite some time.

Cathy Hooley's Pricing System

Cathy Hooley runs a home-based quilting business. She sells T-shirt quilts, memory quilts, wall hangings, baby quilts, pillows, and holiday items. She sells directly to consumers via her Web site, at retail prices.

Cathy uses only 100 percent cotton fabric and thread in her products, a preference of many buyers today. She also uses only cotton batting between quilt layers to accentuate traditional style and look, as cotton batts produce a flatter finish.

Pricing her products fairly and being attentive to the market, Cathy currently uses a pricing system that is based on the actual cost system described earlier in this chapter: Labor, overhead, and raw materials, plus profit, equals her prices.

"Initially I didn't have a pricing system," said Cathy. "I set my prices to what I felt people would pay, without considering how much time and work went into my quilts. I was just happy to sell something. Finally, I realized that I was losing money even when I was selling many items, so I decided to get serious and develop my own pricing system.

"I calculated the cost for every item I made. My cost included the raw materials, my labor at $10 per hour, overhead expenses, and contingency, which I calculated at $2 per hour. Contingencies are basically unexpected costs like machine repairs. My overhead expenses include:

$500 per year: Web site fee
$500 per year: Bank charges
$200 per year: Car and gasoline expenses
$500 per year: Notions, needles, rotary cutters, and other tools
$200 per year: Equipment and repairs
$100 per year: Required subscriptions to keep up to date on the quilting industry

"The price of my quilts was derived by adding these cost elements together," Cathy said. In addition, Cathy devised a contingency plan to test her pricing strategy. She explains: "On larger items I consider a square-foot test and do market comparisons. To be competitive, the price per square foot for my quilts should fall into the $10–$30 range."

"If my formula yields a price that is outside this range, I adjust the price accordingly. If my cost is too high, I determine whether I can make the item using less costly materials or improve my process to save time. If I cannot, I don't make the item. If my cost is lower than the square-foot calculation, I can raise my price.

"After a year, I had a very good idea of what it cost to make my quilts, and what I could charge to be competitive and earn a fair return, but I needed to streamline.

"Studying my costs, I found that 40 percent of the price of each item I sell goes to the cost of raw materials and overhead expenses, and 60 percent is my labor. For example, an item that sells for $100 costs me 40 percent, or $40, in materials and overhead, which leaves $60, and if it takes me six hours to make the item, I make $10 per hour. I have used this system for a couple of years, and find it very accurate.

"To keep tabs on my costs, I periodically divide my total costs by my total sales and make sure it's around the 40 percent figure. I need to keep very detailed records of my sales and expenses, so I use a spreadsheet to track each item I make, the price, the number of hours spent, and use the spreadsheet to calculate my cost and hourly rate." Cathy shares her prices below based upon her pricing system:

> Wall hangings: from $100 for a 28-inch square to $450 for quilts 45 inches square, machine quilted
> Pillows: from $20 to $40, depending on size and complexity, i.e., ruffles and other trims
> Table runners: from $50 to $100, depending on size and complexity
> Table mats: from $40 to $85, depending on size and pattern
> Bed-size quilts: start at $400 for twin-size quilts, while king-size quilts start at $700
> T-shirt quilts: start at $170 for throw size and $475 for king-size quilts

"I use the 60/40 system for everything I make," Cathy says. "I like this system because it gives me a quick, accurate picture of how my business is performing. I know how I arrived at my prices, and I'm continually working at reducing my costs and streamlining my processes."

Just for Fun

Recently, two quilters had a good time determining how to price their quilts. They did some creative figuring, then posted their results on the Web. Their satirical article, "What It Costs to Make A Queen-Sized, Pieced, and Hand-Quilted Quilt," provokes thought for all.

Materials:

Fabric	$170 to $200
Batting	$25 to $40
Thread/Notions	$10 to $20
Total Materials:	$205 to $260

Hours

Piecing	10 to 40
Setting	2 to 10 (also called "laying out designs")
Hand quilting	500 to 950
Total hours:	512 to 950
Total Cost	If paying $1/hour (Would you do this for $1/hour?)

Materials:	$205 to $260
Labor:	$512 to $950
Cost to consumer:	$717 to $1,210
Total Cost	If paying minimum wage: $5.15/hour

Materials:	$205 to $260
Labor:	$3,692 to $4,892
Cost to customer:	$3,897 to $5,152
Total Cost	If paying $20 per hour for skilled labor

Materials:	$205 to $260
Labor:	$10,340 to $19,000
Cost to customer	$10,545 to $19,260!

Woodland Manor's Pricing Schedule

Janet-Lee Santeusanio, owner of Woodland Manor Machine Quilting, kindly granted permission to reprint her very thorough, up-to-date pricing details for her machine quilting services. She overlooked nothing. Her excellent Web site begins:

Woodland Manor Quilting will turn your pieced quilt top into a treasured heirloom. We offer a variety of quilting services, including edge-to-edge designs and custom work, to your specifications. If your quilt top leaves you with more questions than answers, feel free to take advantage of our consultation services. We are available to advise you about the options available.

Quilting Categories

Listed below are the various types of quilting we offer. We have made every attempt to describe each quilting level in such a way to make it easy for you to decide which category best suits your quilting needs.

I. Basting ~$.0075/sq. in. A quick and easy way to prepare your quilt for hand quilting. Edges are stabilized, and the body of the quilt will be basted in a 3–4" grid. Minimum ~$40.

II. Simple Pantograph or Meandering ~$.0125/sq .in. Pantos are rows of quilting done edge-to-edge throughout the entire quilt. All-over meandering is a stipple-like pattern which can be done in soft curves or loop-de-loops. Minimum ~$45.

III. Semi-Custom ~$0.175 to $.0275/sq. in. Includes simple or complex Panto, or continuous border patterns, in the border, and/or free motion designs in each block. Minimum ~$60.

IV. Full Custom Quilting ~$.03 to $.05/sq. in. Includes many different types of quilting: stitch-in-the-ditch, any size meandering, feathers, sashing designs, multiple border patterns, inset blocks, gridwork, and cross-hatching. Minimum ~$75.

V. Heirloom Quilting ~$.04 to $.06/sq. in. This is show-quality quilting for treasured quilts. This level of quilting includes everything in the Full Custom category as well as trapunto, fine background quilting, and patterns designed exclusively for a single quilt. Minimum ~$100.

To Figure Out Your Quilting Cost

Width _____ × Length _____ = _____ Sq. Inches _____

Sq. Inches × _____ per Sq. Inch Cost (from categories above) =

_____ Additional designs for multiple borders ~add $15 per border. (Does not apply to category "Full Custom Quilting" above.)

No deposit is required. Full payment is required upon completion. Any unpaid quilts will be donated to charity after thirty (30) days. Checks returned for any reason are subject to a $25 returned check fee.

Thread ~We have many colors of cotton thread to choose from. Single-color thread is included in the quilting price.

> Monofilament and specialty threads ~available for an extra charge of $15.
> Multiple thread colors ~Primary thread color, no charge.
> Additional thread colors, $2 each.
> Custom design work ~at $20 per hour.

Binding Service: (Optional) ~$.17/linear inch. Includes machine sewing to the front and hand sewing to the back. To figure your binding cost on a 72" × 90" quilt, add 72 + 72 + 90 + 90 = 324, then multiply by .17 = $55.60. Send extra fabric—we'll tell you how much you need.

Hanging Sleeve: ~$7.50.

Batting: ~We use top-quality batting products purchased on the large roll. Some of the battings we have available include: Warm & Natural, Quilter's Dream, Hobbs, Mountain Mist, Buffalo Batt, and many others. Please let us help you make the best possible batting choice for your particular quilt, as there are many weights and thicknesses to choose from.

Return Shipping Charges ~$9 for most sizes. Quilts over 90" long ~$14. $100 insurance included, additional insurance ~$2.50 per hundred.

Please be sure to follow the steps outlined for quilt preparation. Please note: Prices are subject to change without notice.

Quilt Preparation

There are times when machine quilting can be expensive. Please review the following to properly prepare your quilt. In the end it will help us be more efficient and incur fewer costs for you.

Always make sure that you have squared your quilt top and your quilt backing material. If there are lots of pieces in the outside border of the top, be sure to trim it up evenly. We have to pin the top and bottom of your quilt to rollers. If it is not square or trimmed, it will not mount straight, and therefore end up with puckers or little tucks because of excess or uneven fabric.

(Cost to square up quilt top ~$10; cost to square up backing ~$10.)

Pressing your quilt top and backing is also important. If you have properly pressed during the construction of the quilt top, you will have no problem doing a final pressing before sending it to us. Pressing will make your quilt top quilt more easily and look so much nicer. Don't forget to press the backing so that no creases will form on the back.

(Cost to press quilt top ~$15; cost to press quilt back ~$10.)

Some quilts require that the backing fabric be pieced. Remember to remove all the selvedges, as they are not woven in the same way as the rest of the fabric.

(Cost to piece backing fabric ~$15.)

Repairs to poor piecing or rippled borders are charged by the hour. We have a document describing the proper way to measure and sew borders onto your quilt. If you would like one, please e-mail or call us ~603-778-6994.

(Cost for repairs ~$15 per hour.)

Backing and batting must be four inches larger on all sides than quilt top.
Mark the top by pinning a piece of paper at the top of the quilt so we will know where to begin.
Do not pin or baste.
If you have questions, please feel free to contact us by telephone or e-mail.

Summary

We have discussed that everyone who wants to start a small quilting business wants a foolproof, easy system that will guarantee the most profit with minimum wasted resources. As you now know, no such magic formula exists. But I can tell you the four most important points that most business owners who sell their products should know:

1. Sell only products of high quality and excellent workmanship
2. Produce what people *want* to buy, not just what you want to sell
3. Always stay alert for ways to decrease expenses
4. Choose a niche in the quilting world and *never* stop marketing yourself and your business.

Contributors to this chapter:
Cathy Hooley
354 Bogden Road
Broadalbin, NY 12025
(518) 842-8700
Goose Tracks Quilts: *www.goosetracks.com*

Janet-Lee Santeusanio
Woodland Manor Quilting
7 Merchant Road
Hampton Falls, NH 03844
(603) 778-6994
info@woodlandmanorquilting.com
www.woodlandmanorquilting.com

More Ways to Make a Profit

Now that you have read about the many traditional ways to *Make Money Quilting*, let's take a look at a few methods you may not have considered. In this chapter, contributing experts in their fields will explain why they chose their particular field within the industry and how it fits into their status as professional quilters.

Judy Laquidara: Finish What Other Quilters Start

Quilting done on a longarm machine is as relatively new to the quilting industry as the machines themselves. Judy Laquidara has been providing machine quilting services to other quilters since 1998. Having invested in an expensive longarm sewing machine to stitch quilt layers together in a fraction of the time it takes to hand quilt a project, Judy quilts the projects of other quilters. Judy's target market is primarily quilters who are too busy or not of the inclination to do handwork. Working to remain visible in the industry, Judy enters her quilts in shows and quilts for a local quilt shop owner who allows her to display her quilts in the shop.

Judy won a ribbon at A Quilters Gathering in Nashua, New Hampshire, and, more important to her, one of the customers whose quilt Judy quilted won a Best of Show ribbon in an Illinois show. Judy also teaches quilting for community education programs and gives guild workshops in her area.

While Judy was living in Louisiana, a professional machine quilter quilted Judy's quilts. Working full-time, Judy could only make two quilts per year. She easily afforded this service, as she did not have the time to quilt her projects herself.

Relocating to Kentucky in 1997, Judy did not return to full-time employment. Instead, she used her time to make twelve to fifteen quilts per year. Time did not permit her to hand-quilt this many quilts either, so once again she sought out a professional quilter. Unsatisfied with the services of the only two people she could find, she decided to buy her own longarm quilting machine. She was determined to learn to use it for herself, and perhaps for a few others.

"Too many people buy a longarm machine thinking they can make money quickly," Judy points out. "They finance the machine and then panic because they have a loan to pay. Wanting instant profit, they forego the time required to learn and practice on the machine—which is nothing like a conventional sewing machine," she explains. "When new longarm quilters start quilting for the public before perfecting their skills, word gets around. Inexperienced quilters must then overcome a reputation for doing work found to be below standards."

Judy practiced for six months before she felt ready to work on a real quilt. She limited herself to work only on her own quilts for an additional four to five months more. Only then did she feel ready to take on paying customers. "Business snowballed right away," says Judy. "I have been blessed beyond anything I ever imagined with this wonderful enterprise."

"My reputation goes along with every quilt I quilt," says Judy. "So when someone sees a quilt that is puckered and stretched, they may not distinguish whether the maker or the professional quilter is responsible. Though it is hard to reject such a quilt, I explain to the maker that I cannot do a problem-type quilt justice merely because I have a longarm machine. I gain confidence when I turn away such jobs and can avoid worrying about how I would quilt it and what others would say when they see a poorly done quilt associated with me. I want every quilt I work on for others to reflect the maker's skills and my own skill as well." Judy advises others:

+ Practice for several months before accepting work from others.
+ Maintain a clean, secluded area to store quilts and to do the quilting itself.
+ Do not allow pets or little fingers near the quilts.
+ Maintain a professional attitude and establish good business practices.
+ Some quilts are poorly pieced and not square. Do not accept hard-to-quilt quilts.

Patti Foster: Custom Quiltmaker

Quilters who love quilting dream of making quilts for others, and Patti Foster does it. She makes a custom quilt from start to finish for clients. "First, I meet with the potential customers and ask them what they want," Patti says. "Second, I make sure they understand the costs for fabric and other materials. Third, I calculate what my time is worth and stick to that price. If I miscalculate how long it takes me, I feel responsible for my error and never pass that along to the customer," Patti says.

Explaining the type of quilts she makes for others, Patti says, "If I am to make a simple Log Cabin quilt, for example, I do not charge as much as I do for a more detailed quilt. I hand-quilt every quilt I make, so I try to be very clear about that with the customer. I tell them before we begin that my services will cost more than for a machine-quilted project due to the labor-intensive process of hand quilting. Last, before beginning the quilt, I draft a simple contract stating the cost of materials, and then estimate the time it will take before the customer can expect a finished project."

Patti advises others thinking of going into the custom-quilting business. "Do not accept customers who ask you to 'just go to the store and pick out what you think would look good in green and red (or whatever colors).' This is far too risky. Your idea of what the quilt will be like and what the customer expects may vary widely. Instead, meet them at the quilt supply store and help them choose the fabrics. Store employees often help, making the proposed quilt a team effort. This works marvelously well for everyone," she concludes.

Karen McCleary: Maker of Quilt Samples

Making quilt samples for teachers, shop owners, and manufacturers is also relatively new to the quilting industry. Karen McCleary began quilting early in 1980 but did not get serious until 1985, when she began to teach quilting in the evenings while maintaining her day job at a bank. In 1992 she left the bank to pursue quilting seriously. Karen clerked at a local shop and taught quilting for quilt guilds, women's groups, quilting retreats, the Creative Needlework Show, and any group that hired her.

While teaching and working in a local shop, Karen began to make samples of patterns to display in the store. Shop owners and customers alike know if a pattern is made up and displayed in the store, sales of that pattern escalate. At this time, Northcott Silk Inc. offered day classes in the same shop once a month. The fabric manufacturers offered a variety of quilting patterns.

"Attending one of these classes, with my boss, Patti Carey, we could provide two samples worked in two different color ways of each pattern. We found that this practice really expanded the class repertoire," says Karen. "Patti Carey taught the classes and we developed a relationship."

After a year, Karen stopped clerking, feeling she could not teach while spending so much time making shop samples. One day, Karen asked if the shop ever needed samples to be sewn to encourage shop class attendance of other teachers. Patti was happy to have Karen sew samples for the shop, which began a good relationship with Northcott Silk Inc. as well.

Karen describes making samples for a manufacturer as sporadic work, with samples needing to be made in rhythm with the Houston Quilt Market and other trade shows. Most samples were needed immediately. But Karen said she enjoyed the work, as it challenged her to try methods and techniques she would not have needed on her own and to make better use of her time.

Local shops hire Karen to make their samples today, paying Karen $10/hour. Working for Northcott was similar, though Karen had an extra option. She could accept a set fee or could opt to receive compensation in the form of complimentary fabric from the company line. She could also choose to accept a lower fee and have the sample returned to her to keep one year later. Company samples were also paid at the hourly rate of $10/hour.

"Last year, I asked Patti if she would consider allowing me to try designing one of their feature quilts—one that would make use of a specific line of fabric," Karen said. "I tried my hand at a line called 'Wellesley' and made a quilt to show off the fabric. Wellesley had a great striped/border print that adapted itself well to being one of the striped blocks. My quilt was a great success. I have been challenged to make quilts and samples for shops and manufacturers, but working for them helped my quilting skills to stretch and grow, pushing me to do better while learning new techniques simply to keep current."

Marilyn Maddalena: Appraiser, Judge, Historian, Speaker

Appraising is a traditional service, but there are not enough appraisers to go around. Marilyn Maddalena has been a professional quilt appraiser, show judge, quilt historian, and speaker since 1977, and has more work than she can do at times.

Describing her appraisal work first, Marilyn says, "As a quilt appraiser, I give both verbal and written appraisals, for insurance value or donation value, and occasionally, for fair market value. The cost of a written appraisal is $40. The cost of a verbal appraisal is $25. I work independently, but also work with other quilt appraisers.

"Sometimes I appraise during quilt shows, sometimes I do it in my home, and other times, I visit clients' homes. I am in touch with other quilt repair people, and refer this type of work to them if my schedule is too full," she says.

Marilyn's market as an appraiser consists of quiltmakers and quilt owners. Written appraisals are needed for entering quilts in some shows, for shipping quilts, and for insurance coverage.

Judging quilt shows takes Marilyn to many county and state fairs, quilt guilds, and other exhibits. "At times, exhibitors who plan to submit quilts for competition request that I prejudge their quilts to give them tips on improving them before entering them in a show. Prejudging is charged at an hourly rate, while show judging charges depend upon the fee set by the sponsoring organization," she says.

"My buying market as a quilt historian and speaker consists of guilds and groups interested in learning more about quilting," Marilyn says. "I present programs to quilt guilds and other groups and charge a speaker's fee, plus mileage and travel expenses."

Marilyn has a Web site and also distributes business cards and brochures to local quilt shops, remains involved in quilt guilds, and volunteers at museums to keep her name in front of the quilting public. "Articles have been written about me on other Web sites and in quilting magazines and local newspapers. I demonstrate quilting at the California State Fair each year and never come home without valuable contacts and referrals," she says. "Speaking fees are the most profitable for me, and appraisals come next, with judging fees being least profitable.

"I chose quilting as my career because I love quilting, the quilts themselves, the rich history, and most of all, the innate beauty of quilts. I advise others thinking of doing what I do to read everything possible about quilts, to attend every possible quilt show, to become familiar with design and color, and to remain informed on new techniques, lines of fabric, new notions, and anything related to the quilting field."

Marilyn's quilting experiences and skills have recently earned her a month-long, all-expense-paid trip to South Africa aboard a cruise ship. Crystal Cruise Lines was about to launch a new ship, the *Serenity*, and wanted Marilyn and her husband to join the cruise for a special quilting activity. Marilyn will lecture her way at sea about the glories of quilting while she teaches passengers and crew members to create a special inaugural quilt to commemorate the ship's maiden voyage. As a former arts and crafts instructor for Holland America Cruise Lines, I can tell all of you teachers that nothing beats teaching quilting on the high seas!

Nancy Kirk: Quilt Restoration

"Quilt restoration and repair can be a good home-based business for talented quiltmakers who have a special passion for antique quilts," says restoration expert Nancy Kirk. "Basic restoration skills are easy to learn through workshops or home study, but a professional restorer will spend the rest of her professional life learning about antique fabrics and quilts, from dating to dyestuffs, fiber identification, material culture at different historic periods, conservation techniques, and more.

"Restoration is generally a part-time business because it requires long, tedious hours of handwork. Most people find that four hours a day is the maximum they can work effectively at the actual restoration. Some time needs to be allocated to marketing, bookkeeping, and customer service, but finding customers is easy once you let it be known that you are doing this kind of work. Many restorers combine a restoration career with appraising, lecturing, or teaching if they want to work in quilt related fields full-time.

"Restorers generally charge from $15 to $65 per hour, depending on their skills. Our 2004 rates are $40 per hour for basic restoration and $50 for intricate embroidery work. We also charge a $40 evaluation fee to inspect a quilt and prepare a written proposal and estimate.

"Most clients are private parties who want a family quilt restored. Sometimes dealers will want antique quilts fixed, but it rarely works out economically to repair quilts for resale, as the cost of restoration will probably equal or exceed the increase in the retail price.

"Most museums will seek conservators rather than restorers to work on pieces in their collections where the goal is to maintain the piece in its current condition and stabilize it structurally. The goal of most restorers is to return the visual integrity of the quilt to what it was some point before the most recent damage.

"Many restorers finish old quilt tops, but must advise people on the options of using antique versus reproduction versus contemporary fabrics. At times, you may be asked to repair a contemporary quilt after a dog has chewed it. The most important thing is to learn enough about quilt history and conservation to know when to walk away from a job because the value of the quilt will be adversely affected by restoration." Nancy offers her valuable advice to others considering a career in quilt restoration:

Setup

A restorer needs a studio or workspace free from pets and children where client quilts can be stored safely. The work area should be large enough so the quilt can lie flat on a single surface while under repair. Good lighting and ergonomic seating is important, and a well-stocked library is an asset.

Training

Quilt restorers can take workshops, and most learn by doing, working on their own quilts or garage sale finds until they have confidence enough in their skills to work on client quilts.

Marketing

The least expensive and most effective marketing tool is an engraved nametag with your name and the words "Quilt Restorer" on it. Wear it everywhere you go. On every trip away from home, someone is likely to tell you the story of her family quilts. A simple business card with your name, phone number, and e-mail works. Many restorers do not publish their addresses on their cards because they become responsible for unexpected clients' quilts left for repair on their doorstep.

Insurance

Discuss your home-based business with your insurance agent. You may need separate business liability insurance to cover clients who come to your house, and/or a special floater policy to cover other people's quilts while they are in your possession. Some restorers require a written appraisal before they will accept quilts, or ask clients to sign a waiver of responsibility for fire, water damage, theft, or other quilt tragedies.

There are only a few dozen quilt restorers working in the country right now, and we estimate at least five million quilts in need of repair. Consider a career in quilt restoration.

Nancy teaches quilt restoration and has published home study workshops on DVD on the subject—yet another way to profit from quilting.

Sylvia Landman: Consultant

I define consulting as follows: "Renting someone else's brain, resources, research, referrals, information, and experience by the hour." In addition to teaching and writing, I run a consulting practice from my home office. As quilting and craft industries continue to grow, you too can sell your valuable experience to others who need your help.

Before you seek clients, make sure you understand the role of a consultant to a client. You will offer your services, advice, and referrals to another. Consultants are by definition professionals who deal with clients as independent contractors rather than as employees. Consultants usually analyze the needs of the clients and help them develop a system to achieve their goals. People sell their expertise in all fields.

According to Dr. Jeffrey Lant, an expert in the field of consulting, consultants are needed because of the complexity of today's world. There is so much more information now that no one person can know everything. "Do not give people a piece of your mind—instead, sell it to them," he advises.

I began my own consulting practice twenty years ago in response to students' questions. Many called me at home, even after bedtime, asking questions. During all-day workshops and classes, I found it difficult to take breaks or eat meals while trying to continue answering questions from inquisitive students seeking more and more information.

Finally, I formed a separate arm of my craft/quilting business and called it Self-Employment Consultants. I updated my large home office and advertised in the yellow pages of our phone book.

At first, most of my clients wanted to start businesses unrelated to mine, but since I teach classes on self-employment, this was easy for me. Eventually, I began to see increasing numbers of clients who wanted to start a craft business similar to mine. I guided them through the process of starting up or expanding and helped them solve business-related problems. I also see clients with design and color problems and, of course, quilting issues. Here are a few tips from my practice:

1. When the phone rings and the caller begins to speak, write down her name and take notes immediately. Listen attentively while you record information.
2. Ask the callers what their principal concern (*not* problem) is.
3. Ask them to describe their principal needs.
4. Suggest that they make a list of *written* questions before the appointment.
5. Look up everything you can find about their business before they arrive.
6. Prepare a contract for each client. Hand it to them as they arrive. List the date, the time of the appointment, and the hourly fee to avoid disputes over time used or cost. Include the reasons for the appointment and client's full contact information.
7. Provide a second sheet responding to their concerns as stated on the phone. List the tips, suggestions, ideas, referrals, and references relating to their specific business issues.
8. Listen attentively. Having a listener can help clients crystallize their own ideas, priorities, and goals as they bounce them off of you.
9. Let clients know when their first hour is up. Ask if they wish to continue into a second hour, return for another visit, or end the visit. Have a clock that sounds off so clients will know when time is up. I use a cuckoo, which reminds both of us of the time.

10. I make it a practice to *always* disconnect my phone so the time the client pays for becomes dedicated to her.

11. Discuss when you need to spend time on preparing proposals for long-term work and set a limit on how much time you will spend without compensation. You may recall from an earlier chapter that I prepare business plans for many types of businesses.

12. Mention an "extra service" of fifteen-minute free phone consultations during the first month of initial consultation, before new charges accrue, or you may find yourself answering mountains of questions on an ongoing basis.

13. Never promise that dollars spent on consulting will result in specific profits or outcome.

14. Agree on how the time will be spent avoiding small talk and personal conversations during consulting periods.

To find clients, accept offers to teach or speak as an authority on your subject. Refer to clients and give examples of some you served in the past as you talk. Make your brochures and business cards available at every opportunity. Contribute to newsletters and trade journals in your field, even at no fee. The exposure matters most. Write articles, offer tips, give examples, answer questions, and make suggestions. All of this provides credibility for your expertise.

Join trade organizations in your field and participate as visibly as possible. Promote others in exchange for them promoting you. Exchanging Web site links is a modern, practical example of this process. As a quilter, consider publishing designs in magazines. Request that in the contact information provided, reference to your consulting services appears. Send press releases about your services to local newspapers and related groups.

Join non-craft-specific local business groups in your area such as Rotary Clubs, University Women, and the like. Present yourself as a professional consultant, not just a quilter. Join online chat groups and mailing lists. Make sure that the word "consulting" or "consultant" appears in your signature line. Offer limited but frequent advice and ideas on such lists to provide credibility and professional status.

Contributors to this Chapter:
Judy Laquidara
Sunshine Quilts
Highway 1389
Owensboro, KY 42303
Home Phone: 270-281-0369
Studio Phone: 270-685-4786
e-mail: Judy@SunshineQuilts.com
www.SunshineQuilts.com

Patti Foster
1424 May Street
West Sacramento, CA 95605
(916) 371-2883

Karen McCleary
Address #5586 - 10th SR R.R. #1
Egbert, ON
L0L 1N0
Canada
(705) 434-3088
mccleary@look.ca

Marilyn Maddalena
3436 Windsor Drive
Sacramento, CA 95864
Phone: 916-979-9632
mm@marilynquilts.com
www.marilynquilts.com

Nancy Kirk
The Kirk Collection
1513 Military Avenue
Omaha, NE 68111-3924
(402) 551-0386 or (800) 960-8335
Fax: (402) 551-0971
KirkColl@aol.com
www.auntie.com/kirk

Sylvia Landman
create@Sylvias-studio.com
www.Sylvias-studio.com

No one is more surprised than I am to find myself an author of six full-length books and countless magazine articles. I do not have a degree in journalism or writing. English, in fact, is not my first language, but my second.

From my earliest years, I wanted to become a teacher. After teaching in classrooms for thirty years, I realized that writing can follow teaching as a natural next step. Rather than continuing to teach exclusively in person, I found writing afforded me another venue for teaching—on paper, in books, and in articles. It only takes translating the spoken word to the written.

My first editor, an elderly gentleman attending my knitting classes, tactfully explained that he saw much room for improvement in my use of English on my handout sheets. He offered to help, explaining that he was a proofreader and editor for the Smithsonian Museum in Washington, D.C., the U.S. Army's Secret Service, and a seminary in California. I was impressed. My purple mimeographed handout sheets would be safe with him.

He returned my sheets to me, with tactful corrections and suggestions in red pencil. I owe my career as a teacher and writer, in great part, to his teaching me basic writing and editing skills.

"Considering all you know about writing and English grammar," I asked one day, "why haven't you written a book yourself?"

"Because," he gently explained, "I have nothing to say, but you do." This treasured relationship lasted thirty years.

So, if you believe *you* have something to say or valuable information to share, or if others want to know what you know, then consider organizing your thoughts and writing them down. Sprinkle in patience, time, and dedication to not only your topic, but also to this fascinating language of ours, and you too may realize your dream of getting published.

Most quilters enjoy reading quilt magazines. In fact, in the latest quilting survey mentioned earlier in this book, they state that magazines are their principal source of inspiration. If you want to see your designs in the magazines of today, here is how to start.

What Type of Designs Should You Try to Sell?

To make selling your quilt designs and articles profitable, you must make what you enjoy while keeping an eye on what the public wants to buy. Sometimes, you may find that what sells well differs from your personal taste. You do not have to make what you really dislike (though I have done this myself), but you must remain sensitive to the external marketplace if you want to sell what you make.

Let me give you an example. My favorite colors have not changed since I was a little girl. I still reach for anything in yellow, gold, orange, and especially red-orange. However, I always read and study articles and announcements about current color trends in trade journals.

Color marketing experts find that most people choose blue as their favorite color, followed by its variations, such as turquoise, aqua, and recently, rich purple, made by mixing blue and red together. Purple has enjoyed a huge popularity from the late nineties well into 2004. Witness the clothing, yarn, and fabric using purple.

Fifteen years ago, you certainly could not find purple shoes unless you dyed them yourself. Today, even infants' clothing comes in purple, to say nothing of shoes and a certain stuffed dinosaur children love. My favorite colors are warm, tropical hues. These can appear in my personal projects, but I must yield to current color trends if I want others to buy my design articles, and that means designing in blues and purples much of the time.

Consider this principle not only when you choose color, but also when you choose fibers (cotton is hot—polyester is not!), styles, and designs. Victorian designs are hot, while country and folk designs have declined. Embellishments on quilts show no sign of slowing down and seem more outrageous than ever. People favor dimensional work on quilts like stuffed areas, pleats, tucks, metallic threads, ribbon, beads, and lots of strong texture today.

New methods in photosensitive materials allow you to make quilts based upon treasured photographs of family members. Nostalgia is more popular than ever, but start by making things within your own skill level. Move to more sophisticated designs and use of color as you gain more experience and develop your own design style.

Finding Magazines Interested in Your Topics

Quilters often think the only way to generate income from what they produce is to sell the item directly. Not so! You can sell every item you make *and* still get paid to write about its design for craft magazines *before* you sell the item to consumers.

Magazine editors need writers to quench their never-ending thirst for new ideas and designs for their publications. Hobbyists need writers to provide fresh ideas, inspiration, and motivation. Readers learn about the latest trends and techniques from both publications and craft designers.

Suppliers need writers who can put their design skill into words. Companies usually provide free materials so that published designs will encourage readers to try their products. Further, they pay the designer endorsement fees over and above what the designer receives from the publisher. They do this to encourage writers to use a specific product in their published designs. In order to earn the endorsement fee, the writer must list the product in the exact format set by the product manufacturer. Follow the manufacturer's exact specifications when listing or mentioning their product even if it is longer or you do not agree with it.

So, what is a freelance craft designer? Today, the term means "a person who sells work or services without working exclusively or regularly for one employer, but who will sell to anyone who will pay." If you have perfected your technique, consider combining your skill with words. Write about your skills and designs, or provide step-by-step instructions so others can recreate your quilts and other designs. The first step is to find the right magazine for you and for your style.

Magazine editors state regularly in writing magazines that their pet peeve is writers and designers who submit designs without taking the time to learn about the magazine's style, needs, and format. Choose carefully before annoying an editor you wish to impress. Help yourself by reading *Writer's Market*, published annually by Writer's Digest Books. This hefty book describes both the needs and the readership of nearly all American magazines, and even some foreign publications as well.

Look up "craft," "quilt," and "consumer hobbies" in this book. These headers will take you to listings of magazines in this field—a good start for you. The entry for each publication will provide everything you need to know. Read about the magazine's focus and readership, as well as its needs and requirements. You will find contact names of editors and learn the magazine's subscription rates, which in turn determine how well the magazine pays its freelancers.

Learn what rights the magazine wants to buy (literary rights are listed later in this chapter), how long they want articles to be, whether they want photos, how long they take to reply to your first letter, and, importantly, how much they pay writers and when payment is made. Here is a portion of the *Writer's Market* listing for *Quilter's Newsletter Magazine*, providing contact information and the editor to contact.

> **Nonfiction**: "We are interested in articles on the subject of quilts and quiltmakers *only*. We are not interested in anything relating to 'Grandmother's Scrap Quilts,' but could use fresh material." Submit complete manuscript. Pays by the word.

> **Reprints**: Send tear sheet of article or typed manuscript with rights for sale noted and information about when and where the article previously appeared.

> **Photos**: Additional payment for photos depends on quality.

> **Fillers**: Related to quilts and quiltmakers only.

> **Tips**: "Be specific, brief, and professional in tone. Study our magazine to learn the kinds of things we like. Send us material which fits into our format but is different enough to be interesting. Realize that we think we are the best quilt magazine on the market and that we are aspiring to be even better, then send us the cream of the top of your quilt materials."

Study several quilt and craft publications before you select a few appropriate for your work. Match carefully. Send traditional designs to publications that specialize in designs that have borne the test of time, such as *Quilter's Newsletter*, but send contemporary ideas to *Quilting Arts* or others that feature modern quilt designs.

Before submitting your quilt article and design to a particular magazine, study three issues to determine whether your design is appropriate for the publication. Magazines such as *Threads* prefer narrative articles about how a designer works, rather than step-by-step how-tos. *Piecework Magazine* focuses on the historical aspects of quilts they feature. *Professional Quilter Magazine* seeks articles about the business of quilting. *Craft* magazine prefers simple, theme, and holiday quilts and is one of the highest paying craft magazines for freelancers in print today. *Craft* likes quilt designs that incorporate other crafts into the quilt such as painting, stenciling, or photo imaging. Do not send a Christmas project in October when it is needed by March.

Read the information below the masthead in every magazine. A number of quilting publications include wording telling readers that if they send an unsolicited picture of a quilt, the magazine is free to use it without giving either credit or payment, for example.

Selling your designs depends on your ability to choose the proper publication to offer your design idea, but you do not have to limit yourself to submitting quilt designs exclusively. Readers want topically related ideas, too. Recently, I have written articles about:

+ Choosing and collecting fabrics and notions for nostalgic quilts
+ How to organize a sewing studio
+ Color and design basics
+ Hand-painting fabrics
+ Stained-glass quilting techniques
+ How to write lesson plans for quilting classes

Once you have selected a few appropriate publications, write to each and request a set of writer's guidelines. Publishers provide these at no cost, and some allow you to download them directly to your computer from their Web site.

Study the guidelines carefully. Editors and publishers describe exactly what they want, what they need, and how they want designs presented to them. Will they accept your text on paper or require a computer disk? Do they limit article length? Do they pay extra for photos? Will they ask you to send them your quilt for photography or accept your snapshots? Do they require slides?

Note deadlines for each issue. When do they wish to see holiday items? Do they require fabric swatches? Will they accept computer-generated designs? You will receive answers to these questions in the guidelines from each publication.

How to Write a Query Letter

In her book *How to Write Irresistible Query Letters,* author Lisa Collier Cool writes, "A query letter—a combination sales pitch and nonfiction article or book summary—must grab the attention of the editor or agent with a few well-chosen words."

Writers' guilds and clubs and books advise you to say it all, briefly and powerfully, on a single page. Don't be surprised that it takes longer to get your information onto one page than if you ramble over three or four. Avoid losing a busy editor's attention as she tries to find important ideas in overly long queries. It takes time to be brief, but your letter will become more powerful once you extract wasted words.

After studying the guidelines, the next step is to submit a query letter describing your idea. Approach the editor in a businesslike tone in your query. Propose your idea clearly and assertively. The style, grammar, and word usage of your query letter serve as an example to the editor about how you will prepare your articles and instructions. Thus, make your query letter your best effort by using professional letter-writing techniques.

What to Expect When You Submit Work to Magazine Editors

Tell the editor about yourself and your qualifications by including a brochure, business card, or résumé. If you are proposing a quilt design, include a photo or two. All of these enhance your chances of acceptance. Avoid long-winded personal statements not pertinent to the editor, the magazine, or your project.

Editors who find your quilt article or design interesting will either call or write to you, but almost never in less than a month or two. Sometimes, it takes four or five months, and a year's wait is not unheard of, which frustrates designers and writers.

It is aggravating to wait with high expectations for word from an editor for months. When you feel you cannot wait any longer to know the status of your submission, write a *brief* letter stating when you sent the material. Mention your need to have a date for a reply.

Sometimes, even this does not garner a reply. Most editors do not appreciate phone calls, but an increasing number will accept e-mail inquiries about the status of your submission. Learn which works for the editor you are dealing with.

Desperately, after a year without a word of response to my letters, I once sent a "final" letter. Remaining polite, I let the editor know about my previous inquiries, giving the actual date for each one. I closed by saying, "May I assume that if your busy schedule does not allow you to let me know the status of my submission by June 22, I am free to offer this project elsewhere?" Usually this does the trick. Either they reject it and return everything, or they contact you right away to keep you from getting away from them and going to a competitor.

Once they accept your article, editors will write or call to propose an amount they will pay to buy it. Occasionally they will ask you how much you want for the article. Novice writers may feel unprepared when this occurs, having no idea of the going rates.

Save yourself some anxiety and research this issue beforehand. Contact other quilt designers and ask. Join the Society of Craft Designers. Tips in their excellent newsletter can help prepare you for the buying and selling procedures of designs. The newsletter offers regular tips about pricing so you will neither price yourself out of the market nor sell yourself too cheaply. Their Annual Designers' Seminar focuses on the needs of designers such as materials, writing and editing information, manufacturers' complimentary supplies, and design and color trends. The five years I invested in my $135 annual membership paid off handsomely, to say nothing of all the contacts I made with manufacturers, editors, publishers, and other designers that continue today.

Editors can offer to buy your design's already completed project, or can commission you to make or remake the project to their specifications. In the first instance, your selling process is nearly over but in the second, more options come into play.

I have been asked to remake a project in different colors to suit a possible theme in a specific issue of the magazine. When this happens, the manufacturers usually provide the materials after the editor contacts them to place a designer's order.

I have also been asked to resubmit the design in two sections for successive issues in the magazine. This happens when space is limited and/or when the editor does not want to cut down your manuscript, feeling all of it matters. Increased payment follows.

Another frustrating option occurs when the editor asks you to remake the project in the exact color and style but using the goods of another manufacturer. I feel like a traitor switching my allegiance from a company that provided materials to me to the suggested company, with whom I may or may not have a working relationship.

Usually, this happens because the magazine is running a large-size ad—its bread and butter. To please advertisers, editors often seek to publish designs using that particular company's products. Remember, when the magazine's photographers finish working with your quilt, they return it to you unless you have made other arrangements. In this case, you will eventually have two completed projects to sell or to use as samples if you teach classes.

Recently, heated discussions appeared in newsletters and e-mail digests notifying designers about a disturbing trend. Many magazines that formerly supplied fresh, new, and original designs by freelance designers are now opting to cut their costs by featuring in-house designs by manufacturers.

In a recent magazine I noticed that many of the quilts do not bear the name of a designer any longer. Rather, they say something like, "Submitted by So-and-So Fabrics." This means the magazine did not pay a freelancer for an original design, but instead allowed the fabric company space to run what is in effect a free ad for its new product line, disguised as a design.

Some projects are losing their distinctive touch, as they are really designed and made with the thought of consuming as much product as possible. Former sophistication in design elements gives way to the common denominator in public taste. Watch out for this as you thumb through your magazines and see if you can spot such projects. Decide whether or not you think this trend is for the betterment or detriment of the industry.

Simultaneous Submissions

Submit your original query letter to only *one* magazine at a time. You cannot send your query to several magazines at once. If you do, your writing career will receive a serious setback. Unless the magazine specifically says, "simultaneous submissions accepted," assume it is not. Very few magazine editors will look at a submission you have also sent to others. How do they know? It happens when a second editor to whom you sent a query writes to accept your article and you must admit you've already sold it to another publication.

Editors will not be happy to learn they made space in a special issue for your idea, only to learn they wasted their time. Query letters begin a line of communication between the writer/designer and the editor/publisher, but take care to be patient and conform to the power of editors and publishers by submitting only one query at a time. If refused, you are free to offer it to the next magazine on your list.

It is a good idea to keep good records indicating when a query proposal has been submitted and to whom. If an idea is rejected, send it out again, making sure you have a record of where it has been and any reactions or criticisms it receives. Keep rejection letters too. Editors usually tell you why your idea was refused, which helps you refine your ideas, magazine choices, and timing.

Expect rejections when you begin submitting to magazines. My work has appeared in forty-two magazines, but I received rejections from twice that many. Everyone who submits regularly receives them, so use them to learn.

Many rejections have to do with timeliness and are not a reflection of you, your work, or your design skills. Perhaps a quilt with a similar theme or colors is in the works for an upcoming issue. Perhaps what you propose appeared in a previous issue, which is why you should check past copies of the publication. Writers' magazines tell us that if we do not receive rejections regularly, we are not sending proposals to enough publications.

What Is In the Magazine Contract?

Publishers and editors will send you a contract telling you what rights they wish to buy in order to publish your design. Read a contract carefully, as it tells you the deadline when you must submit your work and when they will pay you—on acceptance or publication.

"Acceptance" means you receive payment when the design is accepted even though it may not be published for many months. "Publication" means you will not receive payment until the design appears in print, a practice that delays payment for months or even a year or two.

Most established quilt designers prefer to make a proposal before completing a quilt. Once the editor accepts the idea, the designer makes the quilt on commission, following the guidelines suggested by the editor. When you agree to design a quilted project for publication rather than selling a quilt you had already completed, you must write another letter if the editor does not offer to do so for you. Direct this letter to manufacturers to request complimentary materials.

Approach manufacturers in the same professional manner you used to contact magazine editors. Prepare to tell them how you will use their product and exactly how much you need. Gather supply catalogs from companies with whom you want to deal. Catalog details will help you make selections. Manufacturers want proof of your professional status to separate you from hobbyists seeking freebies. They may ask what professional organizations you belong to and check your membership status with them before agreeing to ship goods to you.

I reassure manufacturers that I will make good use of their products by sending them a copy of the magazine's contract letter commissioning me to design a quilt for them. This establishes beyond a doubt how I will use complimentary products. Once on the mailing list of a specific manufacturer, you will receive updated information about upcoming and new products. Many companies routinely send samples of new products to you in the hope you will use them on your next project.

Publishers and editors buy the rights to a work from a writer or designer in varying forms and degrees. The originator of a work owns all of its rights until he or she decides to sell all or a portion of these rights to another for publication or other public use. Quilt designers and writers must understand the types of rights so they can make sure they receive adequate compensation for their work and understand how much of the original work's rights, if any, returns to them after publication for future additional use.

A book called *Copyright Law: What You Don't Know Can Cost You!* by Woody Young (Joy Publishing, 1988) provides the definitive source of copyright information explaining the following rights:

1. **First Serial Rights** means you offer a magazine the right to be the first publisher of your article or design. Afterward, the rights to the material revert to the writer.
2. **One-Time Rights** differ from First Serial Rights in that the magazine may not be the first to publish the work, and, in any event, it can publish it only once.
3. **Second Serial (Reprint) Rights** give a magazine the opportunity to print an article or design after publication in another magazine. The term also refers to selling a part of a book to a newspaper or magazine after the book has been published.
4. **All Rights**. Some magazines buy all rights, especially designs. Artisans who sell this way may not use the material in its present form elsewhere. If you

think you may want to use the material later (perhaps in book form), avoid selling all rights. Some editors will reassign rights back to the designer after a given period, such as one or two years, but that should be specified in writing.

5. **Simultaneous Rights** cover articles and designs sold to non-competing publications. You may sell, for example, a Christmas quilt to a quilting magazine and to a religious magazine featuring holiday crafts. Advise an editor when your design is a simultaneous submission to another market.

6. **Foreign Serial Rights**. You may resell a design published in the U.S. to an international magazine if you sold only First U.S. Serial Rights to an American publisher.

7. **Subsidiary Rights** appear in a book contract. These may include various rights for audiotapes or videotapes, for example.

Tear Sheets as Marketing Tools

Contracts state which issue of the magazine will contain your design and how many complimentary issues containing your design they will send to you upon publication. Save tear sheets from magazines that have published your work for your portfolio. Use them in the future when you contact manufacturers to request complimentary products.

Tear sheets lend credibility to your status as a designer. Manufacturers who provide complimentary products request tear sheets of your article before paying endorsement fees. Tear sheets prove your endorsement of their product, which in turn triggers an extra payment above the design fee coming from the magazine.

Take care to use a cutter of some sort to remove the pages containing your article cleanly and neatly. Editors do not like you to literally tear up the article, wrinkle it, or tape portions together. Cut neatly, including the extra pages used if your article was extended to additional pages later in the magazine.

Use "real" cut-and-paste techniques when articles appear in many small pieces in the magazine. I retain the first page of the magazine article itself and proceed to make photocopies of additional pages. Then, I cut and paste the fragments of the extended pages to a single sheet of paper, or more if needed. When an editor requires "clips" of my previously published articles, they see the needed color photos from the magazine, but I submit the text on quality photocopies.

It may surprise you to know that each of the publishers that published my books requested up to six tear sheets of my previously published work in magazines. Not only that, but much to my surprise, while I was writing my first book, *Crafting for Dollars*, a stranger called me one morning to tell me he had been collecting tear sheets from magazines where my articles and columns had appeared for two years.

He identified himself as the acquisitions editor for F&W Publications, the prestigious publisher of writing books and magazines. Based on his collection, he asked me if I would consider writing my second book for them, to be titled, *Make Your Quilting Pay for Itself*. He explained that the company was doing a series of business books based on hobbies, and promptly sent me a copy of *Make Your Woodwork Pay for Itself* to persuade me to agree. That is how I came to write both my first and second books simultaneously, with agreement from both publishers. It's also how I learned the value of tear sheets.

How to Write Instructions

Accuracy is prime in writing instructions. Details about how to make templates, cut fabric, and sew the project must leave no margin for error. Write as if your reader is making her first quilt, leaving nothing unsaid.

Note that many magazines specify how many words to use in an article. Write the instructions first, then go back to prune extra words, but do not leave out steps to save space!

Take care to list the steps in proper order, first to last. Sequence is vital for readers at all levels. Though most editors have a staff to edit your instructions, do not rely on them to make corrections or calculations for you. If you make it simple for your editors to work from your instructions, they will be more apt to buy your future designs.

When you have all of your raw materials, begin the project, but do not work straight through to completion. If you plan to sell design articles, you must write instructions as you go. You will develop your own system, or you may follow the procedure I use as I try to write clear, complete, and accurate instructions:

- List all the materials you use in descending order of importance. Add to the list as you go.
- Each time you pick up a new tool or notion, add it to your supply list.
- Provide measurements for the overall quilt, the blocks, sashing, and borders.
- Include cutting instructions.
- Make an outline of each template you used, if any.
- When you have completed one unit of the project, stop sewing.
- Go to your computer and write down every step.
- Print out these instructions and consider them your first draft.
- Make the project again, but this time follow your written instructions, not your memory. Did you include every step?
- Revise and add any missing information. Create a second draft incorporating all changes.
- Working from your instructions only, repeat the sewing and writing process until you have completed the project. Print out a third draft.
- After you have finished writing the instructions, distance yourself from it for a few days.
- Whenever possible, ask a friend to make a design unit following your written instructions, without asking for your help.
- Keep in mind all suggestions made by your friend. Revise, correct, and reword the instructions for the last time. Try to make your instructions stand on their own.

I keep my laptop computer beside my sewing machine rather than jumping up and down to run to my desktop computer in my office on the opposite side of my house. Is this a viable option for you? Even while watching television while I hand quilt, for example, the laptop is there. It enables me to enter little hints as they occur to me or make corrections if needed.

Teachers have an additional method to test their instructions. With the agreement of a particular class, known as a "pilot" class, students agree to test the pattern as a group. Their success in producing the project indicates that the instructions have merit.

However, if the class experiences frustration following your instructions, or if you see that your pattern contains inaccuracies, you know your text requires additional clarification before submitting it to an editor. Consider asking your guild members to come together for such a class. They often agree and give you good feedback about the project and your instructions.

What Do Magazine Designers Earn?

You do not have to guess or ask embarrassing questions of others to answer this question. Go back to the *Writer's Guide* and look up each magazine. Payment is usually listed. Next, study those guidelines you ordered. You will find the information there, along with variations or increased payments based upon each magazine's requirements and requests and your ability to meet them.

Many magazine design freelancers began writing for nothing. I did. Next, I switched to newsletters, which were usually hungry for outside articles but paid little. I used tear sheets from articles I had written for nothing and would propose a $25 to $50 fee to the newsletter editor. They usually accepted.

Some magazines pay by the word, while others pay by the page. Some demand photos and do not pay for them; others pay extra for photos if they are of professional quality. I have been paid from $0 to $750 for my articles. My average payment for freelance articles and my columns today are $150 to $350 each.

During the year, I study my cash flow statement in Quick Books, my bookkeeping software, but look forward to the end of the year, when I can total all the fees I earned from magazine articles alone. Prior to writing six books in eight years, when magazine articles were my writing mainstay, I earned from $4,000 to $6,000 per year from writing for magazines. That is not bad pin money if all you write are articles, but do not overlook the bonus of complimentary supplies and endorsement fees too.

Turning One Article into a Series

The Writer's Digest Book Club published several books about how to take two or more articles and propose a series to an editor. The idea seemed easy enough, so I tried it. First, I reviewed my most successful articles in each magazine I had written for at the time.

Second, I searched through issues and read "Letters to the Editor" columns to see what readers were requesting. When I thought I could respond in a timely manner to multiple letters readers had sent in, I got my nerve up—believe me, it took nerve—to connect with the editor of the magazines whose readership I thought I understood. I offered to solve *the editor's* problem by proposing a modest series of two or three articles to fill the very need readers had sent to the magazine. To tell the truth, I never received a rejection doing this. It is not that everything I write is magnificent. I was simply using a marketing ploy of, "See a need and fill it—first if possible."

Questions or requests from readers seemed to present a need to that particular editor, and I made it a point to make my offer the day I received my copy of the magazine. This way, I hoped to meet the need before anyone else did. Being a non-procrastinator really paid off for me. I prefer to be timely. I even offered to write or design on very short notice should editors find space they needed to fill in their publication. When this happens, editors usually offer a bonus if you will write, design, or create as soon as possible.

Once, I received a frantic call from an editor at a craft magazine explaining that one of her other designers had missed her deadline and she had two pages to fill, preferably over the Thanksgiving holidays—in four days to be exact. She offered me double payment if I could come up with something. I complied and continued to write several series for that publication for a few years. I also received a handsome endorsement fee from three manufacturers that supplied me with overnight shipments of supplies.

Turning a Series into a Column

Once I got a feeling for this, I decided to try to turn a few series into annual columns. Again, I have never been refused. The ploy I used was to ask a few tantalizing questions at the end of some of my articles. I checked with the editor and presented her with my idea. I invited readers to write to send me questions in care of the magazine, promising to answer them in future articles. When editors began to receive readers' comments and questions, generating magazine sales, they agreed to expand my series to a regular column. This is how I wrote my column called "Quilt-as-You-Go" for *Quilt Craft Magazine* for nearly three years.

Read the "Letters to the Editor" column in magazines that contain your single articles or short series. When you see praise letters for a previous article, jump up on your success, contact the editor, and offer to write a regular column in the same vein. This is how I began to write my current column in *Quilting Quarterly Journal*, the quilting magazine of the National Quilting Association. Readers wrote in, happy with one of my interview articles with a talented quilter. I have been writing this column for nearly six years. A bonus for me has been all I have learned from interviewing our famous "quilting superstars."

How to Write & Sell a Column by Julie Raskin & Carolyn Males, *The Craft of Interviewing* by John Brady, and *The Writer's Complete Guide to Conducting Interviews* by Michael Schumacher all became my mainstay reading. How far can you go doing interviews? To Europe! I was sent to England one year and to Scotland and the Shetland Islands two years later to interview European fiber artists. I also paid for a trip to Costa Rica, where I interviewed talented wood artists and cart makers. I then sold my articles upon my return home. Who knows? If you enjoy writing and designing for magazines, one day you may want to write a book—but that is another book in itself.

I began my career in fiber arts as a dressmaker and designer of custom knitting, crochet, and embroidery, working from my home studio. Not long afterward, it became a teaching studio where students came to learn and share skills. I began teaching classes in needlework, quilting, sewing, fiber arts, and color and design for California Community Colleges in 1962.

Curious as to how I made my livelihood in the creative arts, students asked questions like, "How can you make a business from a hobby?" Adding entrepreneurial classes to my schedule, I taught students that they could do it too! I added ten business classes and continue to teach them today.

+ Make Money Quilting
+ Arts and Crafts in the Marketplace
+ Starting a Mail-Order Business
+ Writing for the Crafts Market
+ Couples and Families in Business
+ Time Management and Organization
+ How to Operate a Small Business
+ Starting Your Own Home Teaching Studio
+ The Art of Teaching
+ Getting Published

Today, I design crafts part-time and write about the business side of crafts full-time. I teach for local community colleges and travel throughout the U.S. giving workshops and lectures.

I was privileged to join the faculty of about thirty teachers at Quilt University in 2000. This is an online teaching program that reaches not only students across the U.S., but students around the world. As time allows, I serve as judge in the fields of sewing, knitting, crochet, quilting, color, and design. My favorite classroom was aboard Holland America Cruise Lines, sailing as their arts and crafts instructor.

Defining Teaching Styles

We all recognize the difference between excellent and mediocre in the teachers we meet in classrooms. Those experiences show us that it is not enough to show off your best quilts in your classroom. Teaching others how to make their own is creative, but more difficult to put into words than designing quilts. This is why I call my class for teachers "The Art of Teaching."

When is a class not a class? When it is a seminar, workshop, or lecture. Study the list below and start thinking about which one suits your preferences and brings out the best in you as you prepare to share your quilting skills with others.

A **class** is a group of people who come together for a mutual learning experience under the guidance of a teacher.

A **lecture** is an informational presentation of a subject delivered by a teacher before a group. There may or may not be questions and answers or participation by those attending. Though questions may be taken, lectures do not offer much group participation, but are an excellent way to deliver concise information.

A **seminar** refers to a group of students who come together to share and exchange information and to participate in group discussions led by a teacher. Students may present reports to their classmates. Participation is encouraged and essential.

A **workshop** refers to a class that offers hands-on experience. After the teacher determines that each student has understood the new skill, students practice at home to reinforce the learning experience. In a workshop, good teachers move among students observing and offering encouragement, tips, and suggestions for improvement.

A **demonstration** is when a teacher shows or makes evident how a skill or technique is to be performed.

A **conference** is a meeting for consultation, discussion, and an exchange of views among participants.

Manual skills such as cooking, crafts, and, of course, quilting, lend themselves well to workshops. You can demonstrate fingering techniques on a musical instrument, handling a brush and oil paints on canvas, or how to run a knitting machine or computer. In a workshop, the teacher demonstrates a new skill to a small group. Each class member tries the new skill. Teachers can enhance their class with visual aids: slides and movies, charts, drawings, graphs, and handouts showing step-by-step examples of the skill. Recently, students were asked to describe what makes a good class. Some of the qualities they listed were:

+ Accurate description of class
+ Detailed description of technique to be taught
+ Complete supply list
+ Good meeting times
+ An informed teacher
+ Ample workspace
+ Meaningful handouts
+ Enough time to learn the new technique
+ Good value for the price of registration

Elements of a Class Description

Before schools, shops, and guilds hire you, they need to know exactly what you plan to teach, how you plan to do it, and the class's content. Take time to describe your classes accurately, fairly, and clearly. Choose from the types of classes listed above, then use the list below as a guide in preparing your course description. This is always required by any group hiring teachers. Included in the list is additional information you would include when preparing packets for students who come directly to your home or other location for classes.

1. **Title** briefly identifies topic.
2. **Student level** identifies who should attend (beginner, advanced, intermediate, children, or other teachers and designers). Be specific, such as, "To get the most from this class, you should already know . . ." In non-beginning classes, I say, "Beginning information about how to sew ¼" seams will not be covered in this class. See my beginning class . . ." Unqualified students registering for a class and slowing it down for others are a big problem in quilting classes. I cover this in more depth in the section on difficult students and classroom situations.
3. **Benefits**. Stress the benefits for the students by writing in the second person. Say "you" instead of "student." Point out how much they will learn, how they will learn, and the new techniques they can use for their future quilting endeavors. Consider using testimonials from past classes and/or students if you can get them. Use clearly written sentences, such as: "When you leave this class, you will know how to . . ." Do your best to arouse student curiosity when describing the class and stress benefits such as, "Learn how to hand quilt small, even stitches without frames and hoops" or "Learn to make stained-glass window quilts reflect light like real glass."
4. **List** the topics you will cover.
5. **Format**. State whether your class will be a lecture, discussion, demonstration, hands-on workshop, seminar, or slide show.
6. **Describe** what the student will receive from you in class, such as books, handout sheets, samples, or thread. If you have supplies they may buy in class, above the price of the course itself, list them as optional items. If they must buy a kit, be clear about the kit fee. Students feel cheated when they sign up for a class only to learn they must buy something they did not expect before they can participate.
7. **Required Materials**. List every item participants need to bring. Start with the largest, most important (like sewing machines) and continue to the tiny, less critical things such as thimbles, glue, and pins. Students often come to class without their scissors, needles, or pins.
8. **Provide** your qualifications and professional background briefly. This is not a promotional event, so do not overdo. They want to know if you are competent to offer what you say you will, but do not add information about your cats and grandchildren here.

9. **Time**. State the date, day of the week, and hours that the class will be held. Allow time for meals, if necessary. Many places do not have restaurants nearby. For those locations, underline in the course description the fact that they must bring their lunch.
10. **Location of class**. Provide driving instructions if your sponsoring group does not. Take care to mention the room number of a college where students will find you. Students who become lost looking for your class arrive frustrated and cranky. Include parking information and whether parking fees are required.
11. **Cost**, including discounts such as early-bird registrations (an effective tool, particularly in shop classes) and whether or not you will accept credit cards for registrations.
12. **Registration**. Offer step-by-step instructions on how to register and enroll. Invite inquiries and design an easy-to-use registration form if your sponsoring group does not do so.
13. **Additional information**. Provide your phone number and street address when teaching from your home studio. Always invite interested persons to call for more information. This provides an additional opportunity to sell your class. If you have a Web site, include the URL, and if at all possible, provide a picture of the project there.
14. **Include deadlines** (if any) for late registrations, and whether or not refunds will be made for last-minute cancellations.

Planning and Organizing Your Class

Lesson plans are organized outlines and timelines of what you will offer for each lesson of a particular class. They keep you organized and on track and help you present your information in a logical sequence. Start by listing the subject matter you plan to include in a specific timeframe.

Organize your class by taking all the information you wish to present during the entire class and dividing it by the number of lessons you will have. Furthermore, divide the information you will offer into smaller segments within one lesson. To maintain my students' interest, I break up the lesson time, dividing it into four flexible portions. During each lesson from me, my students can expect:

+ Individual progress reports and answers to questions from the last lesson
+ Formal lecture
+ Group demonstration
+ Show-and-tell

First, I invite individual progress reports from each student as I take roll. Students may ask individual questions about their project at this time. If someone asks a lengthy question that takes us off topic, I write her name on the board and promise to come back to it after all the more formal presentations. I maintain this list on the board and cross off each name as I come to it. This allows the student to see that I will return to her question even though it was not appropriate earlier, and allows me to control the content and pace of the class.

Second, I present a formal lecture from a long list of topics, such as basic pressing techniques, measuring, cutting, or marking fabric.

Third, I hold a group demonstration or technique appropriate for the particular lesson, such as how to hold a needle, how to make a quilter's knot on the thread, or where to position your hands and fingers for hand quilting.

Fourth: show-and-tell. This is when I show related samples of work in class, complete or in-progress. Students are invited to bring their own show-and-tell during every lesson.

Show and refer to the swatch binders and photo albums in the room, and suggest that students may begin their own reference library by starting their own swatch binders. More about this later.

Using Class Time Well

Recently, there was an interesting conversation thread on an e-mail list for teachers. A teacher expressed boredom during slack times in her classroom. She considered remedying the situation by working on her own projects, unrelated to the class, and asked other teachers on the list for their opinion.

One teacher said this practice would send the wrong message to students. "It is one thing to show them how we work if it is relevant to the class topic, but another thing altogether to make students feel like we are too busy to interrupt."

When I accept payment to teach a class of any length, 100 percent of my time belongs to the students. I never work on my own projects other than demonstrating a technique. There are many things that can be done to take up slack time while students work to get to the next step. Here are a few ideas I use and include in my books and classes about teaching:

1. Take your portfolio to class. Invite student questions about anything they see in it. Develop thoughtful answers to their questions.
2. Visit personally with all class members, one on one, and ask how they are doing and if they have any comments or questions. Go around the tables again until you are ready to move to the next teaching point.
3. Take *lots* of samples. Invite comments. If someone does not like your work, invite her to tell you her reasons. If people do like your work, ask them specifically what they like about it. Move into a discussion of design choices and alternatives.
4. Take books and magazines and quote from them or review aloud.
5. Invite unrelated, but pertinent, questions. Where can you buy this? Why did you choose this? How can you organize your supplies better? Why did you choose your sewing machine? In other words, keep the class thinking by giving more of yourself and your personal experiences relating to the subject.

6. Avoid chatting about movies, pets, children, or traffic. Bring every conversation back to issues related to the class topic.
7. Discuss students' fabric and color choices. Encourage them to share opinions while you remain a guiding leader, seminar style.
8. Share your own problems and solutions as they relate to the topic.
9. Try to have students leave feeling they got every minute's worth of the class they paid for.

Another teacher responded, "Working on your own projects in class? NO, NO, a thousand times, NO. Bringing your own work to a class is unprofessional and disrespectful of students. Teaching is a job, not a personal amusement. You are being paid to teach, entertain, and remain engaged with the class. When teaching, your students are your employer."

Creating Informative Handouts

To recognize, accommodate, and encourage individualized learning speeds, I devised a system enabling students to work at their own pace, so that they don't feel they must keep up with others in class. All class materials, instructions, and patterns specific to each level I teach are given to each student all at once during the orientation (first) lesson.

Patterns, template drawings, and instructions for each level take about twenty pages, which I print out and photocopy. I collate each set of pages and put them into report covers with slider spines. This enables students to add more pages or their own notes later if they wish. I refer to them as "workbooks."

Generally, I have four workbooks for each class I teach and for each topic. This means I maintain forty sets of workbooks—four for each of ten classes I presently offer. Using color-coded covers for easy recognition (for me, not them), I have prepared one each for beginning, intermediate, advanced, and designer levels.

During the first lesson, I distribute the workbooks. Colleges allow me to charge $5 per workbook, which they collect for me when the student registers. Some shops do this; others prefer me to collect for these during the first class. Here is a condensed example of the contents of my beginning workbook, which I prepare, copy, and distribute to beginning classes. Each bulleted item represents a page.

+ What is a quilt? What is a quilt-as-you-go quilt? How do they differ?
+ Materials list and shopping tips. Choosing fabric, color, thread.
+ General tips and information for beginners: pre-washing fabric, storing class supplies, fabric grain.
+ A list of the blocks that will be made in class. Details about block size; styles; definition of one-, four-, and nine-patch blocks. Show basic construction in general, not specific terms. There will be time for that when teaching each block.

+ Define sashing strips and when to use them. Choosing color, fabrics.
+ Protractor lesson to make individual templates. Rotary cutting in place of templates.
+ Cutting and marking tools; how to use them; many choices on the market.
+ Making best use of their sewing machines if they plan to use them. Yes, I have students who piece and appliqué by hand, so I include this too.
+ Seaming exact 1/4″ seams, by hand or machine; using a 1/4″ foot; pressing directions; using the iron properly; making a basic template that doubles as an ironing pad.

Exact template drawings for each block that I offer in class are accompanied by brief instructional text. I provide detailed instructions for planning, cutting, piecing, and/or appliqué during the actual demonstration of the new block itself. When appropriate, I provide both rotary cutting and template cutting instructions with accurate line drawings as needed.

Please realize that this list is just a brief outline to give you an idea of how I organize and prepare my class handout sheets. It is not intended to be copied or used as-is. I have not included every topic I cover, or this book would be a thousand pages long. Sharing my list is just to give you an idea of what my workbooks contain. You must develop workbooks that suit your topics and style.

My workbook concept has saved me a lot of time over the years. When I was handing out instruction sheets at each class, absent or late students missed theirs and expected me to remember their absence and bring them next time. They frequently lost single sheets and expected replacements. When I was teaching five to six classes per week, this was frustrating for me.

The students like the system. Fast learners can jump ahead on blocks or instructions they feel they understand without waiting for slower students. The slow folks know that if they fall behind, they have all the information they need to complete the beginning class project at home, at their own speed. If you have students who drop out during the class, you have already recovered your copy costs and a bit of profit for each workbook ahead of time.

If you are concerned that students will copy your handout sheets for others, I will talk about copyright in chapter 14. I deliberately do not cover every construction tip and instruction I give orally in class. Without being in the class, beginning quilters could not complete a quilt independently, with a workbook alone. I use the blackboard in class for actual construction steps that do not appear in the workbooks. My workbooks are just to help students work. They are not meant to be full-length books. I always include my copyright information on the first page of each workbook and take time to explain it.

A last word about workbooks. As you may expect, the workbooks for the other three class levels for each of my classes are similar, but provide more advanced blocks, construction, paper piecing, blind stitching, and other skills non-beginners want to learn. So it goes for intermediate-, advanced-, and designer-level classes.

Here is another tip that has served me well. I keep an extra copy of my workbook for a particular class in my briefcase, which is available at every minute of class time. When students seem to stumble over the same point, I take that to mean I need to revise my handout and make it clearer. If I forget anything, find an error, or receive a constructive suggestion from a student, I pencil it in for future revision before I duplicate the next batch of handouts.

This way, I am constantly updating and improving the information, until at last it seems to suit everyone. (Actually, nothing suits everyone. In every class, you may find a student who will always blame the handout sheets or you for anything not easily understandable to him/her.) Stimulate your students with photos and samples of what they will be making.

Producing Handout Sheets

Here are some timesaving tips for non-computer-users to make producing and continually updating student handout sheets easier. When I began teaching quilting, I designed handouts by carefully outlining the pattern pieces of each block on paper, using my templates. I penciled measurements and protractor readings inside each outlined shape. In the space remaining around these shapes, I squeezed instructions and tips on how to make each block.

I meticulously designed forty such handout sheets. I expected to use my originals for years. My fantasy was that all I needed to do was to photocopy the number needed for each class. The reality was that from the first moment I passed out my handout sheets, changes were needed. A few students requested clearer, more precise wording. I wanted to add or delete instructions as I observed students interpreting my directions.

To my chagrin, there were a few sheets with small errors to correct. Going back to the originals was not helpful. To make even minor changes, I had to redraw every outlined shape, and then I needed to type the text again or to cut and paste. What a waste of time!

Handout sheets nearly always require revision at first. Often there is updating as well, and I had not planned for this. I realized I could save time if I made a master sheet for each block of the outlined pieces, which did not include text or mathematical notations. Instead, I photocopied each master pattern sheet and typed my text onto the copy. Future revisions meant I needed only to make another copy of the master pattern sheet and add new information, without tediously redrawing each pattern shape.

Storing Handout Sheets

I place each master sheet in a plastic page to identify it as the original sheet to be used for photocopies only. The plastic page goes into a manila folder labeled with the name of the quilt block. My supply of handouts for the pattern also goes into the folder.

I file the folders in my cabinet in the order students receive them. For example, Irish Chain is the first block for beginners, Rail Fence is the second.

Each folder contains the master sheet and remaining copies for student handouts. Stored this way, I can see at a glance if there are enough handouts for a particular class. Since my college classes last for eight weeks, and I use ten patterns for each class level and teach four levels, my files have forty such folders.

Each time I need to revise or update handouts, I discard all existing copies in that file folder. This prevents outdated sheets from finding their way to a student. I need only make another copy of my master and add the new text.

Computer Help

It was a miracle to me when I realized I could produce text that flowed around my drawn outline shapes by using my word processing program. Many of you may design templates and outlines for blocks using Electric Quilt software, but I have not mastered it yet. I draw an empty box of the approximate dimensions of each pattern piece, since my word processor allows me to make blank graphic boxes that contain no words. Many other software programs have this capability, too.

As I type in text, it wraps around the box that will ultimately hold the drawn line shapes. After printing the first draft, I hold it up to a window with the master sheet of pattern shapes behind, to see if there is enough room to draw the pieces as the text flows around.

If adjustments are needed, I move the text on the computer screen, then reprint. After printing the text, I trace the shapes onto the empty places on the page. This final sheet becomes the one used to make photocopies for students. You could also have the drawn shapes scanned into the computer as art objects. You could then automatically insert the pattern piece into the text and have the text flow around it—in most word processing programs. That way, you would not ever have to retrace the shapes.

When revisions are needed, I simply reword the text to conform to the space around the shapes, reprint, and retrace, taking only minutes. This is much easier and more professional-looking than Wite-Out, cut-and-paste, or type-over strips. It is wonderful to be able to update as needed without having to produce an entirely new document with every small change. Naturally, all you computer whizzes with quilt software programs need not follow my instructions above, but for students who are like me and have not yet made friends with their graphics programs, this is a good method.

You should put all your quilting, teaching, and business matters into their own subdirectories, or folders. Do not be tempted to save your files to the main directory of your computer, because even if the files are sorted by alphabetical order, you will have to remember what you named every single file in order to retrieve them. It's much better to have everything saved in a specific place.

Computers that are running recent versions of Windows have a folder called My Documents. You can open as many folders in My Documents as you like, name them as you like, and fill them with both documents and graphics. Here is the way I organize my files: In the main directory I have a parent directory called Sylvia's Studio (the name of my business). Under the parent directory, there are subdirectories:

+ Articles
+ Book lists
+ Lesson plans
+ Letters
+ Lists (catalogs, companies, Web sites)
+ Ideas (for future projects)
+ Mailing (those to whom I send regular mailings)
+ My books (my personal list of books in my library, by topic)
+ Resource (people, groups, associations)
+ Subscribe (subscriptions and associations I belong to)
+ Wholesale (listing of wholesale sources)
+ Workshop (all the workshops I offer)
+ Patterns

Is organization worth the effort? If you are unsure as to whether you should take time to organize your teaching business and all of your materials, consider the following equations:

Organizing = less time searching for what you need
Less time searching = more time for designing, sewing, teaching
More time creating and teaching = a more profitable quilting business

Visual Aids

I use swatch binders and other visual aids in my classes, since I teach primarily for community colleges and recreational programs, as opposed to shops. While shops usually have plenty of quilts on every wall, they may not be illustrating the points you wish to make or the color combinations you want to show. You should never rely on the shop samples as your visual aids.

Swatches, books, samples, wall charts, easels with individually mounted blocks and binders of tear sheets are also excellent learning tools for classes. I share mine and explain and demonstrate their use.

In the beginning class, I have assorted sewn samples to illustrate parts of the sample the student will be making. Here are some examples:

+ Construction in progress
+ Smaller versions of what they will make
+ The correct way to make an intersection seam beside another sample that shows what happens when it is done incorrectly
+ A little four-patch square to show how to press in one direction and how to match seams
+ Different sizes of hand stitching and quilting

I keep photograph albums available in class to include photos of my work, student work from past classes, and works-in-progress.

Samples for Your Classes

Samples, meaning completed projects that show potential students what they can expect to make in class, are the most stimulating of all to them (students, that is). Here are a few basics about making class samples to promote your classes or to illustrate procedures for students.

All costs for raw materials you use to make your teaching aids are totally deductible. Making samples is an important part of teaching, but the materials required and the time to make them add up. Keep track of your costs and set a value on each sample you make.

Think about this so you will be ready when a shop owner asks you to make several colorways of one quilt or block for display. You need to be able to set a fair price for making more than one sample for a given class. This may help her sell fabric, but you must be realistic when you set a price to make, sell, or lend your quilted samples to a shop.

Many shops now ask that a sample made with current fabrics be displayed each time a class is offered. In the past, shop teachers assumed that it would take at least one session of the class to recoup the cost of making a sample. If a new sample must be made each time, the preparation costs for the class may eliminate all your profits. You have several options.

You can make a smaller sample to begin with. This allows you to spend less time and less fabric, and it provides a sample more easily displayed than a full-size quilt. Small samples can be quilted if you wish, but those left unfinished allow construction details to be viewed from both sides.

Subsequent class sessions can be promoted by making one new block in current fabrics. This has the benefit of not only satisfying the shop's desire to promote new products, but also of showing that the design can be made in a different style or colorway. For example, if your original sample is made in batiks, make the next one in reproductions prints. Changing the entire style of the sample will appeal to a new group of people. It is amazing how many people can only picture the quilt in the one style you have shown in your sample.

Your Teaching Attitude

If you want your reputation as a good teacher to grow, you must develop a business attitude to help foster a comfortable, productive learning climate that is projected to students in every class. Here are some tips to keep in mind as you develop and maintain a good teaching attitude.

Dress appropriately. Trainers for professional speakers suggest that you dress at a slightly higher level than your students. Take time to appear well groomed, rested, and neat.

Arrive for each class well before it begins so you have completed your setting-up process before the class is scheduled to start. Avoid being a bell-ringer—entering your classroom at the last minute out of breath. Arriving early means you will be relaxed and composed before you start. Absolutely never leave early. Your students deserve your prompt, efficient, and complete attention for the entire period they have paid for.

Show consideration for your students by starting your classes on time. They are always annoyed if you look at your watch and say, "There are two more people in this class. Let's give them ten more minutes before we begin." Consider the students who show up on time first.

Treat students as individuals rather than as a group of people who are all alike. Students do not just come to a class to be taught a specific skill. Think of them as a group of people seeking to increase their knowledge, thinking ability, and competence with your help. Realize that each person has a field of expertise that you may know nothing about. Show respect for each learner's individuality and experience. Do not point out the slowest person's lack of progress to others.

Prove your reliability by keeping your promises to demonstrate a certain technique or bring something of interest to the class when you said you would do so. I keep a notebook in my briefcase for this purpose. I will note that I promised Matilda that I would bring my table topper to show her that oranges and reds can work together, for example. I do not want to apologize for forgetting when she asks again next week.

Make sure your supplies are well organized to avoid shuffling things around on your desk, wasting time looking for misplaced items. Students hate to watch a teacher searching her possessions, saying, "I know it's here somewhere."

Do not overtly try to sell your captive audience books or other products during class time. Some seminars and sponsoring groups forbid the practice and mention it in their contract. Other groups, even shops, encourage teachers to bring hard-to-find items and to show how they are used.

Here is a real example. I was about to teach a class in color and design in a quilt shop. Before the class, I visited to ask the shop owner if she carried color wheels. She pointed out two of them on the bottom shelf of a bookcase, explaining that customers rarely bought or seemed interested in them. During my class the following week, I demonstrated how to use one when shopping. She sold her two immediately, and student/customers wanted more.

From this point onward, she asked me to order them wholesale myself, demonstrate them in class, and sell them at the end of class. I did so, and everyone was happy. She did not have to order them when her staff did not understand how to sell them, students were happy to learn how use them, and I augmented my teaching profit by selling something students wanted. This does not work everywhere, but it worked well this time.

On the other hand, it is unfair of the shop to ask you to take class time to promote new items. Suggest that a display be made and a shop employee be available to demonstrate these during a break or before or after the class.

If you have things to sell, make sure your students understand that purchase is optional and only available during breaks or before and after class.

Such selling is referred to as "BOR," or "Back-of-the-Room" sales. Do it only when allowed by the hiring group. The college where I teach prints in the college bulletin that my books will be available for purchase after class. Thus, I buy my own books at wholesale and sell them at retail when and where it is appropriate. More about this in chapter 11.

Be sensitive to your language to avoid inadvertently offending. Avoid both slang and jargon, which may not be understood by all students.

Be open to different perspectives. Stress that your way is not the only right way, and that usually there are many ways to make a technique work. Focus on what works for the student and do not insist that everyone use your particular method if they are pleased with their own. Use humor such as, "If you place your hot iron on the wrong side of the freezer paper, you will have it bonded to the iron." In this case, students can hear that this would be a mistake, and they know it is not just another method.

Remain patient as you repeat information or techniques. Most students require a lot of repetition to reinforce learning. Think about how you feel when you take a class from a quilting superstar. Regardless of my professional status, when in another teacher's class, I appreciate repetition so that I am sure I am learning. Have more than one way to explain any technique. People learn in different ways. Try to approach things from different angles so that everyone understands.

As a teacher yourself, never move in on another teacher's class by identifying yourself as a teacher, saying something like, "When I teach this in my class, I have the students do . . ." I feel strongly that when I have enrolled in a class taught by someone else, I should leave my teacher's cap at home and behave like the student I am. I have signed up to learn her special techniques or ideas. Resist stealing the thunder from another teacher.

Individualize your instruction and be flexible. Take into account each student's personal needs, experience, and current situation. You can speak louder to a person who is hard of hearing, you can demonstrate the hand quilting stitch with your left hand for a left-hander. Do not let your ego get in the way here, fearing that you will be clumsier than you are with your right hand. The person is already clumsier and slower than you, because she is just learning.

Ask your class at the beginning if there are left-handed students. If so, you should explain any techniques that are different as you go along, such as putting the bulk of the fabric to the left when rotary cutting.

Organize your information so students can follow easily. I provide a syllabus for every class I teach. You will find a sample in this chapter.

Move among students observing, offering encouragement, tips, and suggestions for improvement. My preference is to have a U-shaped classroom configuration, with students sitting on the outside of the U. I use a rolling chair on the inside of the U so I can come face-to-face with each person frequently during a single class session.

In shop classrooms, space is at a premium and you may find it difficult just to get between tables. A full class can mean that students are more crowded than you would like. Look for ways to minimize the congestion, such as setting up ironing stations off to one side. Once the sewing machines are in place, you can set up one or two cutting areas for trim work. This will give people more room around their machines.

The advantage of the small space is that you can actually see all your students at one time. Watch them as they work and be sensitive to confused or irritated body language. Those are the students who need your help!

Avoid taking yourself too seriously. If your attitude implies superiority, it will interfere with your students' learning and your possible future bookings. Be open to untried ideas. Beginners in a class often have wonderful new ideas while approaching issues more creatively or intuitively than you do. Prepare for this and, if it occurs, enjoy it. If taught correctly, each student will learn something of value, depending on her personal needs, experience, and current situation. Believe me, I have learned my share of tips from beginning and intermediate students. When this happens, thank them. Acknowledge that this is new information to you, that you appreciate learning it, and that you are glad they shared it.

Avoid approaching the session with the idea that all students must learn exactly what you think they should learn. Instead, view your teaching as a cooperative venture for learning. Students already may have their own ideas of what they want. Even though some students resist information you know is essential, they have a right to experiment and often come around later.

An example that comes up all the time in my classes concerns 100 percent cotton fabric. Many students recognize that there is often a vast difference in quality from chain stores to quilt shops. There is always someone in every class who announces to everyone how much money she saved from what I told them in the first lesson might be their average expenditures. "But I found this at Bargain-mart for $1.99 per yard, and it is exactly the color and print in the quilting shop further from me," they say. This topic is discussed endlessly online because the issue is so common. After my students hear what I have to say about selecting quality fabric, they also have a right to use a remnant of unknown fiber or seconds purchased at chain stores. They will learn sooner or later.

Adopt a caring attitude and show it. Show concern about the learning experiences and problems of your students as they struggle to absorb new information. I often will rest my hand, however briefly, on a student's shoulder or arm to let her know I care about her needs and her progress. Sometimes, just a reassuring pat on a hand or arm lets them know you care about them as individuals.

Support all student participation by acknowledging the rightness of each person. This does not mean that wrong answers are right. It means that exploration, effort, personal integrity, creativity, and risk-taking should be supported and encouraged.

Develop patience with your students and freely acknowledge that you, too, make errors, rip out, and create do-overs. I will usually rip out something I am working on right in class to illustrate that I goof up, and then follow by demonstrating imaginative ways to make corrections.

Be honest if there is a question you cannot answer, but promise to research the topic and present it for the next class. I just tell my students that it is an absolute fact that I do not know everything about anything, but I am diligent about researching for them and for myself.

Never, but never, bad-mouth or criticize your colleagues and other teachers' methods in class. Not only is this practice unprofessional, but it also damages your perceived ethics with students.

The adage "familiarity breeds contempt" applies to teachers in class. Avoid being overly friendly, being personally inquisitive, or discussing a student's personal problems, so that when you must offer criticism or retain control of the class, you can do so.

I make it a policy to always thank a student for asking a question. If it is a good one or one you had not considered, say something like, "Thank you for asking that excellent question. I appreciate your participation."

I generally maintain a high energy level when I teach. I talk fast and discourage personal conversations unrelated to class. Under no circumstances should students bring children of any age to class. I do not make exceptions unless the child is old enough and interested enough in the class to participate. If that is the case, the child should pay a fee. Bringing family or friends from out of town is very inappropriate for everyone concerned. A class is for learning, and guests, whether they are interested in the subject or not, do not belong in a class for which they have not paid. The only exceptions I make are physical facilitators for a student, such as attendants for wheelchair-bound people or sign language interpreters.

Problem Areas and Difficult Students

This seems the perfect segue into discussing difficult students and situations, so you can be as prepared as possible. Students are human beings, and humans have frailties that show up in class. Here is a partial list of problem areas you may encounter in class. You may be able to add to it from your own experiences.

+ Chronically late students who interrupt the class after it has started.
+ Students who challenge you at every opportunity.
+ Students who interrupt to impress others with what they know.
+ Students who teach others, often incorrectly.
+ Complainers and whiners.
+ Students who continuously jump ahead and try to hurry you to work at their preferred speed, oblivious of others.
+ Rude, hostile, and demanding students.
+ Students who talk so much that they distract everyone, even you.
+ Students with genuine physical, emotional, or learning disabilities. I believe they deserve special attention. Anyone in a wheelchair, learning

English, or with physical disabilities gets plenty of time from me. (I taught a lady with one arm to knit and an MS patient in a wheelchair to crochet. Wonderful experiences for them and me.)

✦ Students who know it all and belittle other, slower students.

✦ Gossipmongers with bad tales about nearly every class, teacher, program, or technique they know about. Some folks just love "horriblizing," as I call it.

All these situations require patience, humor, gentleness, and tolerance. Over time, I have had to ask a few students to step out of the room, to chat with them about a problem they were creating and of which they might not be aware. Half a dozen times, I have had to call seriously disruptive students at home to discuss a problem. Two or three times, I had to call and ask someone to please not return to my class.

We all must develop little tricks to try to keep order and maintain the students' attention. Here are a few tips that you may find helpful to minimize difficult students:

✦ I use a little bell when the din gets so loud I cannot hear myself think. I tell them I will continue when the room quiets down.

✦ I ask noisy, chatting students to please step outside for a little break and visit with their friend until they finish their conversation, then invite them to come right back in.

✦ I look a noisy, disruptive person in the eye until she breaks my gaze and looks down and becomes silent.

✦ I make extra handouts or enlargements of special techniques for students having genuine learning problems. These may include larger photos, restating the information in easier language, diagrams, or other tips.

✦ I use the blackboard to jot down a topic a student brings up out of order or when I am speaking. I tell the class I will get to these topics during the group discussion portion or at the end of class, and continue with the class flow.

✦ Eventually, I taught myself to do all of the crafts I teach left-handed. This makes life simpler for left-handed students and for me when I'm instructing them.

✦ I group students of similar levels together, enabling me to provide mini-group personalized instruction. I ask them to sit together next time, promising I will offer them targeted information at their group level for the remainder of the class.

✦ I assign hands-on tasks to one group while addressing another group of a slightly different learning level or subject.

✦ When tardy students come in and interrupt to demand handouts they missed and an overview of what was covered before their arrival, I tell them tactfully that I will gather what they need at the next break or when no others in class need help, whichever comes first.

I often enlist the help of an employee, teaching assistant, or apprentice. This has been an invaluable tool for me over the years when teaching thirty-five to forty-five students per class in community colleges, though I have done it from my home studio as well.

Very advanced students can become your paid or unpaid assistants. You can ask them to sit with a student who is confused, requiring more care than you can give, without holding up everyone else. A word of caution here. I personally select and train an apprentice and announce this to the class when I introduce her. I do not mean that anyone who thinks of herself as advanced should become a volunteer assistant. I have trained eight apprentices over the years, all of whom are presently working in the craft industry in their chosen capacities.

A teaching technique that works marvelously well for me in day-long classes are what we used to call "buzz sessions," now called "breakout groups." At lunchtime, I suggest that the class break into groups of four students each. I assign them the task of asking one another their most pressing questions and issues of concern and to sit back and learn from the others in their group. All unanswered questions or those needing clarification are brought back to me after lunch. I ask a spokesperson from each class to read their questions and then reply as best I can. The students always tell me that this type of networking is helpful to them, and I am able to deal with the specific issues where they needed more help and information.

Students of Different Levels

Having students of different levels within one class heads the list of frequent complaints from teachers. Beginners who sign up for classes beyond their skill level frustrate their classmates. Frequently, such students demand that you stop the flow of the class to help them learn something they should already have known about when they signed up in the first place.

The easiest way to head this off is to be specific in your course description, stating what skills the student should have before signing up for a class you offer. You can further refine this issue by saying something like, "Please let me remind you that my course description said that students should have the equivalent of . . . before signing up for . . . , since basics are not included in this class."

No matter how much they do not know, let them realize that they may be in the wrong place. If they acknowledge this and insist upon staying, I let them know they will get the same amount of time from me as the others do, but if there are little spurts of extra time in class, I will come back to them. I make it clear they are not entitled to more attention than other students. What I try to do is to place the responsibility for their being in the wrong class on them. I am happy to work out transfers, credits, and changes when appropriate, though this may not be appropriate in a shop setting.

Make your course description as clear as possible. I teach an appliqué class for Quilt University. In my course description, I say that the project is not for the faint of heart, cannot be rushed or done by machine, and should be attempted only by those with experience. Putting this type of notice in the earliest promotions and ads for my classes seems to help.

Recently, *QuiltTeach*, a daily online newsletter for teachers working independently, addressed this issue. By the way, I recommend this free digest to all of you, even if you do not teach quilting yet. Challenges, teaching tips, questions, answers, and advice are shared openly among members, all of whom are professional instructors.

Describing the greatest challenge for hands-on classes, an instructor explained that teachers must focus on keeping more advanced pupils moving at a good speed without losing the slower pupils. "Good handouts and step-by-step examples are invaluable when facing students of mixed ability levels," she says. "The popularity of your classes determines future wages. You will be invited back if your classes are well-organized, warm, and friendly, and if they produce something useful and enjoyable."

Managing students of mixed skill levels has appeared as an ongoing topic on several online digests and at faculty meetings before and after quilt events and seminars. An instructor at Quilt University, Jan Krentz, has written an excellent treatise on this subject. You will find it on her Web site, *www.jankrentz.com*.

Organizing Notes—The Start of Your Lesson Plan

Gather up all those notes you use when you lecture and teach. Here is how to organize them into one sequential lesson plan that is easy to update. Place all notes that refer to a particular topic on a table. Arrange them in the sequence you use when you present your material. If necessary, cut up paper that contains multiple ideas so that each piece reflects one thought. Study your arrangement of ideas and be sure it flows logically.

Stack the pieces of paper carefully in order. When you have all your topics sorted, retype the information, one topic to a page. Since I have made friends with my scanning program, I use that, too.

If space remains at the bottom of a page, leave it blank and begin a new topic on another. Continue until you have entered all your information. Each set of notes can serve as a lesson plan. Use the blank space at the bottom of the sheets to jot down frequently asked questions, requests for additional information, or ideas of your own to improve your presentation.

Periodically revise the notes, incorporating your latest ideas. By using the one-topic-per-page method, even added information remains in order by topic. Can you see how this organization allows you to continually refine your lesson plan until it is as perfect as you can make it?

Creating Your Lesson Plan

Lesson plans are the most critical part of teaching preparation. Presenting information in an orderly way helps you avoid rambling or overlooking something. As you begin thinking of drafting your first lesson plan, ask yourself: How long is the entire class in total hours? How many hours for each lesson? What level of experience do students need for the class?

Here is an example from my quilting lesson plan for beginners, based on a six-week class of two hours each. Of course, you will write your own. Mine is meant only as a guide, not a rigid outline of steps you must follow.

With very large classes, I also state the time I will approach each of the lesson segments below. If someone comes late and misses a segment, I consider it to be their problem. I help when possible, but do not stop the class to help one person catch up.

I distribute class literature, instructions, patterns, and, most importantly, a syllabus for the entire class, so they will know at what point their specific interests and questions will be met. I go over class levels, projects, and topics to be included. I explain that after the introductory lesson, every subsequent lesson will include all of the segments listed below.

Obviously, this is not needed for short shop classes that run three to six hours. In this setting, you can outline briefly how the time will be spent, especially if there is a break. This way, people will know where they should be when the break occurs.

When class begins, I write a brief timeline on the blackboard, whether it is a half- or whole-day class. This way, students can plan ahead if they must leave the room and be prepared to return on time. This is how my all-day sessions look:

Begin 9:30
Break 10:45–10:50
Class 10:50-Noon
Lunch Noon-12:45
Class 12:45–2:00
Break 2:00–2:10
Dismiss 4:00

It is easy to just cut this schedule in half for a partial day of two to three hours. If there is no board or any surface to write on in a shop classroom, consider adding this to one of your handout sheets for each student, or posting a sheet of paper in the room where all can see.

Lesson One

1. Orientation to the facility, hours, meals, parking (very brief).
2. Student introductions.
3. Ask each student to explain why she enrolled in the class and what she hopes to learn.
4. I take about half an hour to orient the students to the course itself, reminding them that we have a total of twelve hours together. (Most of the time, I have more hours and longer classes, but I am using this format here because it is the one used in most shop classes.) If you have only three hours, you will want to do introductions and perhaps ask if they have worked with the specific technique. You cannot spend too much on this step.

5. I explain the teaching format I will use for all the lessons in the class. I tell the students to expect me to deliver my information in the following formats. Details about the definition of each of these comes next.

+ lectures
+ demonstrations
+ hands-on, one-to-one individualized instruction
+ slides
+ book reviews
+ trunk shows
+ combinations of some or all of the above

6. After completing my orientation, I ask everyone if it sounds as if the course they have signed up for contains all the information they came for. If they say "yes," I leave it at that. If they express disappointment that something they wanted may not be included, I tell them I will either include it into the remaining lessons or let them know if other classes will meet their needs.

For example, if someone tells me she came to my beginning quilting class and also wants to know how to get started as a quilting teacher, I gently point out that this is not to be covered in the particular class and explain what other classes—mine or those of other teachers—may meet her needs.

7. I introduce myself and explain my qualifications briefly. (two to three minutes)

8. I distribute class literature and go over class levels, projects, and topics.

9. In closing, I go over a list of the materials required for class in great detail, where they can be found, brand names I may prefer, and why. I require the gathering of needed materials as homework for the next lesson. In a quilting class, I also request that students wash and press all their fabrics before bringing them to the next session.

General Order for All Lessons after One

After the introductory class, I divide each of the next four lessons into four flexible segments. Here are further details about how I define the segments of each lesson.

Formal Lecture

Students learn that I will present one or more lectures during every lesson. I define these as brief presentations to disseminate new information that ties in with the current class, project, or technique. In my beginning quilting class, I describe my way of quilting and why I choose it. For students unfamiliar with quilt-as-you-go methods, I define it, then talk about its advantages and the reasons for making all my quilts this way.

Individualized Instruction

I elicit progress reports from each student as roll is taken; special questions are asked and answered. Hands-on, individualized instruction usually takes at least half of the entire lesson. After the second lesson and every one thereafter, I begin the class by personally visiting with each student to see her work from the week before, to allow individual questions, and to offer personalized tips and hints for improvement.

Group Demonstrations

I explain that during every lesson, I will present a formal demonstration of a technique appropriate for the particular session. For example, I demonstrate how to baste in my second session, how to hand quilt in the third, how to bind the quilt in the sixth. Naturally, you will have to plan your demo sessions to fit your own topic and rate of teaching speed.

Show-and-Tell

I show related samples of work in class and invite students to bring their own. Show swatch binders, giving instructions on how students may begin their own reference library. Trunk shows, bring-and-brag, or show-and-tell—whatever you prefer to call them—are critical for students.

I plan and organize my trunk shows, which are so called because you must take a large suitcase or small trunk when you go to class. Today's rolling carts, dollies, and suitcases are ideal for this.

Giving a trunk show means that you collect a few of your completed or in-progress projects and show them to inspire and motivate students, to reinforce the techniques you have taught them, and to provide real examples of the techniques. Place your quilted items in your suitcase/trunk in the order you will be talking about them.

When I give trunk shows to my own classes or to large guild groups, I do not allow anyone else to extract each item. I prefer to do it myself and talk about it, explaining how/why/when I made the item, and then take questions from the audience. In sequential order, I remove the next item, usually tied to the earlier ones, rather like building a fashion show of what I have brought. I try to save some spectacular thing of special interest as a finale.

When presenting trunk shows for larger groups or your guild, realize that one of its functions is to entertain the audience as well as to visually excite and stimulate them. When doing a one-shot trunk show for a group as opposed to class, you can also showcase your talent, skill, and completed collection of your work, and potentially offer yourself as a future teacher or presenter. Trunk shows, professionally prepared and presented, serve as an entrée into future engagements and marketing exposure for you, which enhances your reputation.

Slides

Not all students like slides, to say nothing of those who fall asleep as soon as the lights dim. I offer one or two slide presentations within a six-week class, limit them to fifteen minutes, and announce that I will show them at the end of class. Uninterested students may then choose to leave, knowing they will not miss anything critical.

Book Reviews

These are a must, though students may not think so in the beginning. I present them during slower or quieter class periods, which may not occur every week. My goal is to introduce them to different books, authors, and designers and expose them to the diverse methods and ideas available to all of us today.

Lesson Two: Sample of a Beginner Class

Lecture: differences between chain-store and quilt-shop cotton fabrics. Individual and group instruction: progress reports of each person's color and fabric choices. Show-and-tell: Show them my quilt samples, completed and in progress, and invite them to show and describe what they may have brought.

Demonstration: can be hand piecing, machine piecing, $1/4$" seams, using $1/4$" foot, walking feet.

I hope these two sample classes will guide you as you make your own lesson plans.

Using a Syllabus

I begin a new class by providing a syllabus—a one-page list of topics presented to students in the order you will present them. My syllabus becomes the first page of each workbook and helps students know at what point their specific interests and questions will be met. If you use your syllabus to start your lesson plan, all you need to do is expand it. Here is one of mine exactly as it appears in my workbooks.

Sample Syllabus for Quilting Business Class
(no tape recording permitted in class)

ENTREPRENEURS IN THE CREATIVE ARTS
Right- and left-brain dominance and the need for integration
Extroverts vs. Introverts. Which personality type will help you succeed?
Benefits of trade organizations: HIA, SCD, others
Your first step: A business plan. Why do you need one?

WAYS TO PROFIT FROM YOUR ARTS & CRAFTS
The "professional quilter." What does it mean?
Consignment or commission? Neither without a contract!
Working with sales representatives
Shows, exhibits, and fairs: consumer or trade?
Selling through crafters' malls, in person or from a distance

Selling arts and crafts via mail order and the Internet.
Selling designs, patterns, and instructions to magazines
Offering your services to the trade
Teaching: from your studio or sponsoring groups and organizations
Giving demonstrations for credibility and exposure

COPYRIGHT LAW, LIMITATION, USAGE, INFRINGEMENT
Duration of copyright
Defining "public domain"
Common-law copyright

FINANCIAL ISSUES
Home office deduction, phone, mileage, and other deductions
Documentation of deductible expenses and bookkeeping
How to buy wholesale. Approaching wholesalers, terms of sale
Ten ways to set prices
Credit card status: Why so difficult to obtain?

YOUR PORTFOLIO AND PROMOTIONAL DOCUMENTS
What goes into a professional portfolio?
Arranging your portfolio

DEFINE YOUR MARKET
Who are they? Where are they? What do they read?
Brief discussion about Internet marketing
Writers', artists', graphic, and photography markets: how to benefit from
requesting guidelines and press release packages to learn more

ADVERTISING (STEPS 1 AND 2)
Classified
Display
Cooperative
Promotional opportunities

LEGAL ISSUES
Business name, bank accounts, credit cards
Profit motive and the IRS: hobbyist or professional status?
Business license, zoning permits, home business use permits

Where Will You Teach?

Teaching from a home studio provides additional income to your quilting business and is the easiest way to begin teaching. Even though you may also teach from a shop, community colleges, park and recreation programs, or other community centers, teaching from a home-based studio provides many advantages:

+ You have fewer expenses than teaching for a shop, school, or other agency.
+ You have fewer federal, state, or local regulations than you would teaching anywhere else.
+ You can teach weekdays, evenings, or weekends, setting your own pace.
+ You do not have to incur childcare, commuting, clothing expenses.
+ You do not need teaching credentials.

Bart Brodsky and Janet Geis pooled over thirty-five years of front-line experience as school administrators, publishers, and entrepreneurs to write *The Teaching Marketplace*. "Two out of every three adults attend some kind of non-credit or continuing education program. Freelance and independent teachers constitute an 'invisible university' larger than any other single teaching institution in many communities. Musicians and artists teach from their home studios. Business experts teach in their offices after hours. Teachers share hobbies such as swimming, chess, creative writing, or cooking from home studios. The list goes on," they write in the book.

Shops versus Adult Education

I have spent over thirty-five years teaching in adult education and community colleges. I recognize that today, many instructors teach in shops instead. There are advantages and disadvantages to both.

Teaching in adult education and community colleges means better wages in most states and more regular classes advertised for you by the institution. Generally, such venues repeat their popular classes, so teachers can count on regularly scheduled predictable classes. Usually, you do not have to continue to produce new samples as you do in shops. On the other hand, adult education classes may be in rooms not normally used for sewing. In addition, you may have to carry your equipment for longer distances, and so will your students.

Teaching in a shop means there are more visual aids, supplies, books, and patterns at hand than are available in adult classes. Also, class sizes are much smaller. While I am used to up to forty students in one class, teachers working in shops have much more intimate numbers (four to twelve students).

Issues of what materials shops will provide for their teachers appear regularly on the professional quilting digests. Some give fabrics to teachers, others do not. Some owners want to keep the projects, others return them to the teacher when the class ends. Controversy about this is ongoing, which is a major reason to read and study these digests. Think of them as targeted online newspapers for the quilting industry.

Both venues I have compared provide valuable feedback if you freely pass out evaluation forms. Responses can go a long way to help you remain informed about your local market. Both should include a formal written contract. Both require your very best preparation as a dedicated, organized, and enthusiastic teacher.

Teaching by Correspondence

Teaching at a distance means you will not face your students in a classroom. In fact, you will not face them at all. You will never hear the sound of their voices or see what they look like. Yet teaching at a distance will reveal a lot to you about your students, and they will learn a lot about you and your ideas.

Unlike person-to-person teaching, students learning at a distance have the opportunity to repeatedly go over the class information and what they have learned. They do not have to rely only on their memory and notes to capture your ideas. Your written class information will become a permanent resource for them. If you have done your job well, they will return to your written word time and time again, so make every page your very best.

People prefer to learn by mail at their own pace for many reasons. Perhaps they have small children, transportation problems, or not enough time. Whatever the reason, students who study at home need instructors who teach from their homes. Why not you? I have taught by correspondence in many different ways:

+ I have developed, marketed, and sold my own courses.
+ My community college offered students the option of taking my courses in person or by mail.
+ A national organization sponsored my courses. I taught a correspondence course for the Knitting Guild of America.
+ I also teach individual courses sporadically from my Web site.
+ I am on the faculty of Quilt University.

Find other organizations that sponsor online classes, such as Barnes & Noble Books, Hewlett-Packard Computer Classes, Phoenix University, and others.

If you are already teaching, you have an advantage if you are considering teaching by correspondence. You probably do not need much time to gather your information together. After all, you are already using it regularly in your classes and workshops, aren't you?

It is vital to begin by writing a comprehensive course outline, which differs from a lesson plan. The latter is for your reference and a tool to help you prepare well. A course outline is a document you send to your potential students to let them know what they will be learning from you.

Describe the complete course content concisely. Explain everything you plan to include. Next, convert all your usual oral instructions into written form, thoroughly and precisely. Arrange your material so students learn in a logical, sensible order.

Group the information into lessons. Decide how many lessons it takes to offer the student a rich educational experience. Be exact about what each person will learn from each lesson in your course. Remember that when you are teaching this way, you do not have to factor in time for the student to sew or complete other tasks.

Preparing a Lesson by Correspondence

I prefer a formal outline to plan my lessons. That is, I use roman numerals to designate each lesson of the course. Beneath each roman numeral, I use capital letters to sketch out the main points contained in that particular lesson.

When satisfied with the contents of your course and how the information breaks into lessons, focus on each lesson individually. Think sequentially. Students must find your ideas flowing from one point to the next. Start with the known before offering something new. I use a review paragraph to help students see how what they already know will tie into the new information. Show how the new skills you will present to them relate to previously learned material.

Be clear about each instruction. Make sure your questions and assignments cause the student to research information using their newly gained skills. I include a reading list with each lesson. I also invite the student to tell me about each book they have on the subject just presented. This tells me a little about their previous experience and interest.

When you have completed all lessons, go over them carefully. Your educational material must be free from errors and perfectly arranged and formatted. It is an excellent idea to have another set of eyes proofread your materials. When you have a perfectly completed document (your class) plus a course outline, you are ready to create a flawless original. Computers are excellent for this purpose. If you do not have one, hire a word processor to achieve a professional image. Remember, the only contact your students have with you is what they read on paper, and you will not be present to determine whether or not students have understood your material. To determine whether the student understands, prepare homework essay questions that they cannot answer with a simple yes or no.

I have a different set of essay questions for each lesson. The real work is to prepare a class for the first time. It takes months to complete each course. It is not an overnight project, but once done, my office photocopy machine produces subsequent classes and lessons in a flash.

When you are ready to market your course, approach your supervisor if you are teaching for an adult program or community college. Show him or her your course outline. Suggest the idea of describing your course in correspondence form along with regular classes. Ask to have it included in the class schedules describing regular classes. In my case, the Dean agreed that offering my correspondence course would enhance the reputation of its own faculty while providing teachers further freelance teaching opportunities.

Be fastidious about record-keeping when students begin to enroll. Begin a file for each person. Record what course each person is taking. Keep track of their progress as they complete each lesson. My policy is to send only one lesson at a time. When the student completes the homework and answers all my questions, I go over every word carefully. I add comments, make suggestions, correct erroneous information, and give them encouragement. Each time a student returns a lesson, I add the information to their file before sending them the next lesson.

I keep copies of all letters, lessons, and samples students send me. Copy machines make it possible for me to record needlework and quilting samples students send me for examination as I photocopy the samples themselves. Since I return the originals promptly, the paper copy provides an excellent record of students' work.

Be prompt about sending answers, information, and subsequent lessons. I did some marketing on the potential of teaching by correspondence. I learned that unexplained delays in getting their work and samples returned to them is the main complaint made by students studying by correspondence.

To reassure my students, I offer a guarantee. It shows up in my course outline, which I send to anyone when they first inquire about my courses. I promise I will always respond within two weeks. No delays! No excuses!

Teaching Online
Online learning for students is taking a class in the privacy of home without the inconvenience of a set time for each lesson. Think of it as independent study similar to what you may have done when you were in college. After students register for a class, they receive weekly lesson handouts via e-mail and study at their convenience, day or night. To get a quick idea of online course offerings, visit *www.QuiltUniversity.com*, *www.VirtualUniversity.com*, or *www.hplearningcenter.com*.

Instructors are only an e-mail away! That is one of the greatest things about online learning. You can be in a class with others while receiving one-on-one attention and feedback from the teacher. Questions, comments, homework, and suggestions all come to you via e-mail. This is also true for teachers like me, who teach from their own Web site.

One way or the other, individual Internet teachers must achieve student/teacher interaction during their courses. Some use a bulletin board from their site, and others favor an electronic mailing list provided by Yahoo or other online providers.

Most online teachers set up password systems so that only paying students can access their classes. Personally, I do not use a password system for my private Internet correspondence courses. Instead, I send and receive each class session as an attachment via e-mail. Because I teach from my Web site individually rather than for a class, this works well for me.

This system is well suited for a one-to-one relationship between teacher and student. When teaching a group of students, as a growing number of Internet programs do today, providing passwords to each student so they can access the class material is better. Otherwise, you would find yourself repeating the same lessons, assignments, questions, and answers continually.

All expenses, from postage to stationery, are deductible when using snail mail (the traditional postal system). The same is true of those important technological tools that enable you to teach via the Web, such as a digital camera, a good graphics program, and your Web hosting and Internet servers.

On the Road—Teaching at Conventions and Seminars

If you decide to teach away from your home studio for part or even most of your working time, consider this: If you operate from your home office/studio, you are still entitled to all the tax benefits previously discussed. This is because your home-based office/studio is still, according to the IRS, the principal place of your business. It need not be your only place of business. If you prepare your classes, answer your business phone, receive your mail, and use your computer in your office/studio, when you teach away from home you are still operating from your home address. If you want to expand your teaching activities to include other locales, decide what type of teaching you want to do.

When you travel to teach at regional or national seminars or in shops other than your own, keep records of the following additional expenses. If you teach from a home studio as an independent, you can take deductions for the expenses listed below when you leave home to teach on the road:

+ Meals
+ Hotel
+ Gasoline
+ Parking
+ Tolls
+ Airfare, bus fare, taxis, and other ground travel
+ Convention expenses

Teaching at regional and national conventions requires thorough preparation, teaching experience, and valuable networking contacts, but how do you land such jobs? Study the major trade journals to become familiar with the national organizations and guilds in your field of expertise. Subscribe to newsletters in your field so you can remain in touch with upcoming conventions, seminars, or events where you may want to teach.

Contact sponsoring organizations many months before the event. Most select their faculties a year or more in advance. List the shows, conferences, and conventions that interest you. Select a few of interest and send them an informational package about you and your programs. Focus on the benefits you can offer their program, rather than providing too much self-serving self-promotion.

Next, prepare your informational package. Include a well-prepared, professional-looking résumé, an attractive brochure providing detailed information about your business, and a list of your available workshops and lectures, briefly describing each one. If possible, include copies of published articles.

Though optional, I also recommend including a one-page bio—a brief biographical statement describing your background, qualifications, and general experience. A mission statement is another optional document. This one-page statement outlines why you do what you do, and, most importantly, why you care about it. Express your personal convictions and end with a paragraph or two about your goals.

You will also want to request a copy of their teachers' guidelines and application forms.

Follow every instruction to the letter, returning the forms by the stated deadline.

National groups ask for a detailed lesson plan, course description, and list of required materials. Actually, this means that if you are accepted, you have prepared your class months or even a year before the class is to be held, so keep a careful record of all you sent. Do not depend on your memory in order to deliver what you promised many months earlier.

Before you teach locally, you must qualify as an expert. This becomes even more critical when you accept teaching assignments away from home. Enthusiasm and technical expertise alone will not qualify you as a good teacher. You must learn teaching and communication skills as well. When you have polished both your craft and teaching skills, consider taking the first step toward becoming a nationally recognized craft instructor.

Prepare thoroughly by teaching a pilot class to local students before offering it to a national organization. Pilot classes help you anticipate the types of questions participants will ask as they experience new techniques. Then you can refine lesson plans, visual aids, and organization of your material. You can clarify and revise handouts if necessary. This practice will prepare your classes and workshops to go on the road at your convenience. You can leave home regularly, seldom, or not at all. This is the advantage of being self-employed!

You need not wait to hear from one group before approaching another. Send as many informational packages as possible to organizations coast to coast. You can decide which offers to accept after reviewing them all. Another idea is to subscribe to all the craft associations in your field of interest. Each lists their guild chapters throughout the country. Choose geographical areas where you will consider offering programs. Contact those chapter presidents. Send them your informational packages. Surf the Web for quilt organizations and contact them too.

Take care to avoid over-booking in the beginning. Long-distance traveling can exhaust anyone. You may to have to spend an entire day traveling to your destination and another to return home. This means time away from your work at home. Two or three back-to-back workshops in neighboring cities or states may be manageable. More than this invites complications with reservations, homestays, hotels, and other arrangements.

After several years of teaching crafts in my own studio, at community colleges, and for other local programs, I approached national guilds and organizations and offered myself as a freelance teacher. Each assignment led to others. I have traveled to more than half the states in the union to teach crafts at national conventions, in addition to teaching aboard cruise ships.

Setting Fees

Everyone wants to know what she should charge. Unfortunately, no rule exists that is suitable for every teacher in the country, as mentioned in chapter 9. Teachers must set their own fees, taking several factors into consideration:

+ The degree of expertise and experience you have in your craft
+ Credentials or other certification you may have
+ Years and training of teaching experience
+ The geographical area where you live
+ Current trends in style, color, and craft techniques
+ What other teachers charge locally, regionally, and nationally
+ If you will accept a flat fee offered by a specific organization for teaching

At times, large seminars and conferences want to be fair and pay each teacher the same amount. Teachers with experience may have to settle for less than their usual fee. Newer teachers may be delighted with a higher fee than usual, but may be unable to demand this same amount when they return home.

I researched my market many years ago to learn which classes were popular, in demand, and well attended. You must do this too. How much do classes cost where you live? Visit local shops. Inquire as to whether they give classes and what they charge. Call your local community college, adult school, or city sponsored recreational classes. Check out their fees. Determine the minimum amount per hour that would satisfy you.

Let us say that a shop you visit charges $20 per student for four classes of one hour each. Let's further assume the adult school or community college offers classes for $15 for ten weeks of two-hour classes with twenty students per class. When you call the city recreation program, you learn that the fee is $25 for five two-hour private classes.

Call a few private teachers who advertise in the phone directory. Ask their fees for individual lessons. Now, sit down and do a little figuring to arrive at a sensible fee for you and your students that fits in with your community.

Analyzing the data above reveals that the highest amount students pay is $20 for four lessons of one hour each, or $5 per hour. The lowest they would pay is $15 for ten classes of two hours each, or 75¢ per hour. The median is $25 for five two-hour lessons, or $2.50 per hour.

The highest hourly payment from each student is for private, individualized instruction. The lowest is for large classes where individualized instruction is minimal. Now you have an idea of the market in your area. Translate this information into setting your tuition fees for classes of two hours each.

Learn what craft instructors earn at your college or city program. Assume an art teacher with a college degree earns $20 per hour. If you do not have a degree, perhaps $20 is too high, but minimum wage is too low. Try averaging.

How about $15 per hour as your minimum? You can set the tuition high to attract a few students at a time and stress the individualized learning available to them. Or, lower student fees, which means you must hold larger classes to reach the same base pay. How about a class for five weeks of two hours each? Four students paying $35 each would bring you a total of $140 per class, or $14 per hour. Such students would be paying $3.50 per each hour of instruction, which is in line with the amounts we discovered were average in a given local area. You also could charge each student $20, require at least seven students per class, and earn the same $140. Remember that one day away from home when traveling out of state counts as three days lost from your regular work.

Also remember that when teaching in a shop, your enthusiasm generates increased sales for the shop owner. Shop owners usually determine the class price and pay a percentage to the teacher—often 80 percent of class fees collected.

Occasionally (though not often), the shop will collect and turn over all class fees to the teacher. The shop owner expects that the class will sell enough products to warrant offering the class. Some teachers insist on setting a price for the amount of actual class teaching time. For example, a three-hour class may cost $50.

A teacher I know gathered information from other speakers and teachers concerning standard fees for teaching in shops versus teaching at seminars and national shows. "How much does experience matter?" she asks. "Should you charge more if you have won awards? Should you base your fees on per-student cost, or use an all-day flat fee?" She found that most shops pay $20 to $30 per hour for instructors and some include mileage.

National seminars have a set budget and often pay all instructors the same flat rate per workshop fee. For example, a half-day workshop may pay the instructor $175 plus travel expenses, while an all-day workshop pays $250 to $300, in addition to travel expenses and meals. A few national shows I have taught at pay whatever fees I asked for in my fee schedule. Some instructors charge $450 for an all-day workshop while others charge $300, even though both perform the job in the same place for the same number of students. With so many variables in earning power, teachers must pay close attention to their contracts and marketing information.

Another teacher uses one of two ways to set prices for her classes:

Flat Rate. The teacher sets an amount regardless of the number of students in a class. In addition to the flat rate, the sponsor pays travel and kit expenses (if any). Flat rates range from $50 to $380, for simple lectures to a small group all the way through all-day or two-day workshops. This arrangement works best for smaller groups that co-sponsor a teacher and share her travel expenses. It also works well for local groups when the only transportation expense is mileage.

Per-Student Rate. A second pricing rate is a per-student rate, based on a minimum and maximum number of students, with a minimum number required. If there are no travel expenses or kit costs, she charges a per-student rate of

$3 to $10 per classroom unit. A classroom unit is equivalent to one teaching hour. Using this system, she charges $5 to $7 per classroom unit for most two- to four-hour classes. Longer classes may have a lower per-classroom unit charge because there are more total units.

The per-unit rate is generally higher for more complex classes or very small classes. If a particular class is determined to be $6 per classroom unit and lasts for four hours, the final per-student cost would be $24. With ten participants in the class, this teacher charges $240. Some sponsoring shops will take up to 25 percent of the teacher's total fee for classroom space and publicity, particularly if the teacher does not provide supply lists and sells her own kits. Check this out before determining the minimum number of students you will accept to conduct the class. You may need to adjust your per-student charge to remain competitive with other teachers' fees in your area.

A machine embroidery teacher charges the price of the class determined by (length of class in hours) × ($6). The teacher determines the minimum number of students she will teach (usually three to four), and the maximum is determined by the size of the classroom (usually eight).

The teacher provides a sample for each class before the schedule is published, and receives 75 to 80 percent of the total paid by the students. In addition, the teacher gets a 20 to 30 percent discount on all purchases and a 30 to 40 percent discount on class-related purchases for her sample/supply/book/pattern requirements.

Example: For a five-hour class, the student pays $30. If eight students enroll, they pay the store $240. The teacher gets $180 to $192 for five hours of teaching time.

For a six-hour class, the cost of the class per student, say, $50 to $60, times the number of students, say six, would generate $300 to $360. Then the store makes the difference, plus sales.

Teaching fees vary wildly depending on whether you are a regular shop teacher or a traveling guest, and your reputation. Some shops pay per hour, and others pay per student. Another teacher I interviewed taught for a local quilt shop for many years and had a large following. When she left that shop to teach at another, she assumed all her students would follow. "How wrong I was!" she confessed. "The next shop, though friendly and nicer, was not as good at business. The moral of the story is, don't underestimate the power of a good shop owner who has a great mailing list! As nice and loyal as your students are, they still rely on newsletters, advertisements, and promotions to get them into a shop. Also, a well-equipped shop with good lighting, adequate electricity, machines, and supplies is critical. Traveling and teaching can be great money, but it is also heavy, hard work."

When discussing fees for teachers who present guild workshops, a program chairperson told me that workshop fees for 2004 range from $250 (for lesser-known teachers) to $350, $500, and even $599 for the bigger-name teachers. For lectures, the fee range was comparable. "We also pay for travel expenses (which range from $125 to $600)," she said. "We try to collaborate with another guild or shop in the area to also book the teacher, so we can share travel expenses. The guilds and shops we collaborate with are not in our immediate area, but are within a few hours' drive to avoid competition among participants. Our guild usually puts the teacher up at a home of one of our members, though bigger-name teachers ask to be put up at hotels. I know some have had some bad experiences staying at people's homes, but with the prices we pay for speakers and teachers, guilds are having a hard time affording the bigger names."

A clothing instructor says, "I set my own fees and am comfortable with presenting them as a standard. Otherwise, I was doing what someone else wanted, with no control over my fees. Today, I charge $15 per student for a three-hour course and $30 per student for a six-hour course, with 20 percent of my class fees going to the shop. I guide my classes to items in the shop such as books, patterns, rulers, and notions. I schedule two three-hour classes per day to minimize my travel expenses."

Another point concerning teaching fees arose on an online business digest. It seems that a teacher was invited to give a three-hour presentation to a guild far from home, only to find a surprise waiting that had not been mentioned in the previously signed contract. The program chairperson explained that the guild wanted a kickback in the percentage of sales after the program, which resulted in lost income to the teacher. She posted her story to the QuiltTeach list to ask for feedback.

Someone wrote, "My husband calculated that I'd need to add $50 to my lecture fee for each 5 percent in kickback a guild requested, in order to come out with the same profit. I have considered noting that on my fee schedule. One national teacher doubles her fee if the guild takes a cut!"

Many teachers responded to this query. Most know the practice is growing. Guilds often feel this is a way to increase their treasury, but teachers resent it bitterly. Teachers agreed that nonprofit quilting guilds should not raise funds by demanding a percentage of teachers' profits.

"One shop where I teach gives me all the class fees," says a quilting teacher. "The owner feels that she makes money on the fabric and notions. Another takes 10 percent, but is going to raise it to 15 percent next quarter. I just raised my prices accordingly to make up the difference coming to me.

"I get 80/20 with a 15 percent discount on my purchases from one shop, 70/30 and 20 percent discount from another, and $20 per hour with a 30 percent discount from a third shop. I am happy with each of these arrangements, except when I have a large class at the third shop. I get paid the same for ten students as for four."

Shop owners, on the other hand, say, "When my guild friends buy directly from a teacher following a class, my shop loses the sale." To avoid disappointment and bitterness, read contracts carefully. If you want to offer BOR sales, arrange for this in advance. The conclusion teachers make about this practice is that when a sponsoring guild demands a percentage of the teacher's sales, the teacher should raise her teaching fee to cover it.

How much of the total tuition for a class to be taught in a shop should go to the teacher, and how much for the shop owner? Should teachers also receive a discount when they buy fabric in the shop to make samples to advertise the class? Read on.

A quilting teacher speaks out as follows: "Here is the agreement I have with the local fabric store, where I teach sewing/quilting classes. The store chooses the project, although they always ask me what I want to teach. I feel that if I'm teaching for them, then classes should be based on products they want to promote. The store provides all the materials for me to make the sample free of charge, with the exception of tools. They choose fabric and colors, and I take the pattern and fabrics home, make the sample, and return it, along with supply lists, to the store. The sample remains in the store from two to four months, or at least until after the last class.

"I set the price and try to keep the price low, so more students can afford it while bringing in more business for the store and more students for me. The store collects the registration fee, and they return 100 percent of it to me.

"The store advertises the classes in their monthly newsletter. I put information about the classes on my Web site. If no students sign up for the class, I get paid nothing. However, I keep the samples after they are taken down from the store walls, to compensate me for the time spent preparing the class."

Teacher Interviews
Linda Hahn

Linda Hahn teaches adult education courses near her home, in addition to teaching regularly at local quilt shops nearby.

What topics do you teach?
I prefer to teach classes that the other shop teachers do not teach, such as machine embroidery and art quilts. I have an extensive legal background and use an outline form as opposed to written lesson plans. I write out the points I plan to make and discuss them at class.

Are you a certified or credentialed instructor? If so, please name the institution.
I am an NQA-Certified Teacher.

Do you offer books, patterns, or other quilt-related products during or after classes?
Yes, I offer specialty and hard-to-find products that I choose carefully to use myself.

What is your advice to others thinking of teaching?
Research and listen to your students. Learn what they like and dislike and what makes a teacher special to them. Observe how teachers you admire yourself

present themselves at classes. How do they present their materials and their visual aids? How do they dress, and what do they bring to class? Notice how they pack their supplies and their quilts.

Cara Gulati

Cara Gulati, a teacher with phenomenal success with optical illusion art quilts, is relatively new to the quilting scene, but has already taught at the Houston Quilt Festival in 2003. She has been teaching for five years, making art quilts for four years, and publishing patterns for a year and a half, with a self-published book released in November 2004.

Where do you teach? Do you like traveling or avoid it?
I teach locally in the San Francisco Bay Area, where I live, and have traveled to Texas. I have bookings in other parts of the country coming up since I like to travel, but I limit myself to leaving home once a month.

Which do you prefer—teaching at home, shops, schools, or seminars?
Seminars excite me the most because there are so many other quilters and teachers to meet. I like teaching in shops and for guilds, too. I do not teach in my home, but have my office and studio there. When I teach, I prefer to go somewhere else to work!

What topics do you teach? Do you teach from a lesson plan?
I teach art techniques similar to my new books about my 3-D explosions. Curved piecing without pins is my specialty, along with embellishments and free-motion quilting. Lesson plans are more like guidelines for me. I have a list of what I want to cover to make sure I get it all in. Then I see how fast the students are going and adjust my timing. If I have a class where the students zip through the material, I give them extra demonstrations on free-motion quilting and binding by machine. I also will teach them any-thing they want to learn, even when unrelated to the class, if I know how to do it myself.

Are you a certified or credentialed instructor?
No.

Do you use a pattern or book written by someone else?
No longer. My favorite books and patterns for teaching are by Kaffe Fassett, but now I teach my own original designs exclusively.

Do you teach using your own designs/work?
Yes. I prefer to design what I want to make, not what I think will sell. This works well for me. I teach from some of my patterns, and also have technique workshops that cover embellishments and free-motion quilting. My most popular workshop is a design class based on my 3-D Explosion series.

Do you offer no-fee classes and programs to your own guild?
When I have time, I volunteer, but the busier I get, the less I can spend free time for volunteer teaching. I have crossed over from hobby to job now. I do what I love, but I have to find a new hobby so that I know when I am not working. It worked well for practicing my teaching skills and was a great way to check the timing for teaching the class.

Do you offer books, patterns, or other quilt-related products during or after classes?
Yes, I offer things for sale after classes and during lunch. The exception is for templates for two of my patterns. After I speak at the beginning of class about choosing colors for the project, cutting, and getting the pieces up on a design wall, students usually want the templates before they begin to cut. This is the time when everyone is getting their fabrics organized into gradations. It usually takes me about five minutes to trade my template sets for checks; then I begin checking fabric choices individually.

Do you have advice to others thinking of teaching?
My best advice is to plan workshop timing for both fast and slower students. Teach so that fast learners will not run out of something to do, and slower students do not feel rushed and feel like they are falling behind. This is a delicate balance, but I feel it is very important in order to keep everyone happy and feeling successful.

Tracey Browning

Tracey Browning has been quilting for fourteen years, teaching for six, and doing custom machine quilting for three years. Her work has been published in Australian magazines for five years, with two of her projects chosen for publication in the U.S. by That Patchwork Place in a recent book, *Fabulous Quilts*. She describes herself as a self-taught Web site author, wife, mother, farmer, accountant, quilter, teacher, and designer.

"The machine quilting industry in Australia is growing fast," Tracey says. "I upgraded my machine eighteen months ago and have been very busy. I was already supplying patterns for machine quilting prior to starting this branch of my business, so it was a natural progression to start concentrating on machine quilting books, patterns, and gadgets both for commercial and personal use. This led me to delve into designing and producing templates and rulers to use with these machines. Before that, the only templates available in Australia were from the USA, and exchange rates ran high. Over the past three years, I designed new templates not available or made by any company in America, and hence have established quite a large customer base in the U.S., Canada, Ireland, New Zealand, and here in Australia."

Do you prefer teaching at home, in shops, in schools, or in seminars?
I prefer to teach from my home studio, where I have everything on hand, but anywhere that is within driving distance is suitable. Traveling by plane

is more cumbersome, as I must bring extra samples and supplies, but I do it if it is worthwhile.

What topics do you teach? Do you teach from a lesson plan?
I developed a number of one- and two-day workshops based on my own designs. Each offers a different quick piecing technique and follows with design options. I have detailed lesson plans for two different beginner quilting courses. One is a traditional course designed to show how to draft blocks and use templates, and how to do hand and machine piecing and quilting. The other is more popular these days—it teaches rotary cutting, machine piecing, and quilting, and offers a variety of quick piecing methods.

Are you a certified or credentialed instructor?
No, I am not certified. No certification course exists here in South Australia at this time. I could complete a course by correspondence interstate, but it requires me to attend their state for certain portions, which is not possible at this time.

Do you use a pattern or book written by someone else?
No, I do not use patterns or books for teaching. I encourage students to see certain books that I believe will expand upon what I am teaching and give them a different outlook on the technique or design I have used.

Do you teach using your own designs/work?
Yes, all my workshops are based on my own designs, most of which have been published in Australian national quilting magazines over the last five years.

Do you offer no-fee or low-cost classes and programs to your own guild?
I offer one or two presentations each year to my local guild—usually a one-hour presentation that they choose. I do not find extra teaching jobs from this activity, but it certainly promotes good will, and many who attend become customers for my machine quilting services.

Do you offer books, patterns, or other quilt-related products during or after classes?
Yes, I offer books and notions after classes. I keep them in sight so students can view them during their breaks or after the class.

Do you have advice to others thinking of teaching?
Be passionate about what you do. Know your subject and be prepared to learn as much from your students as they learn from you!

Linda Schmidt

Linda Schmidt, named 2003 Teacher of the Year by *Professional Quilter Magazine*, has been in business for ten years, and is best known for art quilts designed for large, public spaces.

Describe your buying market.
My customers are cities, hospitals, nursing homes, and private parties.

Which is most profitable for you?
I prefer to create and sell new pieces for new spaces and give talks and workshops for guilds.

Do you do BOR sales after presentations or lectures?
No.

Deb Donovan's Lesson Plan

In my classes and books, I stress the importance of teachers drawing up good, professional class proposals and lesson plans. Deb Donovan, an online student, submitted hers to me for critique. With her permission, I include it here.

Butterfly Dance

A Class Proposal

by:

Deb Donovan   42837 Ledgeview Dr., Novi, MI 48377   (234) 567-8901

Get ready for spring with this butterfly quilt, which can be made in lap or twin sizes.

3-D butterflies dance in curves over your quilt, which uses rotary cut templates. Get shortcuts, hints, and cutting directions not provided in the pattern! Dimensional piecing makes this pattern unique. It uses templates and careful placement of patches to achieve "curves without curved piecing."

Time: 6 hours instruction time (6½ with ½ hour lunch)

Pattern: "Butterfly Dance" by Christine Thresh, winnowing.com (retail $8.50)

Level: Advanced Beginner, comfortable with sewing machine and rotary cutter

Techniques: Template piecing with freezer paper, cutting and sewing bias edges

Technique requires:

Freezer paper

Point turner (I use Checker item number 7097)

Fabric:	Background	2½ yds
	Butterflies	12 FQs OR 6½ yd cuts OR 72 5" × 10" pieces OR 144 5" squares

Sewing machine/thread/basic sewing supplies

Irons/ironing boards (*store to provide*)

Other items that *may* be promoted: smaller cutting board (12" × 18"), magnetic board (Checker item BB-1L), Clover Hi-Tech seam ripper (Checker item 482CV_WHT)

Class Agenda

1. Introduction; show my quilt

2. Help students to evaluate and audition their fabric and color choices

3. Working with freezer paper templates and piecing

4. Sewing butterflies (three options given for sewing/turning, only one in pattern)

   *** Lunch ***

5. Cutting the background (with specific cutting instructions not provided in pattern)

6. Sewing a block

7. Finishing options

Students should be able to complete a half-block during the class period.

Sample available of a completed lap-sized quilt for your review and for store display.

Handout is available for review if you choose.

Butterfly Dance   **Class Supply List**

Level: Advanced Beginner

Class Date: _____

You are expected to understand:

$1/4$" seam allowance

How to use a rotary cutter

You will learn:

Template piecing using freezer paper

Cutting and sewing using bias edges

Tools and Supplies

"Butterfly Dance" pattern. Original pattern required; *no photocopies allowed*.

Lunch

Freezer paper (piece at least 12" × 18")

Point turner

Pencil or permanent fabric pen (i.e., Pigma) that shows up on background fabric

Paper scissors

Fabric scissors

Seam ripper

Neutral piecing thread (for both making butterflies and piecing blocks)

Rulers for rotary cutting (I use a 6 × 24 for cutting strips, a 6 × 12 for cutting blocks, a $12^{1}/_{2}$" square for squaring up blocks, and a 4 × 8 for cutting butterflies)

Rotary cutter (bring 45 mm and 28 mm rotary cutters if you have them)

Rotary cutting mat

Sewing machine (that you are familiar with operating, in good working order)

Fabric Requirements for Class

Background Fabric: $1/4$ yd or one Fat Quarter

✦ No need to precut larger pieces, bring what you have.
✦ All-over print or semi-solid works best.
✦ Make sure that your butterfly fabrics differ in value from your background fabric; you want to show them off.
✦ Take a possible background fabric. Randomly drop another piece of fabric (right sides up!) on top of the fabric. If the second piece is obvious, this will probably not be a good fabric to choose.
✦ Directional fabrics will NOT work.
✦ 2¼ yds required for finished quilt.

Butterfly Fabric: 12 pieces, 5" × 5" or larger, OR 6 pieces, 5" × 10" or larger

✦ No need to precut larger pieces; bring what you have.
✦ Anything goes! Stripes, wild fabrics, pastels . . .
✦ Make sure that your butterfly fabrics differ in value from your background fabric; you want to show them off.
✦ Need a minimum of 6 different fabrics.

A FQ will yield 6 butterflies
Works great with Charm Square Packs (5" or larger squares)
Call with questions! Shop: (123) 456-7890   Deb (Teacher): (234) 567-8901

Sample Contract

Here I include the contract that I use when I work as a speaker or a teacher.

Sylvia's Studio

1090 Cambridge Street
Telephone FAX
E-mail: Create@Sylvias-studio.com

Novato, CA 94947-4963
415-883-4546
http://www.sylvias-studio.com

Contract Form

This contract confirms the understanding between teacher/speaker Sylvia Landman and _____.

I understand I am being hired as an independent contractor, and that I am solely responsible for payment of taxes from my earnings.

Date of program:

Hours of program:

Location of program:

Subject of program/workshop:

Required materials provided by each participant:

Kit cost of materials provided to each participant by teacher:

Contents of kit:

Maximum number of participants:_____Minimum number:_____

Deadline for group to cancel without penalty: 10 days before presentation

Penalty if canceling in less than 10 days: cost of materials/copy costs of printed literature.

Travel by car (for year 2004, 36 cents, IRS allowance, per mile):

By air: airline ticket + ground travel to and from airports:

Meals & lodging: provided by group from: to:

Fee per diem: $400 for full-day program; $250 for partial day or evenings

Fees and expenses: due and payable upon receipt, following presentation.

Nonsmoking homestays are acceptable; hotel required only if private bedroom is unavailable.

Sylvia Landman   Group Representative

_____   _____

Teaching Credentials and Qualifications

If you have a teaching credential, include it in your advertising and résumé and letterhead stationery. Teaching experience and/or credentials add credibility to your teaching status. If you want accreditation and are not a college graduate or have no specific teacher training, look to your State Community College system or University for help, but realize that requirements vary from one state to another.

Teaching from a home studio or nearby shop does not require teaching experience or credentials, but those who have them succeed more often than those who do not.

Individual guilds and associations often offer teacher certification programs. Trained teachers find it easier to inspire students to return repeatedly. Good teachers instill an appreciation for the subject and help students feel confident with their new skills.

Teacher Certification Programs
American Needlepoint Guild
Box 241208
Memphis, TN 38124-1208
www.needlepoint.org

Craft Yarn Council of America
Box 9
Gastonia, NC 28053-0009
www.craftyarncouncil.com
(800) 662-9999

Embroiderers' Guild of America
335 W. Broadway, Suite 100
Louisville, KY 40202
egahq@aol.com

National Quilting Association, Inc.
Box 393
Ellicott City, MD 21041-0393
nqa@erols.com

Contributors to this chapter:
Linda J. Hahn
24 Eliot Rd.
Manalapan, NJ 07726
Lawnquilt@aol.com

Cara Gulati
Business Name: Doodle Press
P.O. Box 508, Nicasio, CA 94946
(415) 662-2121
DesignBear@aol.com
www.doodlepress.com

Tracey Browning
Business Name: Constantine Quilts
RSD 1028, Kadina, SA, 5555
Australia
+61 8 88256214
conquilts@bigpond.com.au
www.constantinequilts.com

Linda S. Schmidt
Business Name: Short Attention Span Quilting
7695 Sunwood Drive
Dublin, CA 94568
(925) 829-4329
shortattn@comcast.net

Deb Donovan
42837 Ledgeview Dr.
Novi, MI 48377
(248) 926 9169

When the time arrives to switch your quilting activities from a hobby to a business, here are a few issues to consider.

Naming Your Business

Choosing a name is the first step to starting your business. This is more complicated than it sounds. Legally, you *must* include your *full* name in the business title *or* file a fictitious name form at the county clerk's office in your county courthouse. You may not call your business "Betty's Quilts" or "Bell's Quilts" because this does not completely identify you. If you want to use one of the two examples above, you must file a fictitious name form. If you call your business "Betty Bell's Beauteous Quilts," you would not need to file the form, because the title includes both your first and last name.

Second, if you find you need a fictitious name form, you will need to state the legal form of the business you have chosen. Full disclosure about who owns your business, its location, and the legal form of your business (proprietorship, partnership, or corporation) must become public information so people in your community can find you readily. If you need help deciding which legal form of business is best for you, contact the IRS to request their free literature comparing the advantages of each.

Third, after you file a fictitious name form, you also must publish the information it contains in a county newspaper in four consecutive issues. Your information becomes a part of the public business record in your county.

You may not select a name in use by someone else in your county, though you may use a name registered out of your county if it is not trademarked. Check existing records in your county clerk's office and prepare ahead of time by having alternative business names in mind. If you find another business exists in your county using your first choice, you can quickly submit the next name on your list without wasting time thinking up another.

Filing fees do not cost much, but renewal is required every five years—though this varies from state to state. You may choose the same name used by a business in a neighboring county or state, which is why we have many "Quilters' Corner"s and "Quilters' Attic"s across the country.

Trademarking your business name is the only way to ensure exclusive ownership in the U.S. Contact the U.S. Patent Office and request or download their free trademark literature. You must complete an application form and pay a $290 registration fee. A trademark search will begin to determine whether the name you chose already exists. If so, you must select another.

City Business License

City Hall is your next stop if you live in an incorporated city. Cities charge a fee for a business license, which permits you to generate income within city limits. While a few cities across the U.S. do not license home-based workers, most do. Call your city hall for information, since rates vary widely. If you live outside the city limits, you may find that your county requires a county business license. Check your city and county business offices to make sure you know what they require.

Those of you who plan to work from home may feel discouraged to learn that not all cities welcome home-based businesses, and some may refuse to license them. Though this policy is changing across the country due to the growth of home-based businesses, resistance still occurs. Your city may insist you operate your new business from a downtown site. Homeowner associations may be sticky to deal with too. Did you sign an agreement when you rented or bought your condo that you would not use the premises to conduct a business?

Home Occupation Use Permits

Across the country, local city and county governments recognize the great increase in home-based businesses. Often they conclude that this national trend can generate additional tax revenues. Many, but not all, cities have instituted the Home Occupation Use Permit. This permit is in addition to a city business license. Cities describe this as a tax levied against home-based workers, granting them permission to generate an income from home. This tax has created great resentment and controversy, but is one you must know about. Contact your city hall to learn whether or not you must pay this tax. The amount varies across the country. Where I live, I pay an annual fee of $90, but within my county, other cities require from $25 to $250.

Zoning Variances

You *may* need a zoning variance. Most homes within city limits are zoned for residential use only. Business districts receive commercial zoning. When you conduct a business from your home, most cities require that you apply for and perhaps pay for a variance to alter the zoning. There may be a one-time fee. Call your planning commission to determine your zoning status and the cost of obtaining a variance. Bear in mind that cities (and your neighbors) want home-based businesses to be unobtrusive, invisible, and otherwise not detrimental to the neighborhood. They are most especially concerned with increased traffic or extra noise.

The Home Office Deduction

The IRS allows owners of small, home-based businesses to write off a portion of their home mortgage payment or rent payment as a business deduction. This frequently misunderstood deduction adds profit to a home-based business. Taxpayers often fear it, not understanding this important tax advantage. Home business owners assume this deduction triggers an IRS audit more than any other issue. Not true! Random selection is responsible for the most tax audits. The home office deduction ranks fifth as a reason for selecting taxpayers for audits, according to most certified public accountants. Major repairs, alterations, modifications, and furnishing expenses for your home office are 100 percent deductible, but always check with your tax professional and make sure.

How the Home Office Deduction Works

The IRS allows home-based workers to deduct a percentage of their rent or mortgage interest payments (by far the largest portion of your monthly mortgage payment), utilities (except for the phone), and real-estate taxes as business expenses. These deductions lower your annual gross income, which lowers the amount of state and federal income taxes you pay.

The vital aspect of this deduction is that you must use the room or space in which you work *exclusively* for your business. Setting up your sewing machine on the dining room table does *not* qualify the area as a legitimate home office. Remove all furniture and personal items that the IRS perceives as non-business-related.

The home office deduction also requires you to use your home as your business headquarters. If you have a business telephone in your home, receive business mail there, and meet clients and customers, you qualify. You should not have any problems if your home is the *primary* location of the business and you spend most of your working hours there.

Note that you do not have to spend *all* of your time at home. Think of home-based gardeners and housekeepers, for example. While they operate their businesses from their home, they must leave it to work. Note that all business-related trips from your home by car also generate a mileage deduction.

Quilters working from home generally qualify for the home office deduction, but consult your tax professional for specifics about your situation. Call the IRS office and request their free pamphlet, number 587, "Business Use of Your Home," to decide whether or not this valuable deduction suits your business and your home.

Other Deductions You Should Know About

Successful home-based business owners realize that being meticulous about taking every deduction to which they are entitled lowers the tax they must pay. Here is a list of common deductions:

1. Office and studio equipment and supplies.
2. Postage and freight charges.
3. Marketing and advertising fees.
4. Licenses.
5. Separate insurance for your business, such as fine-art floaters.
6. Photography costs to promote your quilting business.
7. Entrance fees and booth rentals for shows, fairs, and exhibits.

8. Automobile mileage. Keep a notebook in your car to note every trip to the post office, bank, and wholesalers, plus any other business-related trips.
9. Visual aids, including materials to make samples and display items.
10. Continuing education, including courses, workshops, and books to help you remain informed about the industry. When traveling away from home to attend or work at national seminars, document expenses carefully. Such deductions put money in your pocket when you fastidiously record and document them with invoices and receipts.
11. Dues to professional groups.
12. Subscriptions to newsletters and magazines.
13. Wages you pay to anyone who works for you.
14. Fees paid to consultants, such as attorneys, tax experts, graphic artists, and business advisors.
15. Telephones: If you have only a personal phone in your home, you may only deduct long-distance calls. To deduct your monthly phone bill together with phone services such as call waiting, you must install a second, business-only phone line. A mere extension of your personal phone line does not qualify. You must install a second line with a separate number. Once you have the second number used exclusively for business, it becomes a deduction, including installation fees, the phone itself, and monthly payment.

Buying Wholesale

An advantage of becoming a quilt professional is that you begin buying raw materials your business requires at wholesale prices. Absolutely *never* run your business by purchasing raw materials on sale from a retailer. Hobbyists do that. Professional quilters find manufacturers, distributors, or wholesalers to buy supplies in larger quantities at prices greatly reduced from retail sale prices.

Visit your county State Board of Equalization office to obtain a "Seller's Permit," which is also known as a "Resale License," a "Seller's License," a "Retail License," or a "Wholesale License." Once you receive this permit, you will find it enables you to buy products at wholesale prices in order to sell them at retail to consumers. In addition to allowing you to purchase wholesale items for resale in your business, permits are often required as admission to trade shows that consumers cannot attend. Your permit number identifies you as a business interested in buying. Minor differences exist from state to state, so check the uses and limitations of permits in your area. Many erroneous conclusions exist about Seller's Permits. Here are the two most common.

Misconception #1

New business owners envision buying countless items they have always wanted at wholesale prices. However, this is a misconception. The permit enables you to buy at wholesale only what you will resell to the ultimate consumer—the person who takes the item home. Office supplies, sewing machines, and other tools used to produce your quilts are for business use—not for resale. You may, however, deduct them as business expenses.

When you receive your permit, you must collect state sales taxes on every retail dollar earned from the direct sale of products, except in the few states that do not have sales taxes. The amount of sales tax varies from state to state. Each state office provides free information about the amount of sales tax to collect in each of its counties. You become, in effect, a volunteer tax collector for the state.

Keep sufficient funds on hand so you can pay your sales taxes promptly to avoid penalties. The state office determines whether you must pay your sales taxes annually or quarterly, based upon your anticipated gross income.

Misconception #2

The second misconception about a Seller's Permit that business owners just starting out generally assume is that merely having the permit assures them that all wholesalers will want to sell to them. This may not always be true. If, for example, a nearby shop has a contract with a wholesaler for exclusive selling privileges within a geographical area, the wholesaler will usually be loyal to the established company and exclude you as a new buyer.

Some wholesale vendors guard against selling to hobbyist buyers who just want the lowest prices for personal use, so they set their minimum orders so high that a home-based quilting business cannot afford to buy. However, an increasing number of manufacturers and wholesalers do accept home-based, professional quilters, allowing them to buy wholesale. It will be up to you to ferret them out.

Tips to Help You Contact Prospective Wholesalers

Avoid sounding like a hobbyist by making your application letter brief, businesslike, and to the point. Write a single-page letter on letterhead stationery to identify yourself and to indicate your professional status. Let the company representative (usually found in the marketing division of larger companies) know you are familiar with the company's product line, and explain how you will use their merchandise. Ask about "terms of sale," which means you want information about minimum order amounts and preferred methods of payment. Study their terms carefully. Profit interests vendors most. Persuade them that you will increase their business and tell them the ways their company will benefit from dealing with you.

Business practices vary from one vendor to another. While some require high minimum orders, others sell one item at a time. Some permit you to buy COD and others allow you to order by credit card. Prepare for a few inevitable refusals by contacting more distributors than you need. This way you can still choose from those that offer to deal with you.

Refer to the *Thomas Register*, mentioned earlier in this book, which lists all American manufacturers and wholesalers. Search by subject matter or company name. Here you will find everything manufactured in the U.S., from adhesives to zippers. The Thomas Register is the most comprehensive listing of wholesalers anywhere.

Vendors, distributors, and wholesalers can become the lifeblood of a business selling to the public. Answer correspondence promptly and pay your bills on time. Establish good credit, and as your business expands, your dealings with vendors will too. After all, your business cannot exist without them.

Managing Your Cash Flow

Managing cash flow is critical in managing your business. Choose your bank carefully. Look for a neighborhood bank close to your home, and one that offers help and advice to small business owners. If you need to find startup money to start or expand your business, read more later in this chapter. The head banker at my bank advocated for me to acquire merchant credit card status. She also guided me into making other financial decisions regarding my business. More about this later.

Spreadsheet programs allow you to record financial income and expenses and help you prepare your income tax returns. Use them to record income and expenses. Choose software for your business bookkeeping if you have a computer. Excel, Quicken, and QuickBooks have a good reputation, but you may prefer another program. The important thing is to choose one that can automatically produce a cash flow or profit and loss statement when called upon.

Accounting programs like these create invoices, bill clients, and keep track of what they owe. Other programs allow you to make pie charts and graphs, providing an instant pictorial view of earnings and expenses.

I made an error in choosing my software. I already knew that QuickBooks would be my choice over Quicken because QuickBooks makes it easy to deal with calculating sales taxes (for retail sales). I went to my local large chain store and simply chose the box from the shelf, paid for it, and left. It cost $435. I did not question that, since the name was all I looked at. Later, I learned that I had inadvertently purchased the top-of-the-line version—one recommended for large corporations with many employees, insurance policies, and benefits. It even contained a huge number of business letters for owners not used to writing. As a one-person business owner, I did not need the bells and whistles. As an author and columnist, I did not need a file of boilerplate letters either. I paid $225 more than I needed to.

Commingling Funds

The IRS discourages and may even disallow legitimate business expenses of self-employed people who write both personal and business checks using only one bank account. Do not put off opening a second checking account for your business. If the time comes when your business needs cash from your personal account, establish what the IRS calls a "paper trail" by transferring funds properly.

Write a check on your personal account and deposit it into your business account. Call this a "transfer of funds" in your bookkeeping ledger. When your business can pay your personal account back, reverse the process. Write a check from your business account and deposit it in your personal account to pay back your "loan." Not only will the IRS approve, but your tax expert will appreciate your effort to make your transactions clear.

Your Business Account

Your business account does not have to be an expensive one—an ordinary, second checking account at the same bank will do. For your checks, select a different color of paper from the one you use in your personal account so that you can readily distinguish one from the other. Just as your personal checks states your name, address, and other information you care to add, so can your business account checks. You can also have your legal name appearing at the top of each check with the initials "D.B.A." (Doing Business As), followed by your business name.

Sources of Operating Funds

Scrutinize your present financial situation if you need startup funds. I suggest that you avoid borrowing money, but if you are opening a shop or beginning an enterprise requiring a large outlay of supplies and equipment (longarm quilting comes to mind), you may need to. Do you have enough cash from your savings or personal account to have "staying power" until your business can begin to pay you an owner's draw? If not, consider the following ways to raise money without borrowing until you must. You can:

+ Cash in savings bonds
+ Cash certificates of deposit
+ Sell or refinance real estate
+ Borrow on your credit cards, but consider the high interest rates unless you feel positive that such a short-term loan will pay for itself quickly.
+ For large amounts, take out a home equity loan, enabling you to use part of your home's equity to fund your business. Repaying the loan becomes a business deduction. Take care not to overdo this and jeopardize the security of owning your home.
+ You can also make a short-term bank loan using your CDs, "T" bills, or savings accounts as collateral. All of these methods avoid recording your loan onto your credit report. If none of these ideas work for you, read on.
+ Friends and relatives are also informal ways of borrowing. Don't ask for a "favor." Instead, approach them and ask if they wish to invest in you and your idea. Give a specific offer of the return they will receive for their loan—don't call it a gift. Discuss the offer of paying back the loan with interest. When you agree, draw up an informal written contract.
+ Consider a friend or family member who will co-sign a loan with you. This is easier then getting someone to lend you actual cash. Your repayments are a legal business deduction.
+ Perhaps you can take on a silent partner who will help with startup expenses in exchange for a percentage of your business for a limited time.

Credit Cards

Buying by credit card usually helps your business, but watch co-mingling again! If you plan to pay for business purchases with a credit card, obtain a new one. Separate your personal purchases from business purchases. Your second card need not be made out to the actual name of your business; your own name suffices. Make sure you make all payments for business credit card purchases from your business account.

Obtaining Merchant Credit

Quilt professionals agree that accepting credit card sales from customers increases sales. However, if you work from home without a storefront, you may find it extremely difficult to obtain merchant status from a bank, enabling you to accept Visa, MasterCard, and others from your customers.

Obtaining merchant credit card status from a bank can be arduous, but it is becoming easier than it once was. It is not at all like applying for a business license or a Seller's Permit.

During the college classes in which I prepare hobbyists to become professionals, I tell students that perhaps one in fifty of them may succeed in acquiring credit card merchant status.

A few years ago, I invited my banker and the merchant sales representative for the San Francisco Bay Area to visit my class and talk about merchant credit. Students asked if I was being unduly pessimistic by stating so few would gain credit card status from a bank. My guests replied that probably none of the students would qualify! They explained that banks feel that storefront businesses are more stable than home-based businesses, and shared the banks' perspective below:

✦Banks prefer storefronts to home-based businesses because they feel shops are more stable.

✦ They prefer clients with whom they have a long-term banking relationship.

✦ Usually, you must be in business for one year before becoming eligible for merchant credit card status.

✦ Credit managers want proven business and personal stability.

✦ A home-based business must be in compliance with local and state business regulations, including owning Seller's Permits, business licenses, and zoning variances.

✦ Collateral such as certificates of deposit or savings accounts are not considered by card-issuing banks in deciding whether to grant merchant status.

✦ They will want to see your résumé and business plan.

✦ Bankers want to know your average annual sales as documented by business records.

✦ Bankers will want to see your federal income tax returns for the last three years.

✦ They will need you to show invoices that prove you buy for a business.

✦ Bankers request references from other banks where you have accounts.

✦ They need to know the legal structure of your business.

◆ They will want to see copies of your business license and Seller's Permit.
◆ If applicable, they may request copies of your fictitious name form, partnership agreements, articles of incorporation, brochures, catalogs, or advertising to prove you are in business.

If you take the home office deduction, a bank officer will probably come to check your home office for IRS compliance—as they did in my case. Make sure your quilt business complies with local and state business regulations before you apply for credit card status. In addition to all of the above, my credit manager also requested copies of yellow page advertisements.

Bankers need this information to determine whether you will be a good credit risk for them. Disputes or nonpayment left by a company that goes out of business can become the bank's responsibility—something banks want to avoid at all costs. This, our banker explained, is the reason banks want to make sure that you can prove your stability, good credit, payment history, and permanence in the community. Disgruntled customers may charge back orders to the bank for up to seven years.

You may have to visit several banks before persuading one to grant you merchant credit. Choose smaller local banks as opposed to large, nationally known banks, as they often display eagerness to increase their business.

If you succeed in obtaining merchant credit, you will need to open another checking account at your bank in which to deposit slips verifying credit card sales. Each month you will receive a statement totaling your sales. It will also tell you the total percentage of each sale that is retained by your bank for the privilege of accepting credit cards.

You can choose from several different credit card authorization formats available from banks granting merchant credit card status. The two used most often by small businesses are terminal systems and touch-tone 800 phone numbers. Another method growing in popularity makes use of a program on your personal computer that reports directly to the bank via modem.

Terminal systems plug into a phone line to verify each customer's credit card account at the point of sale. Using an imprint hand machine to swipe cards is another option, but one with a disadvantage. When you are pressed to make sales in a short time, such as after classes and lectures, you may not have time to check each card and may find yourself, as I did, inadvertently having accepted stolen or expired cards. I could not check such cards until the day following the event, which caused frustration for me and the bank.

When you dial the toll-free number your bank provides, a computerized voice asks you specific questions. You respond by pressing numbers on your touch-tone telephone. After providing all the information required, the voice will tell you whether the bank wishes to authorize the sale for that particular customer. If so, it provides an authorization number that you must write at the top of the sales slip.

Remember that the bank will charge you a percentage of each sale. Amounts vary from 2 percent to 8 percent. If you must pay a higher percentage than you would like, you may negotiate after you establish a good record.

Keep your business account running smoothly. Never permit overdrafts on your business checking account. The amount of your credit card sales and the way you handle the authorization process will be a factor in reducing the percentage you must pay later.

If, in spite of your best efforts, no bank will grant you merchant status, consider working with an independent sales organization (ISO). These groups can secure merchant credit for you for a series of fees.

ISOs act as brokers, easing some of the frustration home business owners inevitably feel when they are denied merchant credit. This may cost you more than a bank would charge, since ISO companies set fees for each service they provide. For example, you must pay for monthly bank statements, initiation fees, a fee for each check processed, and equipment rental. You can find reliable ISO companies in your county phone book and online.

Since the problems home-based businesses have with obtaining merchant credit are well known, new enterprises in addition to ISOs have sprung up to meet the need. Their services may cost more than banks because they charge for each service provided. Expect to pay separately for:

+ Monthly statements
+ Initiation fees
+ A fee for each check processed
+ Equipment rental

There are several businesses online to help you acquire merchant credit. Here are a few:

Superior Card Services: *www.superiorcardservice.com*
Buyer Zone: *www.buyerzone.com/finance/credit_merchants/*
The National Association of Electrical Distributors: *www.naed.org/naed/ content*

Using search engines on the Internet, look for companies that provide secure shopping carts, making it easier and safer for your customers to buy directly from you online, such as Monster Commerce at *www.monstercommerce.com/shopping_carts_.asp*.

Employee or Independent Contractor

One of my online students wrote recently to ask about whether or not she had an employer/employee relationship with a large company producing quilting seminars across the country.

The IRS sets guidelines for this. For example: If an employer paid all expenses in connection with the job, provided the tools, set working hours, and other details, then such an individual was an employee rather than an independent contractor.

Other times, the relationship is murky and issues arise as to whether or not an employer is deliberately or mistakenly categorized as an independent contractor just to avoid providing the benefits the same person would be entitled to when classified as a regular employee. At times, employers have abused the practice of classifying and hiring outside contractors as employees. Some owners decide to treat those employees as outside contractors to minimize the amount of paperwork and benefits due to employees.

IRS statutes describe twenty-two factors to help define and separate employees from independent contractors.

Most home-based quilters are independent contractors. Here are some of the issues that define us as contractors rather than as employees: First, we do not receive benefits. Second, we set our own hours. Third, we use our own equipment and tools. Fourth, we have nothing withheld from our earnings. Fifth, we do not report to a superior about how we perform.

There are many more rules spelled out by the IRS that are very critical. See the IRS Web site or call its offices to request free literature explaining this important issue. For now, here are two easy tests that the IRS looks for when making the determination of whether a person is an employee of a business:

Test one: Does the business control the way things are done by the individual? If the business has control, then the individual is an employee. If the worker has control, she is more likely to be an independent contractor.

Test two: Does the individual perform the service for more than one business? If the individual works solely for one company there is a high probability that the IRS might consider this individual an employee. If this person works for several companies, it is more likely that she will be considered an independent contractor.

To avoid problems with the IRS, when a company hires an outside contractor, her status must be made clear to her. An outside contractor is responsible for her own taxes, insurance, and social security. In addition, she is not eligible for unemployment insurance and medical insurance.

In summary, I must say that I often hear quilters considering going professional say that all they want to do is quilt and make money, and not deal with all the legal issues. If they do not want to be attentive to such issues, who will be?

opyright questions concerning both written work and design projects generate more interest, confusion, and misinformation than any other topic among my college and online students. The first thing some ask is how much they can alter the work of another to claim it as their own. Usually, the same individuals express determination to prevent anyone from altering *their* original designs.

Patents and trademarks must be exclusive in order to register them, but not so with designs protected by copyright. Quilters with similar designs may each copyright them even if they look alike. The copyright office calls this "simultaneous discovery."

If each designer proves origination with drawings, sketches, photos, and other supporting evidence, all may apply for copyright. For example: an East Coast quilter may design her interpretation of the ocean shore on a quilt, while a West Coast artist designs one that is nearly identical. Since each one executed a similar original work, both may receive a copyright.

Copyright pirates have received a lot of attention lately as computers and scanners simplify reproducing the work of others. Increasing numbers of violators have gone as far as copying entire Web sites, leaflets, and booklets, then posting and selling them for profit or giving them away at no cost to increase traffic to their site. In effect, this cuts out the legitimate ownership of many writers, artists, designers, and publishers.

National newspapers and magazines have also featured articles describing the attitude of copyright owners to refuse to sit back and take it any more. Millions of dollars have been diverted from musicians, artists, authors, and designers—legitimate holders of copyrighted materials—to those who seek to steal their intellectual property.

What is Copyright?

From the book *Copyright Law of the United States of America*, Title #17, Section #102:

> The heart of the new copyright law is the grant of certain exclusive rights to the copyright owner.
>
> Copyright law saw many changes in 1976 having to do with the duration of protection. The old system of computing the duration of protection was carried over into the 1976 statute with one major change: The length of the second term is increased to 67 years. This means that the maximum total term of copyright protection for works

already protected by federal statute is increased from 56 years (a first term of 28 years plus a renewal term of 28 years) to 95 years (a first term of 28 years plus a renewal term of 67 years). The specific situation for works copyrighted before 1978 depends on whether the copyright had already been renewed or was still in its first term on December 31, 1977. This is known as the "Enactment of Public Law 105–298," extending the second 47-year term an additional 20 years.

For works originally copyrighted between January 1, 1950, and December 31, 1963: Copyrights in their first 28-year term on January 1, 1978, still had to be renewed in order to be protected for the second term. If a valid renewal registration was made at the proper time, the second term will last for 67 years. However, if renewal registration for these works was not made within the statutory time limits, a copyright originally secured between 1950 and 1963 expired on December 31st of its 28th year, and protection was lost permanently and the work becomes public domain.

For works created on or after January 1, 1978, the U.S. copyright law adopts the basic "life-plus-seventy" system already in effect in most other countries. A work that is created (fixed in tangible form for the first time) after January 1, 1978, is automatically protected from the moment of its creation and is given a term lasting for the author's life, plus an additional 70 years after the author's death. In the case of a joint work prepared by two or more authors who did not work for hire, the term lasts for 70 years after the last surviving author's death. For works made for hire, and for anonymous and pseudonymous works (unless the author's identity is revealed in Copyright Office records), the duration of copyright will be 95 years from first publication or 120 years from creation, whichever is shorter.

For more about the duration of copyright protection, see the government Web site, *www.copyright.gov*. Do not listen to the advice of well-meaning friends. This site is the ultimate authority on copyright information in America. People often assume that copyright law is incomprehensible and inconsistent, and reinterpret the law to suit themselves. This has done much to create the confusion we often hear about copyright. See the "Myths of Copyright" section later in this chapter. Here are the rights a quilt designer or writer receives when she copyrights her work:

+ To reproduce the copyrighted work in copies
+ To prepare derivative works
+ To distribute to the public
+ To display her work publicly

The new law (after January 1, 1978) states: "Anyone who violates any of the exclusive rights of the copyright owner is an infringer of copyright. The copyright owner may file an infringement action in federal court against the infringer within three years from the date of the infringement."

Copyright and Quilters

How does copyright apply to quilters? Copyright provides writers and designers the sole right to make copies, reproduce or distribute the work, or prepare derivative works. Others must secure *written* permission before using another's copyrighted work.

Here is a simple example. Jane Doe designs and makes a sampler quilt. Applying the rules above she may:

+ Reproduce her instructions, templates, and designs and distribute them to students who take her workshops. No one else may do this without her *written* permission.
+ Copy her own work into a miniature quilt, thus preparing a derivative work.
+ Give or sell copies of her instructions to anyone she chooses.
+ Present a lecture about her process and show slides of the work.
+ Display the quilt at local, regional, and national exhibits.

Jane cannot copyright the design while the idea remains in her mind. However, the moment she "fixes the work in a tangible medium" (on paper and/or fabric), she has protection by common copyright law. Jane only needs to place the copyright symbol—©— followed by the year, her name, or the name of her business prominently on her work to claim copyright ownership.

Registering her copyright is another matter. Before Jane can take infringement action against Mary, who copied Jane's instructions and distributed them to members of her guild at no charge, Jane must register her copyright with the Library of Congress.

People often assume you may *give* away the work of another as long as you do not make a profit. Not so. The design belongs to Jane, and no one can give it away to others without her permission.

Fair Use of Copyrighted Material

"Fair Use" doctrine also generates confusion for many, but the law is clear. Quoting directly from copyright literature, we learn when we can use the copyrighted work of another without permission: "Fair use allows others to use a small part of your copyrighted work without your permission for: review, comment, scholarship, research, news reporting, and teaching."

That last word, "teaching," brings forth the most controversy. Copying the handouts of another and teaching it to a guild violates the owner's copyright. Quilting teachers, at times, interpret the law to say that they may copy another teacher's handouts because the activity remains "teaching."

Copyright law, section #110, explains that the classroom teaching exemption applies only to nonprofit educational institutions such as primary schools, high schools, colleges, and universities. Guilds, seminars, and conventions may have nonprofit status, but are not defined as nonprofit institutions of learning. The copyright handbook makes this distinction clear.

Since teachers may make copies of patterns for educational use in *nonprofit* settings, a quilting instructor may make copies from a current quilt magazine for each student in her high school class. The *same* teacher may not use the *same* reprint to teach in a local quilt shop or seminar. Why not? Because these are for-profit settings, not to be confused with the nonprofit status of the group (section #107). When groups or individuals photocopy the work of others and distribute them, even for nonprofit purposes, they deprive the legal owner of profiting from her design.

Purchasers of commercial patterns expect to recreate designs according to copyrighted instructions. This is "Fair Use." You can make a baby quilt from a pattern to keep for yourself or to give as a gift. However, if you try to profit from the design or mass-produce the quilt for sale in nearby shops, you would surely hear from the pattern company. They have the right to seek an injunction to stop further production and force you to turn over profits that are legally theirs.

Works in Public Domain

Questions arise when you try to determine the copyright status of a work *before* the new 1978 law took effect. Works published more than 28 years ago but less than 75 years ago received protection for 28 years *unless* the owner filed a renewal. Few designers renewed copyrights during this period, but if they did, they received an additional renewal term.

Suppose you found an unusual quilt block and article in a magazine published in 1963. Without renewal, this material entered public domain in 1991, when anyone could use it. Contact the Library of Congress to see if the writer filed a renewal. You can do the research yourself at certain libraries throughout the U.S., or pay $20 per hour for the Copyright Office to do it for you. Request a free list of research libraries containing copyright, patent, and trademark data from the Copyright Office.

If you cannot determine whether or not a renewal exists, subtract seventy-five years from the current year to be absolutely safe. Anything copyrighted before that date is now in public domain.

What about traditional quilt patterns like *Log Cabin* or *Wedding Ring*? These designs have been in the public domain for decades, and anyone can design a quilt using these patterns. If you design an original quilt based upon *Log Cabin*, for example, you can copyright the quilt's *design*. Recognize that you are not copyrighting *Log Cabin*, but rather how you incorporated a traditional pattern like this into your quilt. Your design copyright covers how you used color, fabric, scale, overall measurements, and borders. Copyright protection also extends to your instructions and template drawings for the quilt.

Get in the habit of documenting your quilt designs. Take a series of photos to show the evolution of the quilt in progress. I usually start by photographing all of the materials I will use after placing them in a pile on the floor or table.

Later, I show the cutting process, followed by basting, piecing, hand quilting, and then finishing the quilt. Placing the dates on photos thus documents the fact that the project originated with me.

Copyright Pirates

Copyright violations are the prime topic debated again and again on online quilting digests. People become adamant about their position and confused about the law, taking advice from friends who know little to nothing about it and pass this misinformation along.

So much rancor has arisen around the subject that a group called "Copyrights Be Damned" (CBD) invites members to join by copying and scanning a published design and sending it by e-mail to the group. This admits them to membership, and they are free to use and copy other designs submitted previously by other members.

The library of pirated designs grew quickly. People participating in this practice were chastised by professionals in the industry, many of whom had had their designs stolen, and flaming wars between the two factions began. I have seen the same process repeated every year or so on all the online lists, including craft, knitting, crochet, painting, needlepoint, and pattern makers.

Because I write and lecture often about copyright, people write to me with complex questions more appropriate for an attorney. Finally, I put a copyright page on my Web site to minimize individual replies. This law may be complex, but it is not as complex as most others, including IRS regulations and sales taxes. Order your own free copy of the booklet called *The Copyright Law of the United States of America*.

Below is a short letter from a program chairperson of a large quilt guild. She and her guild have focused on yet another copyright issue—how copyright affects groups who make opportunity quilts for fundraising. I could not say it better than the policy of the Sun City Quilters does:

> *Dear Sylvia,*
>
> Last August I wrote to you about wanting to share your article on copyright rules with my guild here at Sun City. The result has been educational and rewarding. We have developed a policy that states no opportunity quilt will be made unless there is written permission from the designer or publisher, and a copy of said permission will be kept in the club files. We have also developed a form for our teachers requiring the purchase of patterns for each person attending a class. This form has several parts to hopefully cover the different possibilities. The end result is that we are respecting the hard work of a designer by the fact that each person taking a class is purchasing the commercial pattern. We are also encouraging original designs from our members. Your article has been very helpful in developing our policy and procedure.

Good work, Sun City!

How to File a Copyright

Follow these steps to register your book, manuscript, online work, poetry, or other text.

Step 1

Make sure your work is a literary work. Literary works may be published or unpublished and include non-dramatic textual works, with or without illustrations. Computer programs and databases are also considered literary works.

Step 2

Put into one envelope or package:

A completed application Form TX or Short Form TX (choose which form to use).

A $30 payment to "Register of Copyrights."

Nonreturnable copy of the material to be registered. Read details on deposit requirements.

Step 3

Send the package to:

Library of Congress
Copyright Office
101 Independence Avenue, S.E.
Washington, D.C. 20559–6000
(202) 707–3000

Your registration becomes effective on the day the Copyright Office receives your application, payment, and copy in acceptable form. If your submission is in order, you will receive a certificate of registration in 4 to 5 months.

Myths about Copyright

1. *Myth: Registering a copyright costs $30. Why not save money and merely seal the originals in an envelope, mail them to yourself, and file the unopened contents in the event of future infringement lawsuits?*

   The reality: Lawyers will affirm that such "sealed envelopes" can be easily tampered with and have no legal position in court if there is trouble later.

2. *Myth: Since the copyright law of 1976 states that protection begins immediately upon creating a work, you no longer need to register with the Library of Congress.*

   The reality: Well, not quite. Though the symbol appearing on your instructions announces that you claim the design under common law copyright and that it is not in the public domain, an important reason remains to register your copyright formally. Placing the copyright symbol on your pattern instructions is not the same as registering the copyright with the Library of Congress. Since 1976, a work is copyrighted from the moment you put it on paper. Using the copyright symbol © without registration is a "common law" copyright. It announces your intention to claim the work as yours, preventing it from entering the public domain. Common law copyright serves another purpose too. It protects your design while it goes through the publishing process. Upon publication, the publisher copyrights the entire contents of the magazine, including your article.

Registration is a prerequisite to infringement suits. If someone copies your new booklet of instructions and you never registered it formally, you will have to delay proceedings while you do so. You must pay extra fees to expedite registration. You will find limits on the amount you can collect, even if you prove the design is yours.

3. *Myth*: *Copyrighted designs become yours if you make a certain percentage of changes.*
    The reality: Not so fast. The copyright law states that modifying someone else's design is "preparing a derivative work." Changing colors, stripes, design placement, and other details is not creating an original work. If you alter an existing design, remember, the crafting/quilting world is small. If the copyright holder of the original design sees your copy and takes legal action against you, you must defend the similarities in court. If a judge finds that a design uses a substantial part of a copyrighted design, the copier is in violation of copyright laws. Fines range up $25,000 and can include legal fees.

4. *Myth*: *It's legal to copy photos of quilts from books and magazines to show during any classes I teach or lectures I give.*
    The reality: Sorry—section #102 specifically mentions that copyright protects photographs in books and magazines just like written material.

5. *Myth*: *If it doesn't have a copyright notice, it's not copyrighted.*
    The reality: This was true in the past, but today's law specifies that a work is copyrighted from its inception. Assume that a work is copyrighted, not that it isn't.

6. *Myth*: *Anything that appears on the World Wide Web becomes free for all to copy.*
    The reality: Not so, and attorneys will tell you this. Note the copyright disclaimers on nearly all Web sites to protect their text from reappearing under someone else's name.

7. *Myth*: *Out of print means the same as out of copyright.*
    The reality: Again, this is not so. See details earlier in this chapter about the term of copyright, which applies whether or not the work is in print.

8. *Myth*: *Defend your copyright or lose it.*
    The reality: This is another myth. You only lose your copyright when its term expires, ninety years pass from the death of the copyright owner, or the owner explicitly gives or sells their copyright to another.

9. *Myth*: *Sharing patterns, magazines, and copies of books is friendly.*
    The reality: Sorry, but stealing is still stealing, whether it is friendly or not. Violating the law invites legal action and should be taken seriously.

10. *Myth: I can copyright the name of my business or product.*
    The reality: Names and titles cannot be copyrighted. To protect the name of your business file for a trademark from the Patent and Trademark Office in Washington, D.C. Unlike copyright, trademarks must be exclusive, which means that if someone else has already registered a name you are considering for your business, you may not use it and must seek another.
11. *Myth: When I post the design and instruction of another person on my Web site, I am giving them free advertising, so this is allowed.*
    The reality: Sorry, it is not. People doing this today are finding themselves in court in increasing numbers. Again, you do not have the right to give away the work of another.

International Copyright

International quilters and designers are bound by the same copyright principles as those in the United States. Under the Berne Convention, the United States has intellectual property and copyright reciprocal agreements with nearly every literate country in the world. Thus, an American quilter cannot go to Australia, see a quilt she loves, photograph it, and return home to copy and publish it. The law is the same from one country to another about copyright, as witnessed by the two recent copyright infringement lawsuits brought and won by American quilters against copiers in China.

Before you conclude that it will cost a fortune to register several quilts, consider Form GR/CP. It allows you to cover several works in a series under one copyright and one fee. If you apply for copyright protection, the Copyright Office will send forms at no cost, or you can download them from several Web site resources. You will also receive instructions on how to fill out the forms. Quilters' needs would be covered with one or more of the following forms:

Form TX covers literary works. This includes patterns, instructions, template drawings, articles, and books.

Form VA (Visual Arts) protects creations such as statues, dolls, wall hangings, framed pictures, and so on. The copyright office requires photos of your designs.

Form GR (Group Registration, also called Serial Copyright) covers copyrighting a line of similar items. A series of wall hangings for holidays or a line of paper piecing patterns are examples. Form GR permits you to register similar works with one copyright for a single fee.

The Library of Congress is one of America's most user-friendly bureaucracies. They go to great lengths to help with copyright questions and problems. They offer a large list of free publications. Write for or download the following free circulars from the Library of Congress U.S. Copyright Office:

Circular 1, Copyright Basics
Circular 2, Free Publications on Copyright
Circular 3, Copyright Notice

Circular 4, Copyright Fees
Circular R1c, Copyright Registration Procedures
Circular R15, Renewal of Copyright
Circular 15a, Duration of Copyright
Circular R99, Highlights of the New Copyright Law
Circular 40, Copy Registration for Works of the Visual Arts
Circular 40a, Deposit Requirements for Registration of Claims to Copyright in Visual Arts Material
Circular 96, Material Not Subject to Copyright

Order the handbook from the Library of Congress called *Copyright Law of the U.S.* It is the definitive source of copyright information.

Resources

For patent information, application forms, and free literature, contact: The U.S. Department of Commerce Patent & Trademark Office, Washington, D.C. 20031. Make sure to request their free booklet, *Basic Facts About Trademarks*.

Articles

The May 2001 issue of *Quilter's Newsletter Magazine* provides details about how two famous quilters won their infringement lawsuits against copiers. One of these, Jinny Beyer, has posted the results of her landmark win on her site as well.

Quilter's Newsletter Magazine, "The Price of Piracy," article by the Cactus Punch Co.

"Needlepoint Designers Losing Big as Hobbyists Swap Patterns Online," article by Amy Geier, Associated Press, posted on the Web August 23, 2000

Web sites

Copyright Your Quilt Page *www.lostquilt.com/CopyrightYourQuilt.html*
Jansen Copyright Web site Page for Artists: *http://jansenartstudio.com/Title17.html*
Girl from Auntie Copyright Web site: *www.girlfromauntie.com/copyright/ c_lite8.html*
Copyright Web site: *www.benedict.com*
U.S. Copyright Office, Library of Congress: *http://lcweb.loc.gov/copyright*

Appendix A: *Books*

Consulting
Holtz, Herman. *How to Succeed as an Independent Consultant*. New York: Wiley Press, 1993.

Lant, Jeffrey. *Consultant's Kit*. Cambridge: JLA Publications, 1981.

Copyright
Blue, Martha. *Making it Legal*. Flagstaff, AZ: Northland Publishing, 1988.

The Library of Congress, *Copyright Law of the U.S: The Definitive Handbook on Copyright*.

DuBoff, Leonard. *The Law (in Plain English)® for Crafts*, fifth edition. New York: Allworth Press, 1999.

Fishman, Stephen. *The Copyright Handbook*: *How to Protect & Use Written Words*. Berkeley, CA: Nolo Press, 1992.

Young, Woody. *A Business Guide to Copyright Law: What You Don't Know Can Cost You*! Fountain Valley, CA: Joy Publishing, 1989.

Craft Business
Brabec, Barbara. *Creative Cash & How to Sell Your Arts, Crafts & Know-How*. Naperville, IL: self-published, 1979.

Brabec, Barbara. *Handmade for Profit*. New York: Evans Publishing, 1996.

Landman, Sylvia. *Crafting for Dollars: Turn Your Hobby Into Serious Cash*. Rocklin, CA: Prima Publishing, 1996.

Landman, Sylvia. *Make Your Quilting Pay for Itself*. Cincinnati, OH: Betterway Publishing, 1997.

Long, Steve and Cindy. *You Can Make Money From Your Arts & Crafts*. Scott's Valley, CA: Mark Publishing, 1988.

General Business
Brabec, Barbara. *Homemade Money: Starting Smart*. New York: M. Evans and Co, Inc., 2002.

Brabec, Barbara, *Homemade Money: Bringing in the Bucks*. New York: M. Evans and Co, Inc., 2003.

Crawford, Tad. *Business and Legal Forms for Crafts*. New York: Allworth Press, 1998.

Elias, Stephen and Stewart. *Simple Contracts for Personal Use*. Berkeley, CA: Nolo Press, 1991.

Kamoroff, Bernard. *Small-Time Operator*. Bell Springs, CA: Bell Springs Publishing, 1995.

Whitmyer, Claude, Rasberry, Salli and Phillips, Michael. *Running a One-Person Business*. Berkeley, CA: Ten Speed Press, 1989.

Mail Order

Bond, William J. *Home-Based Catalog Marketing, A Success Guide for Entrepreneurs*. New York: McGraw Hill, 1998.

Kremer, John. *Mail-Order Selling Made Easier*. Fairfield, IA: Ad-Lib Publications, 1983.

Simon, Julian. *How to Start & Operate a Mail-Order Business*, 5th edition. New York: McGraw-Hill, 1993.

Marketing

Brodsky, Bart and Geis, Janet. *Finding Your Niche . . . Marketing Your Professional Service*. Berkeley, CA: Community Resource Institute Press, 1992.

Levinson, Jay Conrad. *Guerilla Marketing*. Boston, MA: Houghton Mifflin, 1984.

Teaching

Brodsky, Bart and Geis, Janet. *The Teaching Marketplace*. Berkeley, CA: Community Resource Institute Press, 1992.

Margolis, Fredric and Bell, Chip R. *Instructing for Results*. San Diego, CA: Lakewood Publications, 1986.

Writing

Brohaugh, William. *Write Tight: How to Keep Your Prose Sharp, Focused and Concise*. Cincinnati, OH: Writer's Digest Books, 1993.

Burgett, Gordon. *Query & Cover Letters . . . How They Sell Your Writing*. Carpenteria, CA: Self-published, 1985.

Cheney, Theodore A. Rees. *Getting the Words Right*. Cincinnati, OH: Writer's Digest Books, 1983.

Cook, Claire Kehrwald. *Line by Line*. Boston: Houghton Mifflin, 1985.

Cool, Lisa. *How To Write Irresistible Query Letters*. Cincinnati, OH: Writer's Digest Books, 1987.

Dowis, Richard. *How To Make Your Writing Reader-Friendly*. Cincinnati, OH: Betterway Books, 1990.

Herman, Jeff and Adams, Deborah. *Write the Perfect Book Proposal*. New York: John Wiley & Sons, 1993.

King, Stephen. *On Writing*. New York: Scribner, 2000.

Larsen, Michael. *How to Write a Book Proposal*. Cincinnati, OH: Writer's Digest Books, 1990.

Poynter, Dan. *The Self-Publishing Manual*. Santa Barbara, CA: self-published, 2000.

Radke, Linda Foster. *Economical Guide to Self-Publishing*. Chandler, AZ: Five Star Publications, 1986.

Ross-Larson, Bruce. *Edit Yourself*. New York: W. W. Norton, 1982.

Ross, Tom & Marilyn. *The Complete Guide to Self-Publishing*. Cincinnati, OH: Writer's Digest Books, 1985.

Zinsser, William. *On Writing Well*, 4th edition. Cincinnati, OH: Writer's Digest Books, 1990.

Individual Magazine Articles from Quilt Magazines

"Cleaning Up Your Act: How to Organize Your Quilting Studio," Sylvia Landman, *Lady's Circle Patchwork Quilts*, #100, August, 1994.

"Creating & Organizing Your Quilting Studio," *Quilting Today*, #72 & #73, 1999.

"Sew Suite," Jeannie Spears, *Quilter's Newsletter*, #279–#282, 1996.

"Space for a Quiltmaker," Wes Hawkins, *American Quilter*, Winter 1994.

"Your Computer Quilting Neighborhood," Betty Roved and Jim Burchell, *Quilter's Newsletter Magazine*, April, 1996.

A.Q.S. (American Quilter's Society)
Publishes how-to articles and pattern books for quilters.
Schroeder Publishing
P.O. Box 3290, Paducah, KY 42002-3290
Book catalog: *www.aqsquilt.com/catalog.shtml*
Orders only: (800) 626-5420, (270) 898-7903; Fax: (270) 898-8890
Meredith@aqsquilt.com, or *editor@aqsquilt.com*

Barron's Educational Series, Inc.
Publishes adult educational, hobby and craft books.
250 Wireless Blvd., Hauppauge, NY 11788
(800) 645-4376 or (631) 434-3311; Fax: (631) 434-3723
fbbrown@barronsedu.com
www.barronseduc.com/info.html

Breckling Press
Publishes illustrated, premium-quality books on quilting and handcrafts.
124 N. York Road, #266, Elmhurst, IL 60126 USA
(800) 951-7836, Fax: (630) 516-0209
service@brecklinpress.com
www.brecklingpress.com

C&T Publishing
Quilt book publisher.
Box 1456, Lafayette, CA 94549
(800) 284-114
Catalog requests: *www.ctpub.com/catalog/catalogrequest.html*

Chitra Publications
Publishes many quilting magazines.
2 Public Avenue, Montrose, PA 18801-1220
1-800-628-8244 or (570) 278-1984; Fax: (570) 278-2223
Editorial Department: *chitraed@pix.net*
Writers' Guidelines: *www.quilttownusa.com/Chitra/guidelines.htm*
www.quilttownusa.com/Chitra/chitra.htm

Dover Publications
Includes sewing, quilting, embroidery books and transfer patterns.
31 East 2nd Street, Mineola, NY 11501-3852
Fax: (516) 742-6953
www.doverpublications.com/family/catalog.html

F and W Publishing, Inc.
Publishes magazines and books for writers and operates book clubs, conferences.
Corporate Office, 4700 E. Galbraith Road, Cincinnati, OH 45236
(513) 531-2690; Fax: (513) 531-0798
www.fwpublications.com

Howell Press, Inc.
Distributor for Quilt-in-a-Day Publications. Authors' guidelines on Web site.
Catalog available. Interested in manuscripts on quilts and quilt history.
1713-2D Allied Lane, Charlottesville, VA 22903
(800) 868-4512; Fax: (888) 971-7204
www.howellpress.com, custserv@howellpress.com

Interweave Press
Publishes instructive titles relating to fiber arts and beadwork.
201 E. Fourth St., Loveland, CO 80537
(970) 669-7672; Fax: (970) 667-8317
www.interweave.com

Krause Publications, Inc.
Publishes periodicals and books, including arts and crafts books.
700 E. State St., Iola, WI 54990
www.krause.com

Lark, Sterling Publishing
Publishes craft books.
67 Broadway, Asheville, NC 28801
(800) 284-3388, (828) 253-0467; Fax: (828) 253-7952
info@larkbooks.com
www.larkbooks.com/book/CraftSupplySources.asp

Primedia Inc.
Publishes quilting books and magazines.
745 Fifth Avenue, New York, New York 10151
Phone: (212) 745-0100; Fax: (212) 745-0121
information@primedia.com
www.primediainc.com/contract

Sterling Publishing Co., Inc.
Publishes illustrated hands-on practical hobby and craft books.
387 Park Ave. South, New York, NY 10016
Phone: (212) 532-7160; Fax: (212) 213-2495
info@Sterlingweb.com
www.sterlingpub.com/contact/AuthorGuidelines.asp

That Patchwork Place/Martingale & Co.
Quilt book publisher.
20205 144th Ave. NE, Woodinville, WA 98072
info@martingale-pub.com
www2.martingale-pub.com

Self-Publishing Web Sites
Cameo Publications
Phone: (843) 785-3770
www.cameopublications.com

Express Media
Phone: (615) 360-6400
www.expressmedia.com

Fidlar Doubleday
Phone: (800) 248-0888
www.fidlardoubleday.com

Para Publishing
Phone: (805) 968-7277
www.parapublishing.com

Trafford Publications
Phone: (888) 232-4444
www.Trafford.com

Xlibris.com
Phone: (888) 795-4274
www.xlibris.com

Trade Journals

Craft & Needlework Age Magazine
Comprehensive trade journal, including quilting and sewing. Magazine and directory for shop owners, professional designers. Free to professionals.
Box 420, Englishtown, NJ 07726
www.krause.com/static/crafts.htm
www.krause.com/subscribe/cn/

Crafts Fair Guide
Comprehensive reviews of fairs across the U.S.
Lee Spiegel, P.O. Box 688, Corte Madera, CA 94976
Phone & Fax: (415) 924-3259
leecfg@pacbell.net
www.craftsfairguide.com

The Crafts Report Magazine
Monthly business magazine for craft professionals.
100 Rogers Road, Wilmington, DE 19801
(800) 777-7098 or (302) 656-2209; Fax (302) 656-4894
editor@craftsreport.com
www.craftsreport.com

Craftrends Magazine
Trade journal serving needlework/fabric/sewing/quilting. Free to professionals.
741 Corporate Circle, Suite A, Golden, CO 80401
(303) 278-1010; Fax: (303) 277-0370
craftrends@primedia.com
www.craftrends.com/craftrends.htm

Professional Quilter Magazine
Quarterly journal covering all aspects of professional quilting.
221412 Rolling Hill Lane, Laytonsville, MD 20882
info@professionalquilter.com
www.professionalquilter.com

Stitches Magazine
5680 Greenwood Plaza, Suite 100, Greenwood Village, CO 80111
(303) 741-2901; Fax: (720) 489-3225
cmcmillen@primediabusiness.com
www.stitches.com

Wearables Business Magazine
5680 Greenwood Plaza, Suite 100, Greenwood Village, CO 80111
(303) 741-2901; Fax: (720) 489-3225
cmcmillen@primediabusiness.com

The Quilting Professional™
The Sewing Professional
The Embroidery Professional
These magazines are distributed to sewing and quilting dealers, manufacturers, and distributors internationally.
2724 2nd Ave., Des Moines, IA 50313
(800) 4-SEWING or (515) 282-9101, Fax: (515) 282-4483
beth@vdta.com
www.quiltingprofessional.com

Consumer Magazines
American Patchwork & Quilting
Published by Meredith Corporation
1716 Locust Street, Des Moines, IA 50309-3023
(515) 284-3000, (800) 678-8091
jbento@mdp.com
www.meredith.com

American Quilter Magazine
Published by the American Quilting Society
P.O. Box 3290, Paducah, KY 42002-3290
(270) 898-7903, Fax: (270) 898-1173
Toll-Free (Orders Only): (800) 626-5420
www.aqsquilt.com/magazine.shtml

Art Quilt Magazine
P.O. Box 630927, Houston, TX 77263-0927
artquiltmg@aol.com

Computer Quilting Bytes Newsletter
Sponsored by Soft Expressions for quilt software users.
1230 N. Jefferson Street, Suite M, Anaheim, CA 92807
USA and Canada: (888) 545-8616 (toll free) or (714) 630-7414;
Fax: (714) 630-8970
info@softexpressions.com
www.softexpressions.com/help/newsletters/index.html

Craft Magazine
14901 Heritagecrest Way, Bluffdale, UT 84065
(801) 984-2070; Fax: (801) 984-2080
editor@craftsmag.com

Fabric Trends Magazine
Published by All-American Crafts Inc.
243 Newton-Sparta Road, Newton, New Jersey 07860
(973) 383-8080; Fax: (973) 383-8133
www. fabrictrends.com

Down Under Quilt
A magazine about Australian quilts, quiltmakers, guilds, and quiltmaking
businesses.
Box 645, Rozelle NSW 2039, Australia
+61 2 9555 9322; Fax: +61 2 9555 6188
info@pridepublishing.com.au
www.duquilts.com.au/DownUnderQuilts/index.html

For the Love of Quilting Magazine
Fons Porter Designs
Box 171, Winterset, IA 50273
(515) 462-1020
mailbox@fonsandporter.com
www.fonsandporter.com/smqmag.html

McCall's Quilting Magazine
Published by Primedia Magazines.
741 Corporate Circle, Suite A, Golden, CO 80401
(303) 278-1010; Fax: (303) 277-0370
mcq@primedia.com
Customer Service e-mail: *mccallsquilting@palmcoastd.com*
www.mccallsquilting.com

McCall's Quick Quilts (see above)
Published by Primedia Magazines, Inc.
Customer Service e-mail: *quickquilts@palmcoastd.com*
www.quickquilts.com

Miniature Quilt Magazine
Chitra Publications
2 Public Avenue, Montrose, PA 18801
www.quilttownusa.com/Chitra/mq.htm

Quilt Magazine
Published by Harris Publications, Inc.
1115 Broadway, New York, NY 10010-3450
(212) 807-7100; Fax: (212) 807-1479
jeanann@quiltmag.com
www.quiltmag.com

Quilt Works Today Magazine
Chitra Publications
2 Public Avenue, Montrose, PA 18801-1220
(800) 628-8244 or (570) 278-1984; Fax: (570) 278-2223
chitraed@epix.net

Other Chitra Publications: *Fabric Showcase Special Magazine* and *Miniature Quilt Magazine*
Quilter Community Online Quilting Information Source
Stewart, FL Office: Dori Hawks: (864) 421-5679
dorihawks@thequiltercommunity.com
Austin, TX Office: David Hawks: (512) 771-9171
www.thequiltercommunity.com

Quilter Magazine
Published by All-American Crafts, Inc.
243 Newton-Sparta Road, Newton, NJ 07860
(973) 383-8080; Fax: (973) 383-8133
editors@allamericancrafts.com
www.thequiltermag.com

Quilter's Newsletter Magazine
Published by Primedia
Box 4101, Golden, CO 80401-0101
741 Corporate Circle, Suite A, Golden, CO 80401-5622
(303) 278-1010; Fax: (303) 277-0370
www.qnm.com/ or *www.quiltersnewsletter.com*

Quilter's World Magazine
Published by House of White Birches
Box 9025, Big Sandy, TX 75755
(800) 829-5865; Fax: (888) 848-4414; e-mail:
customerservice@whitebirches.com
www.whitebirches.com
www.quilters-world.com

Quilting Arts Magazine
Box 685, Stow, MA 01775
(866) 698-6989
www.quiltingarts.com/home.html

Quilting Quarterly Journal
Published by the National Quilting Association
Box 393 Ellicott City, MD 21041-0393
Fax: (410) 461-3693
nqa@erols.com
www.his.com/queenb/nqa

Quiltmaker Magazine
Published by Primedia Magazines, Inc.
741 Corporate Circle, Suite A, Golden, CO 80401
(303) 278-1010; Fax: (303) 277-0370
www.quiltmaker.com

Sew News Magazine
Published by Primedia Magazines, Inc. (see above)
sewnews@sewnews.com
www.sewnews.com

Threads Magazine
Published by Taunton Press, Inc.
63 South Main St., P.O. Box 5506, Newtown, CT 06470-5506
(203) 426-8171; Fax: (203) 426-3434, Order only: (800) 888-8286
th@taunton.com

Writing Magazines

ByLine Magazine
A monthly magazine for writers.
Box 5240, Edmund, OK 73083-5240
(405) 348-5591
www.bylinemag.com
Writers' Guidelines: *www.bylinemag.com/guidelines.asp*

Writer Magazine
Customer Sales and Service
Kalmbach Publishing Co.
21027 Crossroads Circle, Waukesha, WI 53187-1612
(800) 533-6644; Outside the U.S. and Canada: (262) 796-8776 Ext. 421
Fax: (262) 796-1615
www.writermag.com

Writer's Digest Magazine
F&W Publications Inc.
1507 Dana Avenue, Cincinnati, OH 45207
Editorial Queries: 4700 E. Galbraith Road, Cincinnati, OH 45236
(513) 531-2222
writersdig@fwpubs.com
Writers' guidelines: *www.writersdigest.com/wdguidelines.asp*
www.writersdigest.com provides database of writers' guidelines and online ranking of publishers.

Writer's Market
Book containing up-to-date information about publishers, editors, writing contacts, magazine listings.
www.writersmarket.com

Writer's Journal
Box 25376, St. Paul, MN 55125
Writers' Guidelines: send self-addressed stamped envelope
Box 394, Perham, MN 56573
(218) 346-7921, Fax: (218) 346-7924
www.writersjournal.com

Appendix D: *Organizations*

Business
Color Marketing Group (CMG)
Latest color and design trends under "Press Releases" on Web site.
5904 Richmond Hwy., #408, Alexandria, VA 22303
(703) 329-8500; Fax: (703) 329-0155
cmg@colormarketing.org
www.ColorMarketing.org

Home Business Institute, Inc.
P.O. Box 480215, Delray Beach, FL 33448
HBI Technical Center, 3418 N. Ocean Blvd., Ft. Lauderdale, FL 33308
(561) 865-0865; (888) DIAL HBI; Fax: (561) 865-8448
info@HBIweb.com
www.HBIweb.com

Small Business Service Bureau, Inc.
SBSB, national small business organization of 50,000 members.
554 Main St., P.O. Box 15014
Worcester, MA 01615-0014
Membership application: e-mail *membership@sbsb.com* or call toll-free:
(800) 343-0939

Quilting- and Craft-Related
Alliance for American Quilts
P.O. Box 6251
Louisville, KY 40206
Phone/Fax: (502) 897-3819
info@quiltalliance.org
www.quiltalliance.org/index1.html

American Craft Council (ACC)
Publishes *American Craft Magazine*, provides craft show calendar.
Emphasis on contemporary arts.
www.CraftCouncil.org

American Quilter's Society
Box 3290, Paducah, KY 42002-3290
Supports the Museum of the American Quilter's Society, conventions, events, awards for quilters. Helps preserve history of American quiltmaking. Offers quarterly publication, *American Quilter*.
(270) 898-7903; Fax: (270) 898-1173; toll-free (orders only) (800) 626-5420
info@aqsquilt.com
www.aqsquilt.com

American Sewing Guild
Sponsors seminars, workshops, demonstrations, fashion shows, vendor malls.
9660 Hillcroft, Suite 516, Houston, TX 77096
(713) 729-3000; Fax: (713) 721-9230
info@asg.org
www.asg.org
Chapter listing: *www.asg.org/html/chapters.html*

Association of Crafts & Creative Industries (ACCI)
Merged with Hobby Industry Association. See below.
Association of Pacific Northwest Quilters
Box 22073, Seattle, WA 98122-0073
(206) 622-2826
info@apnq.org
www.apnq.org

Belgian Patchwork Association
Started in 1989 with the purpose of promoting patchwork and quilting in
Belgium.
www.belgiumquilt.be

Canadian Quilt Designers Web ring
http://k.webring.com/hub?ring=canadianquiltdes

Canadian Craft & Hobby Association (CCHA)
#24 1410 40th Ave NE, Calgary, AB Canada T2E-6L1
(403) 291-0559 or (888) 991-0559; Fax: (403) 291-0675
info@cdncraft.org
www.cdncraft.org or *www.dcncraftretailer.com*

Contemporary Quilt and Fiber Artists
Over 100 quilters living in the San Francisco Bay area, interested in surface design, dyeing, embellishment, fabric painting, soft sculpture, quilting,
and tapestry.
www.cqfa.org

Contemporary QuiltArt Association
Box 95685, Seattle, WA 98229-2188
www.contemporaryquiltart.com

Crazy Quilt Society
P.O. Box 19266, Omaha, NE 68119
(800) 398-2542 or (402) 551-0386
kirkcoll@aol.com
www.crazyquilt.com

Creative Sewing & Needlework Festival
15 Wertheim Ct, Ste 502, Richmond Hill, ON L4B-3H7 Canada
(905) 709-0100 or (800) 291-2030 (N. America) Fax: (905) 709-0079
Information: *info@csnf.com*
www.csnf.com

Hobby Industry Association
See earlier note about HIA merging with ACCI.
319 East 54th St., P.O. Box 348, Elmwood, NJ 07407
(201) 794-1133; Fax: (201) 797-0657
hia@hobby.org
www.hobby.org

International Machine Quilters' Association (IMQA)
For longarm and shortarm machine quilters worldwide.
www.imqa.org

International Quilt Association, International Quilt Market & International
Quilt Festival
7660 Woodway Dr., Ste. 550, Houston, TX 77063
(713) 781-6882; Fax: (713) 781-8182
shows@quilts.com
www.quilts.org, www.quilts.com

Mayflower Quilters Guild in Nova Scotia
Box 22068, Bayers Road RPO, Halifax, Nova Scotia, B3L 4T Canada
www.chebucto.ns.ca/~ae862/ns_quilt.html

National Craft Association
"The information and resource center for the professional arts and crafts
industry."
2012 E. Ridge Rd., Suite 120, Rochester, NY 14622-2434
(800) 715-9594 or (585) 266-5472, Fax: (585) 785-3231
www.craftassoc.com

The National Needlework Association (TNNA)
P.O. Box 3388, Zanesville, OH 43702-3388
(740) 455-6773 or (800) 889-8662; Fax: (740) 452-2552
tnna.info@offinger.com
www.tnna.org

National Online Quilters (NOQ)
Noqquilt@noqers.org
www.noqers.org

National Quilting Association, Inc.
Box 393, Ellicott City, MD 21041-0393
(410) 461-5733; Fax: (410) 461-3693
Publishes *Quilting Quarterly*, sponsors quilt shows, exhibits, and workshops, provides certification and judging programs, newsletters for quilt teachers and judges, plus grants and scholarships.
   nqamailbox@yahoo.com
   office: *nqa@erols.com*
   www.nqaquilts.org

Sewing, Quilting & Craft Exposition Company: Sew-Quilt Embroidery Festival
5655 Riggins Ct #10, Reno, NV 89502
(775) 826-8812; Fax: (775) 826-2746
pcmg@juno.com
www.sewquiltcraftexpos.com

Society of Craft Designers (SCD)
Promotes and educates career growth within the craft design industry.
P.O. Box 2188, Zanesville, OH 43702-2188
scd@offinger.com

Stitches/International Craft & Hobby Fair (ICHF)
Dominic House, Seaton Rd, Highcliffe, Dorset, England, UK BH23 5HW
01425-272711; Fax: 01425-279369
info@ichf.co.uk
www.ichf.co.uk

Studio Art Quilt Associates: SAQA
Exhibits, conferences, workshops.
Box 2231, Little Rock, AR 72203-2231
(501) 490-4043; Fax: (501) 490-4036
director@saqa.com
www.saqa.com

#1 Quilting Accessories Emporium
29 Wayne Ct., Burbank, WA 99323
Unique handcrafted quilt racks, hangers, ladders, and frames in choices of styles and woods.
woody@bossig.com
www.galaxymall.com/handcrafted/quiltingracks/

100 CraftLinks.com
Links to craft-related sites.
craftlinks100@yahoo.com, sewinglinks100@yahoo.com
www.100craftlinks.com
www.100sewinglinks.com

A-1 Quilting Machines, Plank Manufacturing
32232 E. Evans Rd., Springfield, MO 65804
(800) 566-4276, (800) LONG-ARM, (800) 566-4276, Fax: (417) 833-2883
Info@800longarm.com
www.long-arm.com

ABC-embroidery-designs.com
Machine embroidery designs in various techniques for most sewing machines.
www.abc-embroidery-designs.com

A Quilter by Design
Debby Kratovil's pattern site.
www.quilterbydesign.com

A Quilter's Legacy
Published by Brasswind Publishing
Journal created by Shelley Michel for thousands of quilt owners and collectors to document information and stories about their quilts.
2910 Camille Dr, Dept. CM, College Station, TX 77845
(409) 693-3522, Fax: (409) 693-5514
quiltjournal@brasswind.com
smichel48@aol.com
www.brasswind.com/quiltjournal/
Phone/Fax: (979) 693-3522

ALJO Mfg., Co.
Supplier of textile dyes.
81-83 Franklin St., New York, NY 10013

(212) 226-2878; Fax: (212) 274-9616; Toll-free: (866) 293-8913
sales@aljodye.com
www.aljodye.com/main.html

America Sews with Sue Hausmann
Information about the PBS sewing programs.
www.husqvarnaviking.com/education/americasews/americasews.html
www.americasews.com

America's Quilting History
Explores the history of quilts and the women who made them. AQH has
a monthly *Quilt History Newsletter.*
www.womenfolk.com/historyofquilts

American Craft Malls, Inc.
American Craft Malls operates consignment malls for crafters.
Box 799, Azle, TX 76098-0799
(817) 221-1099; toll-free (800) 335-2544; Fax: (817) 221-4556
plcoomer@ntbb.net
www.ProCrafter.com

American Professional Quilting Systems (APQS)
Hand-guided quilting machines.
23398 Hwy 30 East, Carroll, IA 51401
(800) 426-7233 or (515) 267-1113; Fax: (515) 267-8414
sales@apqs.com or *service@apqs.com*
www.apqs.com

American Quilts!
Wearable art patterns and quilting.
Box 370831, Las Vegas, NV 89137-0831
(877) 531-1619 (toll-free); (702) 247-4200
sales@americanquilts.com, support@americanquilts.com
www.americanquilts.com

Antique Sewing Machine Info
Information, photographs, and illustrations of old sewing machines, by
manufacturer.
www.geocities.com/claw.geo/#manufac

Appalachian Needleworks
Lists Civil War and 1930s reproduction fabrics and patterns.
212 E. Bone Rd., McConnelsville, OH 43756
(740) 962-5059
info@appalachianneedleworks.com
www.appalachianneedleworks.com

Appliqué Society (TAS)
Provides daily mailing list, patterns, a magazine, and national convention listings.
Box 89, Sequim, WA 98382-0089
Phone/Fax: (800) 597-9827
tas@theappliquesociety.org
www.theappliquesociety.org

ARDCO™ Templates by QuiltSmith, Ltd.
Manufacturer and retailer of precision metal non-skid Quilt Templates.
252 Cedar Road, Poquoson, VA 23662-2112
(757) 868-8073 OR (800) 982-7326; Fax: (757) 868-3866
sales@ardcotemplates.com
www.ardcotemplates.com

Art and Craft Market
Collection of Internet links, downloads, discussion forums.
www.artcraftmarket.com

AvLyn Creations, Inc.
Fabric manufacturer. See patterns online.
(866) 564-5426; Fax: (866) 564-5427
info@avlyn.com
www.avlyn.com/index.htm

Barbara's Quilt World, Norway
Ute-Barbara Skjønberg, designer/owner
Quilt patterns and books from Norway and Scandinavian and EQ5 lessons.
barbaras@online.no
http://home.online.no/~barbaras/news.htm

Benartex, Inc.
Fabric manufacturer.
1359 Broadway, Suite 1100, New york, NY 10018
Phone: (212) 840-3250; Fax: (212) 921-8204
info@benartex.com
www.benartex.com

Block Central
Searchable directory of block links to patterns.
noblin@alaweb.com
www.blockcentral.com/links.php
www.blockcentral.com

Bottle Quilt Co., Inc.
P.O. Box 675763, Rancho Santa Fe, CA 92067-5763
Fax: (858) 759-4072
bottlequilt@cox.net
www.bottlequilt.com
www.hoffmanfabrics.com/quilts/bq.html

Brensan Studios
"Wholesale Quilt and Wearable Arts Patterns, Retail Arts and Crafts Supplies"
#532, 8912 E. Pinnacle Peak Road, F-9, Scottsdale, AZ 85255
(480) 471-1123; Fax: (480) 471-1124
www.brensan.com/Patterns/patterns_home.html

Brewer Sewing Supplies
Wholesale distributor of sewing notions, patterns, books, machines, and cabinets.
3800 W. 42nd St, Chicago, IL 60632
(774) 247-2121 or (800) 444-3111; Fax: (800) 999-9639
www.brewersewing.com

Cabral, Jan
Computer graphics instructor to quilters and fiber artists. Partner in Key to the Web, Ltd., a professional web development firm.
www.keyweb.com/high_tech_quilting/aut2.html

Checker Distributors
Patterns, notions, fabrics, books, gifts. Sells wholesale *only*.
400-B.W. Dussel Drive, P.O. Box 460, Maumee, OH 43537
(419) 893-3636 or (800) 537-1060; Fax: (419) 893-2422
bgoliver@checkerdist.com
www.checkerdist.com

Clothworks, a division of Fabric Sales Company
6250 Stanley Ave. South, Seattle, WA 98108
(206) 762.7886; Fax: (206) 762.8809
e-mail: *textiles@ix.netcom.com*
http://clothworks-fabric.com/

Clotilde, LLC
Sewing notions, patterns.
P.O. Box 7500
Big Sandy, TX 75755-7500
Orders only: (800) 772-2891
Catalog request: (800) 545-4002 or online at *www.clotilde.com/cl/request catalog.asp*

Coats & Clark
Consumer Services
P.O. Box 12229, Greenville, SC 29612-0229
(800) 648-1479
Professional Crafters: If you produce crafts for sale and have a business license and a tax ID number, contact:
Coats & Clark Customer Service
8 Shelter Drive, Greer, SC 29650, (800) 241-5997
www.coatsandclark.com

Colonial Crafts
Assortment of historical fabrics from 1700.
479 Main Street, Route 20, Sturbridge, MA 01566
(800) 966-5524 or (508) 347-3061; Fax: (508) 347-4985
e-mail: *info@colonialcrafts.com*
www.colonialcrafts.com/shopcart/fabric/indexhisfa asp

Colorado Wholesale Dye Corp.
Supplies for dyeing, dyeing instructions, and blank T-shirts.
5325 S. Broadway, Littleton, CO 80121
Phone: (800) 697-1566 or (303) 763-8774
customerservice@bestdye.com; questions@bestdye.com
www.bestdye.com
Online catalog: *www.bestdye.com/CAT_Dyes.asp*

Connecting Threads for the Busy Quilter
General quilting products.
Box 8940, Vancouver, WA 98668-8940
13118 NE 4th Street, Vancouver WA
Corporate offices: (360) 260-8900 x103 or toll-free (U.S. or Canada): (800) 574-6454
Fax: (360) 260-8877
www.connectingthreads.com/ct/default.asp
Ohio distribution center: 2235 SW Boulevard Ste D, Grove City, OH 43123
Catalog: *www.connectingthreads.com/ct/cart/catorder.asp,* or call: (800) 574-6454

Contemporary Quilting Fabrics
P.O. Box 3307, Bridgeport, CT 06605
Phone: (203) 576-0591
info@contemporaryquilting.com
www.contemporaryquilting.com/index.html

Cotton Club
Quilting fabric and books, 20% off list price.

Box 2263, Boise, ID 83701
Phone: (208) 345-5567; Fax: (208) 345-1217
cotton@micron.net
www.cottonclub.com

Country Quilter
Pattern company featuring whimsical quilt designs, classes, books.
344 Route 100, Somers, NY, 10589
(914) 277-4820. Toll-free: (888) 277-7780
Fax: (914) 277-8604
info@countryquilter.com
www.countryquilter.com

CraftCanada.com
Lists Canadian shows, suppliers, shops, associations, magazines.
1743 Teakdale Avenue, Ottawa, Ontario K1C 6M8 Canada
Fax: (613) 837-4002
CraftCanada@sympatico.ca
www.craftcanada.com

Craft Gard
Museum archival storage solutions, acid-free textile care products.
Box 1785, St. George, UT 84771
(435) 634-8036; (888) 878-1212; Fax: (435) 634-1046
info@craftgard.com
www.craftgard.com/site/craftgard_index.cfm

CraftNet.Org
Lists links to craft-related Web sites, opportunities and newsletters.
info@jewelrysupply.com
www.craftnet.org; www.craftsupply.com

Crazy Quilts Online
Source for resources and information about crazy quilting.
Submissions: *www.cqmagonline.com/submissions.shtml*
Mailing List: *http://groups.yahoo.com/group/CQMagOnline/,*
www.CQMagOnline.com

Debbie Mumm, Inc.
Books, fabrics, embroidery cards.
1116 E Westview Ct, Spokane, WA 99218-1384
(888) 819-2923 (USA & Canada), (509) 466-3572
Fax: (509) 466-6919
www.debbiemumm.com

Dharma Trading Co.
Fabric dyes, paint, clothing blanks, bags, fire-retardant spray, chemical safety equipment.
Box 150916, San Rafael, CA 94915
1604 Fourth St., San Rafael, CA 94901
Main number (415) 456-7657, Toll-Free (USA & Canada): (800) 542-5227
Fax: (415) 456-8747
service@dharmatrading.com
www.dharmatrading.com

DMC Corp.-USA
shopcustservice@dmc.fr
www.dmc-usa.com

Dover Street Booksellers, Inc.
Quilting books, clipart.
10 Bells Lake Drive, Turnersville, NJ 08012
Fax: (856) 232-0816
doverst@ix.netcom.com
www.doverstreetquiltbook.com/index.html

Down Under Quilts Online
Magazine offers articles and projects, and lists Australian Quilt Guilds.
www.duquilts.com.au/DownUnderQuilts/index.html
Dritz-Prym Corp.
Manufacturer: quilting rulers, rotary supplies, comprehensive notion selection.
Box 5028, Spartanburg, SC 29304
www.dritz.com

Dyes for Fabrics
(See the complete listing for the following companies elsewhere in this appendix for contact info):
Colorado Wholesale Dye Corp.
Dharma Trading Co.
Fabrics To Dye For
Gecko Gully (Christine Abela)
Pro Chemical & Dye

Eagle Pattern Depot (Internet sales only)
Pattern distributor.
Box 370, Eagle, NE 68347
(800) 536-1728 pin 4024, Fax: (402) 780-6656
www.eaglepatterndepot.com

Embellishment Village
Wholesaler: embellishment supplies, patterns, kits.
15165 SW 100th Ave, Tigard, OR 97224
(503) 639-9820
sales@embellishmentvillage.com
www.embellishmentvillage.com

EZ Quilting by Wrights, Wm. Wright Co.
Quilting tools, templates, tutorials, free patterns.
South Street, West Warren, MA 01092
(800) 660-0415
djzim@prairie.lakes.com
www.ezquilt.com

Fabric Depot, Inc.
Sewing and quilting supplies, patterns, sewing classes.
700 SE 122nd Avenue, Portland, OR 97233
(503) 252-9530 or (888) 896-1478, Fax: (503) 252-9556
info@fabricdepot.com
www.fabricdepot.com

Fabric Manufacturers
See the complete listing for the following companies elsewhere in this
appendix for contact info.
AvLyn Creations, Inc.
Benartex, Inc.
Clothworks
Cranston Village
Daisy Kingdom (a division of Springs Industries, Inc.)
Hancock's of Paducah
Hoffman California Fabrics
In the Beginning Fabrics
Kona Bay Fabrics
Lunn Fabrics, Ltd.
Marcus Brothers Textiles, Inc.
Moda Fabrics/United Notions
Debbie Mumm, Inc.
P & B Textiles
RJR Fabrics
South Sea Imports (Fabrics)
Seattle Bay (a division of Kona Bay Fabrics)
Springs Industries Fabrics
Timeless Treasures Fabrics, Inc.
United Notions & Fabrics/Moda

Fabrics.Net
Assists in locating fabrics, publishing of information about fabric.
507 E. 10th, Spokane, WA 99202
(509) 624-4795, (800) 483-5598
www.fabrics.net

Fabrics to Dye For
Jacquard fabric dyes, textile paints.
67 Tom Harvey Road Westerly, RI 02891
(401) 348-6000, Orders only (888) 322-1319, Fax: (401) 348-6580
www.fabricstodyefor.com/jacquard/dyes_and_pigments.htm

Fabric Shop Network (Sponsor of the FabShop Hop)
Trade organization for independent quilt shops, fabric retailers, design studios.
Box 820128, Vancouver, WA 98682-0003
(360) 892-6500, Fax: (360) 892-6700
fabshophet@aol.com
www.fabshopnet.com

FabShop FabSearch
Helps consumers locate and purchase products.
www.fabshopnet.com/fabsearch.asp

Fairfield Processing
Corporate Office
Box 1157, Danbury, CT 06813-1157
Retail: (800) 980-8000, Wholesale (800) 243-0989
info@poly-fil.com, Wholesale: *sales@poly-fil.com*
www.poly-fil.com/index.asp
How to choose batting: *www.poly-fil.com/info/HowToChooseBatting.asp*

Fazely, Lucy A.
Designer, teacher, lecturer, watercolor-by-number quilts.
P.O. Box 492, Oscoda, MI 48750
lucy@lucyfazely.com
www.lucyfazely.com/index.html

FiberArt.Net
Provides links to fiber artist business resources.
www.fiberart.net

Flynn Multi-Frame System
Quilt frames, stands, tools, patterns, quilting books by John Flynn.
1000 Shiloh Overpass Rd, Billings, MT 59106

Order Toll-free: (800) 745-3596
www.flynnquilt.com
Online catalog: *www.flynnquilt.com/cgi-bin/Store/store.cgi*

FreeQuilt.com
Free quilt pattern links, quilt tips, mailing list.
freequilt@yahoo.com
www.freequilt.com

Gammill Quilting Machine Co.
1452 W. Gibson St., West Plains, MO 65775
(800) 659-8224 (US and Canada), (417) 256-5919, Fax: (417) 256-5757
Gammill@townsqr.com
www.gammill.net

Gecko Gully (Christine Abela)
Patterns, textile dyeing supplies.
Box 1201, Werribee Plaza, Victoria 3030, Australia
Phone/Fax: Australia (03) 9749-5068; Overseas: +61 3 9749 5068
christine@geckogully.com
www.geckogully.com

GetCreativeShow!
Online craft, sewing, quilting, needlework, wearable art.
info@getcreativeshow.com
www.getcreativeshow.com

Giesbrecht, Myrna
Quilt artist, instructor, author, specialist in designing and organizing studio
spaces.
183 Castle Towers Drive, Kamloops, BC, Canada, V2E 1Z9
Phone/Fax: (250) 828-6734
Myrna@press4success.com
www.press4success.com

Gray Wind Publishing
Quilting books and patterns, including foundation paper piecing.
308 W. US. Hwy 34, Phillips, NE 68865
(402) 886-2281
www.graywinddesigns.com

Hancock's of Paducah
Fabric, notions, batting, tools, books.
3841 Hinkleville Rd., Paducah, KY 42001
Toll-Free (800) 845-8723; International: (270) 443-4410
www.hancocks-paducah.com/cs.html

HandmadeQuilts.net: A Quilting and Quilters' Resource
Books, information on quilt design, construction, care.
www.handmadequilts.net/home.asp

Handi Quilter Company, Inc.
Home machine quilting frames, quilting machines.
322 East 500 North, Centerville, UT 84014
(801) 292-7988
sales@handiquilter.com
www.handiquilter.com

Historic-American Quilts
Fine antique quilts with descriptions, photos.
4775 S.River Rd., Hanover, IL 61041
(815) 777-2009; Toll-free (Chicago area): (888) 880-2009
haq@galenalink.net
www.historic-american.com

History of Quilting
Illustrated discussion on quilting history from Middle Ages.
rasp@xmission.com
www.raspberrylane.com/quilt_it/history.html

J. Hittle: Wholesale Sewing Supplier
Discounted retail and wholesale sewing notions, books.
11703 Pierce Way, Louisville, KY 40272-5062
(502) 937-1503, Toll-free: (877) 805-2616
john@happythoughtstoo.com
jhittlesewing.funoverload.com/sewing/catalog.php

Hobbs Bonded Fibers
200 South Commerce Dr., Waco, TX 76710
(254) 741-0040, Fax: (254) 772-7238
Sales@HobbsBondedFibers.com
www.hobbsbondedfibers.com/default.htm
Product Highlights: *www.hobbsbondedfibers.com/Retailhighlights.htm*

Hoffman California Fabrics
Retail stores, specialty manufacturers.
25792 Obrero Drive, Mission Viejo, CA 92691
(800) 547-0100, Fax: (949) 770-4022
Manufacturers: (800) 527-8050 Fax: (949) 770-5747
info@hoffmanfabrics.com
www.hoffmanfabrics.com

Home Sew
Catalog: sewing, craft supplies.
Box 4099, Bethlehem, PA 18018-0099
(800) 344-4739, Fax: (610) 867-9717
www.homesew.com

House of White Birches
Quilting patterns, books, quilting supplies, catalog.
306 East Parr Road, Berne, IN 46711
(260) 589-4000, Fax: (260) 589-8093
customer_service@whitebirches.com
www.WhiteBirches.com

How 2 Books/Quiltbooks
Wholesale books distributor.
790 West Tennessee Avenue, Denver, CO 80223
(303) 778-8383, Fax: (303) 778-6516
quiltbks@aol.com
www.how2bks.com

I Quilt For You
Valdani thread distributor (wholesale/retail), Nolting Longarm dealer.
bev@iquiltforyou.com
www.iquiltforyou.com

Iowa Star Quilts and Iowa Thread Company
Valdani threads.
534 2nd Street, Traer, IA 50675-1139
(319) 478-2738
iowastar@netins.net
www.iowastarquilts.com/about.html

In the Beginning Fabrics
8201 Lake City Way N.E., Seattle, WA
www.inthebeginningfabrics.com

Irisworks
"Art Quilts, Liturgical Vestments, Technique Workshops"
11-542 Platt's Lane, London, Ontario, Canada N6G 3A8
(519) 858-4344
irisworks@mb.sympatico.ca
www.mts.net/%7Erevbr/

Jinny Beyer Studio
Box 488, Great Falls, VA 22066
(703) 759-0250, Toll-free: (866) 759-7373

Fax: (703) 759-0739
Inquiries: *info@jinnybeyer.com, sales@jinnybeyer.com*
Hilton Head Quilt Seminar: *seminar@jinnybeyer.com*
www.jinnybeyer.com

JudaiQuilt
"Quilting Techniques to Create Judaica"
ajwcjp@aol.com
www.Judaiquilt.com

Just It!
Wholesale quilting store supply.
480 Draycott Street, Coquiltlam, BC, Canada V3K 5K3
(604) 931-3586
Fax: (604) 931-3505
info@justitdist.com
www.justitdist.com

Keepsake Quilting
Catalog: patterns, books, notions, fabrics.
Box 1618, Center Harbor, NH 03226
(800) 525-8086
Fax: (603) 253-8346
customerservice@keepsakequilting.com
www.keepsakequilting.com

Kirk Collection
Antique/reproduction fabrics, 1850-1950 quilts, wool/silk battings, books, notions.
1513 Military Avenue, Box 19266, Omaha, NE 68111
(800) 398-2542 or (402) 551-0386, Fax: (800) 960-8335 or (402) 934-9970
KirkColl@aol.com
www.kirkcollection.com

Kona Bay Fabrics
1637 Kahai Street, Honolulu, HI 96819
(800) 531-7913, Fax: (808) 841-2458
konabay@konabay.com
www.konabay.com

Lost Quilt Come Home Page
Displays lost or stolen quilts, information on protecting quilts.
maria@lostquilt.com
www.lostquilt.com

Lunn Fabrics, Ltd.
317 East Main Street, Lancaster, OH 43130-3845
(740) 654-2202, Toll-free: 880-1738 (USA & Canada), Fax: (740) 654-3949
www.lunnfabrics.com/gmail.htm
www.lunnfabrics.com

Marcus Brothers Textiles, Inc.
980 Ave. of the Americas, New York, NY 10018
(212) 354-8700, Fax: (212) 354-5245
lshepard@marcusbrothers.com
Customer Service: Indra Rampersaud: *indra@marcusbrothers.com*
www.marcusbrothers.com

Maywood Studio (a division of E.E. Schenck Co.)
Fabric warehouse.
6000 N. Cutter Circle, Portland, OR 97217
(503) 284-4124; Toll-free: (800) 433-0722
Fax: (503) 288-4475 (Local); (800) 433-0723 (toll-free)

California Warehouse:
4561 Maywood Ave., Vernon, CA 98858
(323) 584-8820; Toll-free: (800) 237-6620
Fax: (323) 584-8847 (Local); (800) 255-9594
insp@maywoodstudio.com
www.maywoodstudio.com

Missing Fabrics Page
Site helps quilters find missing fabrics, books, patterns, tools.
2700 E. Valley Pkwy, #264, Escondido, CA 92027
webmaster@missingfabrics.com
www.missingFabrics.com

Moda Fabrics/United Notions
Dallas Office:
13795 Hutton, Dallas, TX 75234
(972) 484-8901 (Local), (800) 527-9447
Fax: (800) 468-4209
Denver: 4945 Lima Street, Denver, CO 80239
(303) 371-0660 (Local), (800) 843-1236
Fax: (800) 525-0109
Customer Service: *service@unitednotions.com*
www.modafabrics.com

Mountain Mist Batting/Stearns Textile
Mountain Mist
2551 Crescentville Road, Cincinnati, OH 45241
(513) 326-3912 or (800) 345-7150
Fax: (513) 326-3911
mountainmist@leggett.com
www.stearnstextiles.com

Needlecrafter's Computer Companion by Judy Heim
Tips from Judy's book, columns about craft-related computer software.
www.catswhoquilt.com/judy.html
www.catswhoquilt.com/tutorials.html

Netcrafts Online Gallery and Magazine
Trends, show guides, classifieds, online classes, market news, links to supply sources.
info@netcrafts.com
www.netcrafts.com/index.sht

New England Quilt Museum
Library, including travel questions, pattern requests, and research inquiries.
18 Shattuck Street, Lowell, MA 01852
(978) 452-4207 Ext.15
www.nequiltmuseum.org/Library_Asking.shtml
www.nequiltmuseum.org/

New England Quilt Supply
Quilt supply warehouse. (Wholesale only)
158 Center Street, P.O. Box 633, Pembroke, MA 02359
(888) 293-6401 Toll-free
Fax: (781) 294-0040
NEQS@juno.com
www.newenglandquiltsupply.com

New Pathways into Quilt History
Antique quilt fabric dated, described; quilt history, quilt development timeline.
quiltdating@jetlink.net
www.antiquequiltdating.com/index.html

Newark Dressmaker Supply
Catalog: sewing/craft supplies.
Box 20730, Lehigh Valley, PA 18002
(610) 867-3833
Fax: (610) 867-9717
www.newarkdress.com

Newport Quilt and Gift Co.
Watercolor flower blocks, landscape and building materials, fabric by mail.
644 SW Coast Hwy, Suite B, Newport, OR 97365
(541) 265-3492, Toll-free: (888) 286-4777
Fax: (541) 574-6870
www.newportquilt.com

Notions Marketing and Crafting Supplies
1500 Buchanan S.W., Grand Rapids, MI 49507
(616) 243-8424; Toll-free: (800) 748-0250
Fax: (800) 678-3400
www.notionsmarketing.com

NZQuilters Online
New Zealand quilters' and guilds' links.
Box 39-152, WMC, Wellington, New Zealand
Phone: +64 25 572 164
christina@nzquilter.org.nz
http://nzquilter.org.nz/christin.htm

Ontario Quilting Connection
Official Web Site linking guilds throughout Ontario, Canada.
www.ontarioquilting.org

P & B Textiles
1580 Gilbreth Road, Burlingame, CA 94010
(650) 692-0422
Fax: (650) 692-4908
Sales Reps: *www.pbtex.com/html/salespeople_list.html*
www.pbtex.com

PBH Foundation Patterns
Vintage Pattern Lending Library: collection of over 3,000 patterns from 1840 to the 1940s.
C/O Vintage Pattern Lending Library
1617 Ashby Avenue, Berkeley, CA 94703
www.vpll.org/services/checkout.html

Patched Works
Longarm Quilting, quilting lessons online, books, patterns, rulers.
13330 Watertown Plank Road, Elm Grove, WI 53122
(262) 786-1523, Fax: (262) 786-1562
Trudie Hughes: *trudie@wi.rr.com*
www.trudiehughes.com
Information-only site: *www.patchedworks.com*

Patches from the Past
History of women and their quilts.
www.historyofquilts.com

Pattern Peddlers
Consignment.
701 Walsen Avenue, Walsenburg, CO 81089
(719) 738-7271
Fax: (888) 756-0585

Pattern Showcase
Sewing patterns, books, notions—primarily fashion items.
Managed by *www.sewingpatterns.com*
service@patternshowcase.com
www.patternshowcase.com

Pieces of Dreams
Hand-painted, space-dyed fabrics, sashiko patterns, supplies.
Saundra Seth, Designer/Lecturer
Box 298, Running Springs, CA 92382-0298
(909) 867-3764
pcsofdreams@earthlink.net
www.piecesofdreams.net/free2.htm

Petersen-Arne
Wholesale Distributors: craft/sewing supplies.
3690 West First Avenue, Eugene, OR 97402
(541) 485-1406, Toll-free: (800) 547-2509
Fax: (541) 485-3459
sales@Petersen-Arne.com
www.petersen-arne.com

Pine Tree Quilts of Vermont
Pine tree quilts.
c/o Frank and Barbara Pespisa, Corinth, VT 05039
vermontquilts@lycos.com
www.geocities.com/ptquilts

Pro Chemical and Dye
Textile dyes supplier, catalog.
Box 14, Somerset MA 02726
Orders only: (800) 228-9393, Technical Calls: (508) 676-3838, Fax: (508) 676-3980.
promail@prochemical.com
www.prochemical.com

Professional Quilter Publications
Quarterly publication: books, leaflets, resources for professional quilters.
22412 Rolling Hill Lane, Laytonsville, MD 20822
(301) 482-2345
info@professionalquilter.com
www.professionalquilter.com

Quakertown Quilts, Inc.
Fabric, books, patterns, notions, classes, services.
180 S. Friendswood Drive, Friendswood, TX 77546
(281) 996-1756, Toll-free: (888) 464-7845 (USA)
Fax: (281) 648-9090
www.quakertownquilts.com

Quilt Academy of Sweden
Forum for information, education, development, socializing about quilting.
http://home.swipnet.se/~w-58758/

Quilt Block Names: History of quilt block names. Part of the WWQP (World Wide Quilting Page).
http://ttsw.com/History/BlockNames.html

Quilt Broker Internet Service
Sells new/previously owned quilts to interior designers, collectors.
907 Columbia Road, Fort Collins, CO 80525
(970) 484-7055
Heidi Hoff Wurst: Design Plus, owner
Customer Service: (866) 456-9800
www.quiltbroker.com
Quilt submission guidelines: *www.quiltbroker.com/guidelines.pdf*

Quilt Doctor at the Vienna Quilt Shop
Quilt repair/preservation, appraisals, commissions, sales (Washington, D.C., area).
396 Maple Avenue East, Vienna, VA 22180
(703) 281-4091, Toll-free: (800) 281-4010
QuiltDoctor@msn.com
www.quiltdoctor.com

Quilt Guilds Worldwide
Lists quilt guilds, quilt shows, quilt-related links, member of the quilt guild web ring.
www.quiltguilds.com

Quilt in a Day (TV quilter Eleanor Burns' site)
Quilting books, patterns, classes, sewing tools.
1955 Diamond Street, San Marcos, CA 92069

(800) 777-4852, Fax: (760) 591-4424
customerservice@quiltinaday.com
www.quiltinaday.com

Quilt Index
Home of the Mall Crawl, index to patterns, links, quilt shops, guilds.
www.quiltindex.com

Quilt Pox
www.quiltpox.com
Info on quilting, care, immersion dyeing, comprehensive quilter's dictionary.
www.quiltpox.com/dyeing/
Additional dyeing links: *www.fibreartsonline.com/fac/surface/dyeing.htm;*
http://ttsw.com/FAQS/FabricDyingFAQ.html; www.dyeingartstudio.com/
Books_Dyeing.html

Quilt Professionals Quilt Shop Directory
Lists quilt shops, quilts for sale, teachers, guilds.
www.quiltprofessionals.com/

Quilt Shop
Online quilting source: hand-dyed, vintage, imports, domestic, appliqué
patterns.
Box 60, Richmond, TX 77406
Fax: (281) 232-7737
tqs@pdq.net
www.thequiltshop.com

Quilt University
Online quilting-related classes, national teachers, library, student lounge,
book reviews.
dean@quiltuniversity.com
www.quiltuniversity.com/registrar.htm
Class catalog: *www.quiltuniversity.com/catalog.htm*
www.quiltuniversity.com

Quilter's Cache (Marcia Hohn)
Traditional and original quilt block designs, many free to download.
www.quilterscache.com

Quilters Dream Batting
100 percent cotton batting, poly batting, pure cotton stuffing.
589 Central Drive, Virginia Beach, VA 23454
(757) 463-3264, Toll-free: (888) 268-8664
Fax: (757) 463-3569, Toll-free Fax: (800) 626-8866
quiltbat@juno.com
www.quiltersdreambatting.com

Quilters Dream Inc.—Illinois
384 Lake Street, Antioch, IL 60002
(847) 395-1459, Toll-free: (877) 405-7421
dreamquilter@core.com
www.quilters-dream.com

Quilter's Husband: Handyman Solutions for Quilters
Unique items that make a quilter's job easier.
5435 South Abbott Road, Armor Plaza, Orchard Park, NY 14127
(716) 648-2660, (888) 248-3484 (Orders Only), Fax: (716) 648-2660
assistance@quiltershusband.com
www.quiltershusband.com

Quilter's Online Resource (QOR)
Online mailing list for quilters.
Box 30184, Albuquerque, NM 87190-0184
qor@nmia.com
www.nmia.com/~mgdesign/qor/

Quilters' Resource Inc.
Catalog: quilting books, supplies, fabric, notions (wholesale only).
Box 148850-CM, Chicago, IL 60614
(773) 278-5695, Fax: (773) 278-1348
qripatches@aol.com
www.quiltersresource.com

Quilter's Rule International, LLC
SewFit products, quilting rulers.
817 Mohn Avenue, Waterford, WI 53185
(800) 343-8671
www.quiltersrule.com

Quilter's Warehouse
Source for locating leading quilt pattern designers on the Internet.
107 N. Second St., Box 458, Cissna Park, IL 60924
(815) 457-2867, (800) 391-2867, Fax: (815) 457-2577
CEO: John F. Bruns
www.quilterswarehouse.com

Quilter's Wizards
Quilting products
Box 7777, Tempe, AZ 85281
(480) 446-0900, Fax: (480) 446-9251
qinquiry@paradigm-eng.com
www.paradigm-eng.com/products

Quilting at About.com
Susan Druding's free quilt patterns, resources, tips, chat, clipart.
http://quilting.about.com

Quilting Books Unlimited
Betty Boyink: quilter, teacher, and author informs quilters about quilt-making supplies.
13772 Cottage Drive, Grand Haven MI, 49417
(616) 842-3304, (800) 347-3261
qbu@inil.com
www.qbu.com/index.html

Quilting from the Heartland
TV quilter Sharlene Jorgensen's Web site: patterns and templates.
9015 Hwy NW, Montevideo, MN 56265
www.qheartland.com

Quilts and Other Comforts
Catalog available.
Box 1250, Eustis, FL 32727-1250
Shipping/invoices: 100 South Bay Street, Eustis, FL 32726
Samples/catalog submissions:
Attn: Suzan Ellis, 947 N Donnelly Street, Mount Dora, FL 32757
(352) 383-9956, Toll-free: (800) 881-6624, Fax: (352) 383-9956
www.quiltsonline.com

QuiltShops.com
Quilt store search engine: over 100 shops listed.
www.quiltshops.com

QuiltSites.com
Lists quilt guilds, shops, teachers, shows, custom quilters, pattern designers, vendors.
www.quiltsites.com

QuiltSmith, LTD
Metal, non-skid quilting templates made by ARDCO.
U.S. Distributor: 252 Cedar Road, Poquoson, VA 23662-2112
(757) 868-8073, (800) 982-7326, Fax: (757) 868-3866
sales@ardcotemplates.com

QuiltSmith, Box 73, Broadway NSW 2007, Australia
(02) 96929300 (within Australia), +61 2 96929300 (outside Australia)
www.quiltsmith.com.au

QuiltSource Canada
Wholesale distributor: quilting related items to the Canadian marketplace.
Unit 8H, #1 Rosetta Street, Georgetown, ON, Canada L7G 3P1
(905) 873-6661 (Local), Toll-free: (888) 778 4343, Fax: (905) 873-3336
info@quiltsource.ca
www.quiltsource.ca/

QuiltWoman.com
One of the most comprehensive quilting services directories, plus a quilt
linking system
3822 Patricks Point Drive, Trinidad, CA 95570
(707) 677-0105, Toll-free: (877) 454-7967, Fax: (707) 677-9162
ann@quiltwoman.com
www.quiltwoman.com

Quiltwork Patches
General quilting supplies.
212 S.W. 3rd St., Box 724-TA, Corvallis, OR 97339
(541) 752-4820
www.quilterssafari.com/quiltworkPatches/quiltworkPatche.htm

QuiltZine Free Magazine Online
Quilters magazine: free projects, quilt galleries, free quilt patterns, news
for Quilters.
QuiltZine list by *auntie@auntie.com*
www.quiltzine.com/

ReproductionFabrics.com
Cotton reproduction fabrics for costumers and quilters, newsletter.
25 N. Willson Ave., Suite A, Bozeman, MT 59715
(406) 586-1775, Fax: (406) 586-8847, Order line (within USA): (888) 728-
2495
staff@reproductionfabrics.com
www.reproductionfabrics.com

RJR Fabrics
2203 Dominguez Street, Building K-3, Torrance, CA 90501
(310) 222-8782, (800) 422-5426, Fax: (310) 222-8792
info@rjrfabrics.com
www.rjrfabrics.com

Rubenstein and Ziff/Quiltworks (RandZ/The QuiltWorks)
Wholesale to quilting/sewing stores/manufacturers only, catalog: books,
patterns, fabrics.
1055 E. 79th Street, Minneapolis, MN 55420-1460

(952) 854-1460, Fax: (952) 854-7254
ssmolarek@r-and-z.com
www.r-and-z.com

Schoolhouse Enterprises
Gridded Geese products, catalog, online shopping cart service with Planet Patchwork.
PMB 173, 2103 North Decatur Rd., Decatur, GA 30033-5305
(877) 558-3660 (toll-free), Fax: (800) 808-4002 (toll-free)
rholland@planetpatchwork.com
www.planetpatchwork.com/storefront.htm

Sewing Machines Past to Present
French site with English translation providing an interesting history.
mcha.smpp@wanadoo.fr
http://perso.wanadoo.fr/buisson/english/index.html

Sewing With Nancy
TV program with Nancy Zieman.
www.nancysnotions.com

Skydyes
Hand-painted cotton and silk fabrics.
Box 370116, West Hartford, CT 06137-0116
(860) 232-1429, Fax: (860) 236-9117
fabrics@skydyes.com
www.skydyes.com/index.html

South Sea Imports Fabrics
www.southseaimports.com

Soft Expressions
Quilting Software source and reviews.
1230 N. Jefferson Street, Suite M, Anaheim, CA 92807
(714) 630-7414, Toll-free (USA and Canada): (888) 545-8616, Fax: (714) 630-8970
info@softexpressions.com
www.softexpressions.com/help/newsletters/index.html
Computer Quilting BYTES Newsletter *http://softexpressions.com/sharla/*

Springs Industries Fabrics
Springs Industries, Inc.
Manufacturer: Spring Maid, Wamsutta, Burlington House, Daisy Kingdom, Bali, Nanik.

Box 70, Fort Mill, SC 29716
(803) 547-1500
www.springs.com/

Starwood Wholesale
Box 217, 13700 S.W. Butler Road, Suite #203, Rose Hills, KS 67133
(316) 733-1035, Toll-free: (800) 371-1035 (Orders Only), Fax: (316) 733-1052
sales@starwoodpatterncompany.com
www.starwoodpatterncompany.com

Sulky of America
Stabilizers, decorative and quilting threads, transfer pens, project books,
free projects.
3113 Broadpoint Drive, Punta Gorda, FL 33983
Fax: (941) 743-4634
info@sulky.com, Questions: *asksulky@aol.com*
www.sulky.com/

Sylvia's Studio
Sylvia Landman, teacher; certified, NQA
Quilt University teacher, CCD/SCD designer, author, columnist.
Create@Sylvias-studio.com
www.sylvias-studio.com

Thomas Register
Provides Internet searches for company names, brand names, and products.
Customer Service: Attn: TR User Services, Five Penn Plaza, 12th Floor,
New York, NY 10001, (212) 290-7277
www.thomasregister.com

Timeless Treasures Fabrics, Inc.
483 Broadway, New York, NY 10013
(212) 226-1400, Fax: (212) 925-4180
www.ttfabrics.com

To Be Quilting
B-Line Home Quilting System
6904 Pioneer Avenue, Agassiz, BC, Canada V0M 1A2
(604) 796-3632, Fax: (604) 796-3612
info@tobequilting.com
www.tobequilting.com

Trend-Tex Fabrics, Inc.
Milt Jorgenson, President
1317 Kebet Way, Port Coquitlam, BC, Canada V3C 6G1

604-941-4620, Fax: (604) 942-4035
mail@trendtexfabrics.com
www.trendtexfabrics.com

United Notions & Fabrics (Combined with Moda Fabrics)
Dallas Office/Warehouse:
United Notions/Moda Fabrics
13795 Hutton, Dallas, TX 75234
(972) 484-8901 (Local), (800) 527-9447, Fax: (800) 468-4209
4945 Lima Street, Denver, CO 80239
(303) 371-0660 (Local), (800) 843-1236
Fax: (800) 525-0109
Customer Service: *service@unitednotions.com*
www.unitednotions.com/modahome.nsf/home

Unlimited Possibilities
Newsletter for Longarm Machine Quilters
Published quarterly.
2570 N. Walnut (location), Box 362 (mailing), Rochester, IL 62563
(217) 498-9460, Toll-free: (888) 744-0070, Fax: (217) 498-9476
dtaf@aol.com
www.kmquiltingsupply.com/booksvideos/ms/marciastevens2.shtml

USA-Quilts
Web quilting directory.
www.usa-quilts.com/top/index.html

Virtual Quilt (TVQ)
Newsletter for computing quilters from Planet Patchwork.
40 Ridley Circle, Decatur, GA 30030-1117
 Copies viewable at: *http://planetpatchwork.com/tvqmain/vq10main.htm*
or *http://planetpatchwork.com/passtvq/tvq42/*.

Virtual Quilt Co. (Part of the Planet Patchwork site)
 Patterns, guild listings, book reviews, galleries, teacher listing, block
exchanges. List of non-commercial quilting and other textile links from Planet
Patchworks. *www.tvq.com/thelist.htm*
 www.tvq.com

Warm Company
 Products: Warm & Natural, Steam-A-Seam, Beads-2-Fuse, Warm Window.
 Corporate Office: The Warm Company, 954 E Union Street, Seattle,
WA 98122
 (206) 320-9276, (800) 234-WARM
info@warmcompany.com
www.warmcompany.com/wnpage.html

WebPaige.com
Information on developing quilt business web sites.
www.thewebpaige.com/w4qs/w4qs12.html

Whole Cloth Quilting Tips (Provided by Raspberry Lane)
rasp@xmission.com
www.raspberrylane.com/quilt_it/tips.html

Wonder Cut Ruler
1020 E. 17th Street, Burley, ID 83318
(208) 678-1317
awalter@pmt.org
www.wondercutruler.com

Woods, Kaye: TV Quilting Teacher/Designer
Contact: Kaye Wood, Inc, Box 456, West Branch, MI 48661
e-mail discussion list: *http://groups.yahoo.com/group/kayewoods-quilting-friends/*
www.kayewood.com

World Wide Quilting Page (WWQP)
Quilt site index: instructions, patterns, show/store/guild listings, bulletin board.
www.quilt.com/MainQuiltingPage.html

Appendix F: *Online Quilting Groups*

A Craft Biz Connection
acraftbizconnection@yahoogroups.com
www.craftassoc.com

AussieQuiltaHolics
aussiequiltaholics@yahoogroups.com
Subscribe at: *aussiequiltaholics-subscribe@yahoogroups.com*

BAQL, British Appliqué Quilting List
Appliqué and quilting from the British and European perspective.
BAQL@yahoogroups.com; Subscribe at: *BAQL-subscribe@yahoogroups.com.*

DesignersBiz,
Needlework, beading, quilt designers.
designersbiz@yahoogroups.com
Subscribe at: *designersbiz-subscribe@yahoogroups.com*

Info-EQ, sponsored by Planet Patchworks
For users of software from The Electric Quilt Company.
Subscribe at: *http://planetpatchwork.com/Mailinglists.htm*

Home Quilting Systems
Quilting systems, sewing machines, accessories.
homequiltingsystems@yahoogroups.com
Subscribe at: *homequiltingsystems-subscribe@yahoogroups.com*

Planet Patchwork Paper Piecing
Sponsored by Planet Patchwork list for paper foundation piecing method.
Subscribe at: *http://planetpatchwork.com/Mailinglists.htm*

QuiltArt
E-mail list for contemporary art quilters.
info@quiltart.com
www.quiltart.com

QORC
Sponsored by QOR (Quilters Online Resource).
qorc@majordomo.nmia.com

QuiltBiz
Professional Quilters and Quilt Shop Owners site.
quiltbiz@lyris.planetpatchwork.com

Quilt History
Quilt history and antique quilt care.
www.quilthistory.com

Quilt Pattern Designers Collective
quiltdesigners@yahoogroups.com
Subscribe at: *quiltdesigners-subscribe@yahoogroups.com*

Quilt Teach
New and experienced quilt and craft teachers share ideas, class topic information.
QuiltTeach@yahoogroups.com
Subscribe at: *QuiltTeach-subscribe@yahoogroups.com*

Quiltopia
Sponsored by Planet Patchwork for all quilters
http://planetpatchwork.com/Mailinglists.htm
QuiltPro Software Support Group
www.groups.yahoo.com/group/quiltpro/

Appendix G: *Other Helpful Web Sites*

Barbara Brabec's World
(630) 717-4188
www.barbarabrabec.com; e-mail: *barbara@barbarabrabec.com*
Ms. Brabec is a leader in the home-business industry, and the author of several books on how to profit from a home-based business.

Display Away
Zellerwood Originals LLC
P.O. Box 54289, Cincinnati, OH 45254
(888) 487-7233
www.displayaway.com/

Standard Rate & Data Service
Lists TV stations, radio, newspapers, magazines, and trade and business publications, alphabetically and by category. Includes rates, size, and cost of advertising space and display ads, plus deadlines.
http://infotree.library.ohiou.edu/single-records/2858.html

Writer's Digest Magazine
Information about writing books and magazine articles.
www.writersdigest.com

Writer's Toolbox
www.writerstoolbox.com

CompuQuilt
PMB # 116, 2791F No. Texas St., Fairfield, CA 94533
(707) 422-1529; Fax: (707) 422-1529
http://compuquilt.com; e-mail: *LindaB@compuquilt*
Information for the computerized quilter, patterns, and QuiltPro software.

The Electric Quilt Company
419 Gould Street, Suite 2, Bowling Green, OH 43402-3047
(toll-free sales order line): (800) 356-4219; Tech Support: (419) 352-1134
Fax: (419) 352-4332
www.electricquilt.com
e-mail: *techsupport@electricquilt.com; sales@electricquilt.com; customerservice@electricquilt.com*

PCQuilt for Windows
PCQuilt support:
75 Sherwood Avenue, Ossining, NY 10562
Orders: (800) 731-8886; tech support: (914) 944-0744; Fax: (914) 944-3555.
www.pcquilt.com; e-mail: *antze@pcquilt.com*

Quilt-Pro
Windows and Mac drawing program to create quilts. Quilt-Pro: Free downloadable QuiltPro Demo at this site: *www.quiltpro.com*
Technical Support: *www.quiltpro.com/tech/contact.shtml*
QuiltPro creator's consulting business.
www.sheilawilliams.com/qpsheets/QP.html
Contact: Sheila Williams (e-mail: *quilting@SheilaWilliams.com*)

Computer and Quilting Software Consulting
P. O. Box 891085, Temecula, CA 92592
Phone: (909) 302-9864; Fax: (909) 302-9864
QuiltSoft, formerly Quilter's Design Studio.
5441 Brockbank Place, San Diego, CA 92115
(619) 583-2970, Fax: (619) 583-2682
www.quiltsoft.com/

Vquilt 2
Quilt design software. Runs only under MS-DOS or Windows.
Computer Systems Associates, Box 129, Jarrettsville, MD 21084-0129
(410) 557-6871; Fax: (410) 557-7928
www.vquilt.com
Contacts: General Information: *info@vquilt.com*, Sales: *sales@vquilt.com*
Customer Support: *support@vquilt.com, webmaster@vquilt.com*

Appendix I: *Government Resources*

Federal Trade Commission
Division of Legal & Public Records, Washington, DC 20580
Request free booklet: *A Business Guide to the Federal Trade Commission's Mail-Order Rule.*

Fiber Content Labeling
www.apparel.ca/government/label.html
Canadian regulations: *http://strategis.ic.gc.ca/SSG/cp01090e.html*
Label compliance guidelines for fiber content, bilingual requirements, dealer identity, application of labels.
United States Regulations: *www.ftc.gov/bcp/conline/pubs/buspubs/thread.htm*

International Trademark Association (INTA)
Check the correct spelling of nearly 4,000 trademarks and service marks, and get the correct generic terms.
www.inta.org

IRS (Internal Revenue Service) Forms and Publications
www.irs.ustreas.gov/formspubs/index.html

SBA (Small Business Administration)
Headquarters Office
409 Third Street, SW, Washington, DC 20416
(800) U-ASK-SBA
www.sbaonline.sba.gov; Site Map: *www.sba.gov/map.html*

SCORE (Service Corps of Retired Executives)
www.score.org
Counselors to America's Small Business is a nonprofit association dedicated to providing entrepreneurs with free, confidential, face-to-face and e-mail business counseling.

State Sales Tax Links
Source of links to all U.S. state sales tax information.
Information available at: *www.fiberart.net/links/taxlinks.htm#tax*

Uniform Code Council, Inc. (UPC/Bar Code info)
UCC Customer Service
7887 Washington Village Drive, Suite 300, Dayton, OH 45459
(937) 435-3870; Fax: (937) 435-7317
www.uc-council.org; e-mail: *info@uc-council.org*

U.S. Copyright Office
101 Independence Ave. S.E., Washington, D.C. 20559-6000
Phones: Public Information Office: (202) 707-3000
Forms and Publications Hotline: (202) 707-9100
Fax-on-Demand: (202) 707-2600
TTY: (202) 707-6737
www.copyright.gov

U.S. Patent and Trademark Office
USPTO Contact Center (UCC). Provides dozens of free booklets.
Crystal Plaza 3, Room 2C02, P.O. Box 1450, Alexandria, VA 22313-1450
Customer Service: (800) 786-9199 (in USA or Canada) or (703) 308-4357
www.uspto.gov/main/trademarks.htm
www.uspto.gov/web/menu/search.html

United States Postal Service (USPS)
www.usps.com
Domestic and international postage rate calculator, zip code lookup.

Index

ACCI. *See* Association of Craft and Creative Industries
action boards, 10–12
action lists, 10–12
adult education, 149–150
advertising
    classified ads, 41–42
    instructors, guidelines for, 80
    magazines, 41
    newsletters, 42
    newspaper, 42
    telephone book display ads, 42
    trade journal, 42
all rights, 120
Alofs, Betty, 51–52
American Craft Council, 73
American Quilt Retailer, 53
American Quilting Society (AQS), 48–49
The American Quilter, 53
Anastasio, Ann, contracts and, 77–78
Anderson, Ann, 29
annual quilt shows, 74
AQS. *See* American Quilting Society
Association of Craft and Creative Industries (ACCI), 50

Back-of-the-Room sales, 138
Barnes & Noble Books, 150
Better Home & Gardens, 41
Bissett, Kathleen, contracts and, 76–77
Blanchet, Ruth, 31
Books, 190–195
boutiques, 69–70
Brady, John, 125
brochures
    marketing plan, professional image in, 44
Broken Dishes Repertory Theatre, 77
Browning, Tracy, 161–162
www.bryerpatch.com, 81

budget proposal, 18
business
    buying wholesale, 173–175
    cash flow management in, 175–176
    city license for, 171
    credit cards, 177
    employees and, 179–180
    general, books on, 190
    home occupation use permits, 171
    home office deduction, 171–173
    independent contractor for, 179–180
    IRS and, 1–2
    merchant credit, 177–179
    motivation, 3, 9
    naming of, 170
    organizations, 202
    personal tasks and, 3
    private, instructors, guidelines for, 80
    self-discipline, 3
    working from home and, 2–3
    zoning variances, 171
Business & Legal Forms for Authors & Self-Publishers and Business and Legal Forms for Crafts, 75
business cards, 43
business plan
    budget proposal, funds required, 18
    business objective, 18
    cash flow, statement, 18
    company background, 18
    defining of, 13–14
    executive summary, 17
    implementation startup timetable, 18
    industry data, 19
    legal structures, 17
    marketing plan, 18
    mission statement, 17
    monthly expenses, 18

outline of, 16–20
    owner information, 17
    personal history, 17
    prior cash floe statement, 19
    product benefits, 18
    product description, 18
    proprietary rights, 19
    reasons for, 14
    success road map, 14–16
    table of contents, 16
    title page, 16
    type of, 17–18
Buyer Zone, 179
www.buyerzone.com/finance/credit_merchants/, 179

Canadian QuiltDesigners, 53
Canadian Quilter, 53
Carey, Patti, 106
Carr, Wheat, 7
cash flow
    business account, 176
    co-mingling funds, 175–176
    management of, 175–176
    operating funds source for, 176
    statement, outline, business plan, 18
CBD. *See* Copyrights Be Damned
Certified Professional Demonstrator program, 50
Certified Teacher Training program, 50
class, teaching styles of, 127
classified ads, 41–42
Collector's Christmas Tree, 30
Color Marketing Group, 40
color, trends, 23–24
www.colorassociation.com/site/mailinglist.hml, 24
www.colormarketing.org, 24

commission, retail,
56–60
conference, teaching styles
of, 127
consignment, retail,
60–61
consulting books, 190
consumer magazines
periodicals, 197–200
contracts
Anastasio on, 77–78
Bissett on, 76–77
importance of, 75
of Landman, 166–167
letter of agreement,
81–86
magazines and articles
writing of,
119–121
sample, 166–167
Scott on, 78
Cool, Lisa Collier, 117
cope, 9
copyright
books on, 190
definition of, 181–183
fair use of, 183–184
filing of, 186
instructors, guidelines
for, 81
international, 188–189
myths about, 186–188
pirates, 185
quilters and, 183
resources, 189
works in public domain,
184–185
*Copyright Law of the
United States of
America,* 181
*Copyright Law: What You
Don't Know Can Cost
You!,* 120
Copyrights Be Damned
(CBD), 185
www.copyright.gov, 182
Craft, 116
craft business books, 190
craft fairs
definition of, 68
selling at consumer,
68–69
craft meals, retail, 61
Crafting for Dollars, 121

Crafts Fair Guide, 69
Crafts Magazine, 49
Crafts 'N Things, 49
The Crafts Report, 61,
69, 70
The Craft of Interviewing,
125
creativity, 26–27
credit cards, 177
Crystal Cruise Lines, 108

D.B.A. *See* Doing Business As
deductions, 171–173
demonstration, teaching
styles of, 127
design
creativity and, 26–27
idea flow and, 27
new materials and,
25–26
profitability and, 24
protecting of, 24–25
selling of, 27–32,
113–114
trends, 23–24
direct mail (mail order),
62–65
distributors, 206–231
Doing Business As
(D.B.A), 176
Donovan, Deb, lesson plan
of, 163–166
dyes, fabric, 212–213

e-Bay, 66
Electric Quilt software, 134
Electric Quilt User Software
Group, 53
employees, 179–180
*Encyclopedia of
Associations,* 42
energy level, observation
of, 4
entrepreneur, characteristics
of, 8–9

fabric dye, 212–213
fabric manufactures,
213–231
FabShop Network, 52
Fabulous Quilts, 161
Fallert, Chryl Bryer, 81
*Federal Trade Commission
(FTC),* 63

first serial rights, 120
foreign serial rights, 121
Foster, Patti, 105–106
FrontPage for Dummies, 67
FrontPage software, 66
FTC. *See* Federal Trade
Commission

Gendron, Ruth Sparrow, 31
Gerards, Paul, 69
goals
achieving of, 8
defining of, 8
knowing, 9–10
government resources,
236–237
Greig, Daphne, 52–54
Gulati, Cara, 160–161

Hahn, Linda, 159–160
Hewlett-Packard Computer
Classes, 150
HIA. See Hobby Industry
Association
Hobby Industry Association
(HIA), 49, 50–51, 72
hobby, quilting as, 1–2
home boutiques, selling at,
69–70
home, working from, 2–3
Hooley, Cathy, pricing system
of, 97–99
*How to Sell What You Make:
The Business of
Marketing Crafts at
Fairs, Boutiques, and
Exhibits,* 69
*How to Write & Sell a
Column,* 125
*How to Write Irresistible
Query Letters,* 117
*www.hplearningcenter.
com,* 152
Hughes, Trudie, 28–29

ideas, 27
incentives, creating, 8
independent contractor,
179–180
independent sales
organization (ISO), 179
INRG. *See* International
Needlearts Retailers
Guild

instructors, guidelines for,
78–81
advertising, 80
class materials, 81
class size, 79
copyright issues, 81
exclusivity, 80
material lists, 80
private business, 80
room setup and
take-down, 80
samples, 80
scheduling, 80
teacher discount, 79
Internal Revenue Service
(IRS), 1–2
home office deduction and,
171–173
International Needlearts
Retailers Guild
(INRG), 32
International Quilt
Festival/Market, 51
Internet Explorer, 66
*Internet Marketing Secrets
for Dummies*, 67
IRS. *See* Internal Revenue
Service
ISO. *See* Independent sales
organization

www.jankrentz.com, 143

Kirk, Nancy, 108–109

labor, pricing, basics
of, 89
*Lady's Circle Patchwork
Quilts*, 49
Landman, Sylvia, 109–111
sample contract of,
166–167
Lant, Dr. Jeffrey, 110
Laquidara, Judy, 104–105
*The Law (in PlainEnglish)®
for Crafts*, 75
lecture, teaching styles
of, 127
lesson plan, 143–147
book reviews, 147
of Donovan, Deb,
163–166
formal lecture, 145
group demonstrations, 146

individual instruction, 146
organizing notes, 143
show-and-tell, 146
slides, 146–147
letterhead stationary
marketing plan, professional
image, 44
Levoy, Gregg, 86
loan, business, 14
Longshore, Lani, 77
Lynch, Alice, 30–31

Maddalena, Marilyn,
107–108
magazines
advertising with, 41
articles, writing of,
113–124
column, 124–125
contract with, 119–121
designer earnings, 123
individual articles
from, 192
multiple articles for,
123–124
selling designs in,
113–114
series, 123–124
submission of article for,
117–119
tera sheets, 121–122
type of articles for,
114–116
writing instructions for
articles in, 122–123
writing query letter, 117
mail order books, 191
mail order. *See* direct mail
Mail-Order Rule, 63
*Make You Woodwork Pary for
Itself*, 122
*Make Your Quilting Pay for
Itself*, 121–122
Males, Carolyn, 125
marketing plan
advice on, 51–54
books on, 191
creativity and, 34–35
products benefit, 43
promotional ideas, 47–48
marketing plan, advertising,
41–42
classified ads, 41–42
magazines, 41

newsletters, 42
newspaper advertising, 42
telephone book display
ads, 42
trade journals, 42
marketing plan, networking,
48–51
trade association value,
49–51
marketing plan, professional
image, 43–47
brochures in, 44
business cards in, 43
letterhead stationary
in, 44
portfolio in, 45–47
marketing plan, selling and,
35–38
competition, 38
customers, 35–36
shops, 37–38
marketing plan, written,
39–41
creating, 39–40
research techniques, 40–41
strategies, 40
materials, new, 25–26
McCall's Quick Quilts, 53
McCleary, Karen, 106–107
merchant, credit, 177–179
mission statement, 17
Morton, Jo, 29–30
motivation, 3, 9

www.naed.org/naed/
content, 179
National Quilting Association
(NQA), 48, 74, 124
The National Association
of Electrical
Distributors, 179
Netscape, 66
networking, marketing plan,
48–51
newsletters, advertising
with, 42
newspaper advertising, 42
NQA. *See* National Quilting
Association

one-time rights, 120
online quilting groups,
232–233
online teaching, 152–153

organizations, 202–205
original design
  defining of, 21–22
  selling more than one of,
    22–23
overhead, pricing, 89
owner information, 17

patterns, selling of, 37–32
PayPal, 67
periodicals, 196–201
personal tasks, business
    and, 3
Phoenix University, 150
Piecework Magazine,
    62, 116
Porcells, Yvonne, 35
portfolio
  articles in, 46
  brochure in, 45
  business card in, 45
  chronological order, 46
  magazine covers in, 46
  marketing plan,
      professional image
      and, 45–47
  mission statement in, 45
  photographs in, 45, 46
  résumé in, 45
  short biography in, 45
  style, 47
  tear sheets in, 45–46
  technique, 47
*Prairie Hands Patterns in
    Nebraska*, 29
pricing, 89–90
  adjustment of, 94
  competition and, 95
  demand-oriented, 96
  example of, 96–97
  Hooley, Cathy, system for,
    96–9787–99
  labor, 89
  mark-up, 90
  overhead, 89
  profit, 90
  profit increase and,
    95–96
  raising of, 95
  range, 93
  raw materials, 89
  retail, 89
  template, 93–94
  value, 89

wages, 89
wholesale, 89
  by Woodland Manor,
    100–102
pricing, methods of,
    90–94
  break-even point,
    90–91
  direct labor, 90
  by hour, 91–92
  mark-up pricing, 90
  pricing range, 93
  pricing template,
    93–94
  profit system, 91
  shortcut, 91
  by spools of thread, 92
  by square inch/foot/
    yard, 92
  by yardage consumed,
    92–93
priorities
  ability to, 9
  setting of, 10
professional image, 43–47
  brochures for, 44
  business cards for, 43
  letterhead stationary
    for, 44
  portfolio for, 45–47
  résumé for, 45
*Professional Quilter
    Magazine*, 116, 162
profit
  pricing, basics of, 90
  reportable, 1
Publish Your Patterns, 31
publisher's books,
    193–195
Purney-Mark, Susan,
    52–54

quality, of work, 55–56
QuickBooks, 175
Quilt Craft, 49
Quilt Craft Magazine, 124
quilt shows
  annual, 74
  selling at, 70–71
Quilt University, 31–32
Quilt-as-You-Go, 124
Quiltbiz, 52
QuiltDesigners, 53
QuiltDesigners@yahoo.com, 71

QuiltDesigners@yahoogroups.
    com
Quilter's Newsletter, 116
*Quilter's Newsletter
    Magazine*, 62, 71, 115
A Quilters Gathering, 104
*www.quiltersvillage.com/
    qinamer03/*, 21
Quilting Arts, 116
Quilting in America
    study, 21
*Quilting Quarterly
    Journal*, 124
Quilting-and Craft-Related
    organizations,
    202–205
QuiltTeach, 53
QuiltTeach, 143
www.QuiltUniversity.com, 152

Raskin, Julie, 125
raw materials, pricing, 89
reliability, 9
Restuccia's, Nancy, 31
résumé, 45
retail
  commission, 56–60
  consignment, 60–61
  craft meals, 61
  direct mail (mail order),
    62–65
  pricing, basics of, 89
  selling at, 56–67
  web site, 65–67
  wholesale, 73–74
rights
  all, 120–121
  first serial, 120
  foreign serial, 121
  one-time, 120
  reprint, 120
  second serial, 120
  simultaneous, 121
  subsidiary, 121

sales representative, 68
Santeusanio, Janet-Lee
  pricing schedule by,
    100–102
SCD. *See* Society of Craft
    Designers
Schedule C, 1, 2
schedule, work week, 4
  sticking to, 4–8

Schmidt, Linda, 34,
162–163
Schumacher, Michael, 125
Scott, BrendaLou, contracts
and, 78
second serial (reprint)
rights, 120
self-discipline, 3
self-motivation, 9
self-publishing webs
sites, 195
selling
at consumer craft fairs,
68–69
at home boutiques,
69–70
quilt shows, 70–71
sales representative
and, 68
at trade shows, 71–72
work quality and,
55–56
selling, marketing plan and,
35–38
competition, 38
customers, 35–36
shops, 37–38
selling, retail, 56–67
commission, 56–60
consignment, 60–61
craft meals, 61
direct mail (mail order),
62–65
web site, 65–67
and wholesale, 73–74
selling, wholesale, 67–68
and retail, 73–74
shops, 67–68
seminar, teaching styles
of, 127
Serenity, 108
serial rights, 120–121
shops, adult education versus,
149–150
Simmons, Judy, 34
Simple Contracts for
Personal Use, 75
simultaneous rights, 121
Society of Craft Designers
(SCD), 49, 118
The Society of Craft
Designers (SCD),
49–50
software, 235

Spiegel, Lee, 69
subsidiary rights, 121
Sun City Quilters, 185
Sunset, 41
Superior Card
Services, 179
www.superiorcardservice.
com, 179
suppliers, 206–231
syllabus, 147–148

tasks, order of, 4
teacher interviews,
159–163
Browning, Tracy,
161–162
Gulati, Cara, 160–161
Hahn, Linda, 159–160
Schmidt, Linda,
162–163
teaching
books on, 191
at conventions,
153–155
by correspondence,
151–152
credentials of, 167–168
online, 152–153
qualifications of,
167–168
at seminars, 153–155
teaching, setting fees,
155–159
flat rate, 156
pre-student rate,
156–157
teaching, styles of,
126–127
attitude, 136–140
class description elements,
128–129
class time used well in,
130–131
computers, 134–135
difficult students with,
140–143
environment with,
148–155
handouts in, 131–134
lesson plan, 143–147
organization, 128–136
planning, 128–136
problem areas in,
140–143

samples, 136
syllabus, 147–148
visual aids, 135–136
The Teaching
Marketplace, 149
tear sheets, as marketing
tools, 121–122
Tech TV, 66
telephone book display
ads, advertising
with, 42
That Patchwork
Place, 161
This Business of
Writing, 86
Thomas Register, 174
Threads, 116
time, management of,
9–10
goals, 9–10
prioritize, 10
trade journals
advertising with, 42
periodicals, 196–197
trade shows, 71–72
Tresch, Christine, 30

value, pricing, basics
of, 89
www.VirtualUniversity.
com, 152
Vlack, Barbara, 28

wages, pricing
basics of, 89
web site, 24, 81, 143, 152,
179, 182
choosing name for, 66
creating presence
with, 66
financial consideration
with, 67
retail, selling at,
65–67
self-publishing, 195
signature line in, 66
Wegert, Susanne
(Sue), 31
What It Costs to Make
A Queen-Sized, Pieced,
and Hand-Quilted
Quilt, 99
wholesale
buying, 173–175

pricing, basics of, 89
retail and, 73–74
selling at, 67–68
shops, 67–68
Woodland Manor Machine
    Quilting, pricing
    schedule by, 100–102
workaholics, 6–7

workshop, teaching styles
    of, 127
Writer's Guide, 123
Writer's Market,
    42, 115
*The Writer's Complete Guide
    to Conducting
    Interviews*, 125

writing, books on,
    191–192
writing magazines periodicals,
    200–201

Yahoo, 66
Young, Woody, 120

Books from Allworth Press

Allworth Press is an imprint of Allworth Communications, Inc. Selected titles are listed below.

Creative Careers in Crafts
by Susan Joy Sager (paperback, 6 × 9, $19.95, 272 pages)

Selling Your Crafts, Revised Edition
by Susan Joy Sager (paperback, 6 × 9, $19.95, 288 pages)

Creating a Successful Crafts Business
by Rogene A. Robbins and Robert Robbins (paperback, 6 × 9, 256 pages, $19.95)

Crafts and Craft Shows: How to Make Money
by Philip Kadubec (paperback, 6 × 9, 208 pages, $16.95)

Business and Legal Forms for Crafts
by Tad Crawford (paperback, 8 ½ × 11, 176 pages, $19.95)

The Law (in Plain English)® for Crafts
by Leonard DuBoff (paperback, 6 × 9, 224 pages, $18.95)

The Fine Artist's Guide to Marketing and Self-Promotion, Revised Edition
by Julius Vitali (paperback, 6 × 9, 256 pages, $19.95)

How to Grow as an Artist
by Daniel Grant (paperback, 6 × 9, 240 pages, $16.95)

Legal Guide for the Visual Artist, Fourth Edition
by Tad Crawford (paperback, 8 ½ × 11, 272 pages, $19.95)

The Business of Being an Artist, Third Edition
by Daniel Grant (paperback, 6 × 9, 352 pages, $19.95)

The Artist's Complete Health and Safety Guide, Third Edition
By Monona Rossol (paperback, 6 × 9, 416 pages, $24.95)

Licensing Art & Design, Revised Edition
by Caryn R. Leland (paperback, 6 × 9, 128 pages, $16.95)

Please write to request our free catalog. To order by credit card, call 1-800-491-2808 or send a check or money order to Allworth Press, 10 East 23rd Street, Suite 210, New York, NY 10010. Include $5 for shipping and handling for the first book ordered and $1 for each additional book. Ten dollars plus $1 for each additional book if ordering from Canada. New York State residents must add sales tax.

If you would like to see our complete catalog on the World Wide Web, you can find us at
www.allworth.com.